Junior Cycle English
Second and Third Year

Raseanna Brooker

GREAT EXPECTATIONS 2

Catherine Leddin

educate.ie

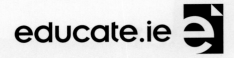

PUBLISHED BY:
Educate.ie
Walsh Educational Books Ltd
Castleisland, Co. Kerry, Ireland
www.educate.ie

DESIGN & LAYOUT:
Kieran O'Donoghue

ILLUSTRATORS:
Emma Kenny (EMK Illustrations)
Eva Dünzinger (Beehive)
Tim Hutchinson Illustration

PERMISSIONS:
Lynn Harding
Síofra Ní Thuairisg

PRINTED AND BOUND BY:
Walsh Colour Print, Castleisland

ISBN: 978-1-910052-85-3

Acknowledgements

Sincere thanks to my students, fellow teachers, friends and family for advice on compiling book two. In particular, heartfelt thanks to Sinéad, Lynn, Julie, Kieran, Paula, Jim and the fantastic team working in Educate.ie.

Catherine Leddin

Table of Contents

Extended Table of Contents

Chapter 4: Non-Literary Texts 216

Chapter 5: Drama 310

Chapter 6: Film: An International Language 400

Podcasts

Icon Key

 CD

 Numeracy Questions

 Did You Know?

 Oral Language

 Writing

 Pairwork

 Visual Literacy/Drawing

 Peer Assessment

 Group Work

 Portfolio

 Listening

 Reading

 Literacy Questions

 Research

RAFT

With any form of creation/writing you need to consider the purpose of the piece and structure it accordingly. To do this it is useful to consider the RAFT strategy or approach.

Role of the writer	Who are you as the writer? A movie star? The President? A novelist?
Audience	To whom are you writing? Your fans? The public? A company?
Format	In what format are you writing? A diary entry? A newspaper? A blog?
Topic	What are you writing about?

Introduction

For the Teacher

Welcome to *Great Expectations 2*. This book is designed to meet the requirements of the new English specification in an enjoyable yet thorough way. Your package includes:

- Textbook and free ebook
- Teacher's Resource Book and ICT Handbook
- Teacher's CDs

In line with the new English specification, the focus is on developing skills in oral language, writing and reading competence. Grammar is weaved into each chapter with plenty of practice exercises in the book and in the Student Portfolio.

A popular feature of *Great Expectations 1*, Pairwork, appears again in our Second- and Third-Year book, while we graduate to Group Work for many tasks to encourage team thinking and figuring out.

A beautiful selection of poems, short stories and drama extracts aims to entice students of all abilities. Step-by-step guides are provided on How to Research, How to Do a Presentation, How to Write a Speech and How to Write a Personal Essay.

Chapter 1	Welcomes the student and focuses on Personal Writing with an enjoyable selection of memoirs, blogs and diaries. It also shows students how to research, paragraph, proofread and write a personal essay.
Chapter 2	Focuses on Novels and Short Stories, encouraging students to understand how elements of fiction such as plot, setting, narration, atmosphere and characterisation combine to tell a story.
Chapter 3	Provides a rich selection of Poetry, beginning with a revision of poetic styles and terms encountered in *Great Expectations 1*. It offers an opportunity to study poems by theme (e.g. World War I, relationships/childhood) or by poet (e.g. Kavanagh, Heaney) and provides a focus on new Irish poetry (Ní Chinnéide) and modern American poetry (Blanco).
Chapter 4	Presents a wide variety of Non-Literary Texts from the worlds of media, advertising and travel writing, as well as offering students plenty of opportunity to practise oral language with step-by-step guidance on writing speeches and doing presentations.
Chapter 5	Looks at extracts from seven Dramas from the prescribed list, including *The Shadow of a Gunman*, *Blood Brothers*, *Romeo and Juliet* and *The Merchant of Venice*, as well as offering old favourites such as *The Field*, and a completely new play, *Leaves*.
Chapter 6	Offers students the tools and vocabulary to study and analyse Film, as well as improving their non-literary writing, with a focus on film posters and reviews.

Features of *Great Expectations 2*

Learning Expectations are stated at the beginning of each chapter

Tasks are clearly laid out under recognisable headings, such as **Literacy**, **Numeracy**, **Research**, **Pairwork**, **Group Work** and **Writing**

Grammar is integrated into each chapter and reinforced in the topics and tasks

Writing tasks offer guidance and encouragement on redrafting to help students prepare for their **Collection of Texts Task**

Each chapter has an **end-of-chapter assessment**, which can be completed and stored in the Student Portfolio

Oral Language, Research and Presentation tasks help students to prepare for the **Oral Communication Task**

How To sections inserted throughout chapters teach students valuable skills such as researching, working in groups, presenting, preparing speeches and debates

A Note on Differentiation

The material, questions and tasks in *Great Expectations 2* are aimed at Ordinary and Higher Levels. Therefore, you pick and mix what suits your own particular class group. You skip past what you consider to be too challenging or too easy. A topic that your class might find interesting, another class might find boring – thus you select what is most suitable for your class.

The Student Portfolio

The Student Portfolio provides opportunities for students to practise their writing across a broad range of genres and to improve their skills gradually. It includes assessment tasks for each chapter and practice exercises to keep students learning. It also features a bank of templates to allow students to build up their knowledge of the plots, key themes, characters and quotes in their prescribed texts.

Teacher's CDs

The CDs that accompany *Great Expectations 2* contain a wide range of audio material to help your students to understand a variety of registers used for a range of purposes.

As in *Great Expectations 1*, we have provided a CD containing a selection of fiction extracts, poetry and drama. Recorded non-literary texts include radio ads, interviews, vox pops and a documentary. We are delighted that a number of the original authors of extracts, such as Ivan Yates and Wil Wheaton, have recorded their own audio for us so that your students may hear the original writer delivering their piece.

The CD icon in the textbook indicates where there is listening material you can incorporate into your lesson.

Teacher's Resource Book

The Teacher's Resource Book clearly:

- Outlines the requirements of the new English specification
- Lists the 39 learning outcomes
- Gives templates on yearly planning, term planning and lesson planning
- Explains the Oral Language Assessment task in Second Year
- Explains the requirements for the two Written Texts in Third Year
- Explains the more complex learning outcomes

In addition, it includes the following materials:

- Extra photocopiable resources
- Tips for assessment
- Transcripts for podcasts
- Crosswords and wordsearches

Good luck and enjoy!

Catherine Leddin, April 2015

What is your Story

Getting Started

~A Student's Guide to JCSA English~

In this section I will:

- **Learn** all about my English course for Second and Third Year
- **Understand** the three parts of my English assessment
- Get ready to start **reading**, **writing**, **speaking** and **listening**

Getting Started

Welcome to *Great Expectations 2*, your Second- and Third-Year textbook, which completes your course in JCSA English. As you may have discovered in First Year, Junior Cycle English is all about improving and developing your skills in reading, writing, speaking and listening. *Great Expectations 2* is here to help you do this.

Great Expectations 2 comes with:

- A Portfolio, where you can complete the **PORTFOLIO** tasks in your textbook
- A free ebook and digital resources (use the code on the inside back cover of your textbook to access these)

Great Expectations 2 has a wide variety of material to suit all interests and abilities. Listen to interviews on the CD. Read about hurling, Taylor Swift or Robbie Henshaw, or read a good piece of fiction. Write an opinion piece, an article or a blog post. Create your own radio or TV ad, or act in a drama. Whatever you do, enjoy it and have fun!

In Second and Third Year, your assessment for JCSA will take place. There are three parts to your assessment. You will get marks for each part. Here's when they take place:

What	When
Oral Communication Task	End of Second Year
Collection of Texts Task	Christmas of Third Year
Final Written Exam	End of Third Year

Oral Communication (60 Marks)

The first part of your assessment is Oral Communication. This involves choosing a topic, doing some research on it, and delivering a presentation to your class.

Your Oral Communication Task is due at the end of Second Year. Three quarters of your marks (45 marks) will be awarded for your presentation. The other quarter (15 marks) will be awarded for research (including a Student Reflection Note).

Great Expectations 2 helps you to get ready for your Oral Communication Task with:

- An Oral Communication Task FAQ right here at the start of the book (page XVI) telling you exactly what's involved and how to get started.
- How to Research (page 36) and How to Do a Presentation (page 243) sections to develop your researching and presenting skills.
- Plenty of Oral Language tasks throughout your textbook, so that you can practise preparing topics and speaking in front of an audience.
- Plenty of Research tasks throughout your textbook, so that you can gain all the skills you need to research your Oral Communication Task topic.
- A dedicated Oral Communication Task section in your Portfolio, with templates for writing up your research, presentation notes and Student Reflection Note.

Collection of Texts Task (100 Marks)

The second part of your assessment is your Collection of Texts Task. This involves selecting some of the written pieces you have worked on in Second and Third Year and redrafting them to make them even better.

You will choose two texts to submit for assessment at Christmas of Third Year.

Great Expectations 2 helps you to get ready for your collection of texts task with:

- A Collection of Texts Task FAQ right here at the start of the book (page XVII) telling you exactly what's involved and how to get started.
- Plenty of Writing tasks throughout your textbook, with lots of opportunities to redraft and revise your work, so that you can gain all the skills you need to choose and improve your selected texts for your Collection of Texts Task.
- A dedicated Collection of Texts section in your Portfolio, with templates for writing up your drafts and your Student Reflection Note.

Final Written Exam

The final part of your English assessment at Junior Cycle is the written exam at the end of Third Year.

Your exam will be two hours long and there will be just one paper. You may choose to sit your exam at either Ordinary Level or Higher Level. If you choose to do your exam at Higher Level, you will need to study Shakespeare as part of your drama course.

Texts for Junior Cycle English

In Second and Third Year you will study:

- Two novels
- Two dramas (or one full drama and one extract or extracts from other drama)
- A selection of poetry
- Short stories
- A film OR a biography OR a travel text OR a documentary

Your teacher will let you know what texts you are going to study. *Great Expectations 2* will help you to study your texts with:

- A Novels and Short Stories chapter that helps you to understand all of the different features of fiction and helps you to analyse your own texts.
- A Drama chapter that features extracts from many of the plays available to study on your course and focuses on the different features of drama to help you understand how to study a play.
- A Film chapter that helps you to understand all of the important features of film so that you can analyse your own film (if you are studying one).
- A dedicated My Studied Texts section in your Portfolio with templates for keeping track of plots, key themes, characters and quotes.

If you read, write and speak regularly, you will gradually build up your skills in English and be well prepared for your final assessment.

At the end of each chapter of *Great Expectations 2* you will find Read and Enjoy or Did You Know? sections that are there to give you the chance to read for pleasure (no assignments!).

Good Luck!

Oral Communication Task FAQ

What's it all about?
Your Oral Communication Task involves choosing a topic, doing some research on it and delivering a presentation to your class.

Do I have to do it on my own?
You can work with your classmates to choose and research a topic, just remember that even if you work in a group you still need to prepare and present your own part of the Oral Communication Task and you must write your own Student Reflection Note. You are also marked individually on it.

When?
It's due at the end of Second Year.

How long does it need to be?
It should last for about three minutes, this includes any time set aside for engagement with your audience, such as questions from your teacher.

What kind of topic can I choose?
Something that is of interest to you! It can be anything from a speech about a sportsperson, writer or musician you are interested in, to a presentation about a book you have read. You could come up with a question you want to answer (e.g. 'Why do we need school uniforms?' or 'Do celebrities make good role models?') or put together a talk about one of your hobbies.

What should I think about when choosing my topic?
The following questions should help you pick a suitable topic for your Oral Communication Task:

- Will I be able to find sources to research this topic?
- Will I be able to do my research and preparation in three weeks at most?
- Can I speak comfortably about this topic in front of my class?
- Will I be able to speak on this topic for three minutes?

How do I research for it?
Once you have decided on your topic, do lots of reading about it from different sources. Use the How to Research guide on page 36. When you have learned lots about your chosen topic, select the most relevant parts and put them in a logical sequence in order to inform your audience about your topic. Make sure it is in the correct format – e.g. if you are doing a speech you should begin by introducing yourself and saying what you are going to talk about.

What format do I use?
There is no set format. You can use a range of approaches, such as interview, presentation, performance, speech and so on.

Do I have to learn it off?
No. You can speak with or without notes or use a prepared script. However, do remember that one of the signs of a good presentation is standing up straight and looking out at your audience. So, if you do use notes, you should still practise so that you don't need to look down at them throughout your presentation.

Can I use props?
Yes, just check with your teacher that they're suitable!

What is the Student Reflection Note?
As part of your preparation for the Oral Communication Task, you must complete a written Student Reflection Note. This must include:

- A title
- An account of the materials/sources you used to research your topic
- An account of how you prepared for the task
- A brief personal reflection

What's involved in a personal reflection?
These are your thoughts about the task. How you felt it went for you. Things you enjoyed. Parts you found difficult. What you might do differently next time. If perhaps you learned anything about yourself or gained any skills during your research or presentation.

Collection of Texts Task FAQ

What's it all about?

Your Collection of Texts Task involves selecting some of the written pieces you have worked on in Second and Third Year and redrafting them to make them even better. You should keep at least four pieces of work (texts) from four different genres (e.g. an opinion piece, a letter, a diary entry, a newspaper article, a poem, a film script, a story).

When do I redraft them?

Once you have your collection of texts, you should narrow them down to the best two. These are the ones you will redraft. They can't both be from the same genre (e.g. two letters or two diaries). Your teacher will help you pick the best two pieces to use.

When are they due?

They're due at Christmas of Third Year.

How do I redraft them?

Redrafting just means rewriting what you have to improve it. Tips for redrafting include checking things like spelling, grammar and punctuation. You should also see if there is anything you can do to make the piece read better, such as reorganising the information, better structuring the paragraphs, making it shorter or longer, or making the opening more interesting.

What exactly do I need to submit?

For each of your two pieces you should submit a draft, your final piece and your Student Reflection Note.

What is the Student Reflection Note?

This is where you write a brief note on each of your chosen texts. It should include:

- The title or genre
- A brief note on why you chose the genre/piece
- A reflection on the piece

What's involved in a personal reflection?

These are your thoughts about the task. How you felt it went for you. Things you enjoyed. Parts you found difficult. What you might do differently next time. If perhaps you learned anything about yourself or gained any skills during your research or presentation.

CHAPTER 1

Me and My World

My Learning Expectations

In this chapter I will:

- **Read** and **respond** to a variety of personal texts such as memoirs, diaries and blogs
- **Read/listen to** and **analyse** a variety of texts
- **Improve** my skills in **descriptive writing**
- Use and revise: **capital letters, nouns** and **adjectives, spelling, grammar** and **writing full sentences**
- **Learn** how to plan and **carry out** research
- **Develop** my teamwork skills doing group work
- **Improve** my essay-writing skills, particularly writing **personal essays**
- **Learn** how to use **paragraphs** and to **structure** my writing
- **Reflect** on how I learn and **identify** my strengths and weaknesses in English
- Set my own **learning goals** and identify my learning expectations
- **Evaluate** my own work and compare it to the work of my peers
- Read for enjoyment

Me and My World

Meditation XVII *by John Donne*

No man is an island, entire of itself; every man is a piece of the continent, a part of the main; if a clod be washed away by the sea, Europe is the less… Any man's death diminishes me, because I am involved in mankind; and therefore never send to know for whom the bell tolls; it tolls for thee.

The above text by the poet John Donne was written almost 400 years ago, but it is still relevant today. In *Great Expectations 1,* you may remember, we focused on learning about ourselves. We talked about our schools, our lives and books and films we enjoyed, and we recorded our personal responses to a variety of texts. In *Great Expectations 2*, we will continue this work but we will begin to explore the world around us by engaging with texts by writers from different places, backgrounds and cultures. We will see examples of other worlds that writers have imagined and experienced. We will investigate the history of our world through literature, ranging from drama extracts from the time of Shakespeare, to poetry written during wartime and to fiction written recently. By reading, analysing and responding to stories and personal accounts from other writers, we can learn how to reflect on and write about our own experiences.

You are one person in over 4 million living in Ireland, one in 742.5 million living in Europe and one in 7.125 billion in the world. Think of how vast the universe is. Think about a boy or girl the same age as you living in Manila, Bangkok, Montreal, New Orleans, Moscow, Sofia, anywhere… What are their lives like? What are their hopes, fears, dreams and challenges? What kinds of things influence their life? What do they do for fun and relaxation? What do you have in common with teenagers in other parts of the world? By thinking about these questions, we can begin to explore our place in the world.

A. Listening

Listen to the teenagers chatting on the audio clip and write a description of each person.

B. Oral Language

Discuss the following questions with the person beside you.

1. What are the top three countries that you would like to visit? Why?
2. Are there any countries you would not like to go to? Why?
3. Do you have relations or friends in other countries? Have you learned anything about those places?
4. How do you feel about travelling abroad? Do you like or dislike it?

C. Research

Choose five countries and fill in details about them in your copy. Use the headings in the table below, add in more headings if you wish. The first one has been done for you.

Country	Language	Capital	Food	Other aspect
India	Though 41% of the people speak Hindi, India has 22 official languages.	New Delhi	Mango	The national animal of India is the tiger.

Find the answers to the following questions and write them into your copy. Use capital letters where necessary.

1. Name three continents.
2. Name four countries in the eastern hemisphere.
3. What is the capital of China?
4. Japan is made up of four main islands. Name them.
5. Name three deserts in the world.
6. Name the longest river in the world.
7. What is the capital of Iceland?
8. List the languages spoken in Canada.
9. List the five counties in Connaught.
10. What is the largest ocean in the world?

D. Writing

While it is great to travel abroad, it's good to appreciate your home country also. Think about somewhere that you really like in either your home country or your native country. On **page 6** of your **PORTFOLIO**, write one paragraph explaining what makes it so appealing and attractive to you, including details about your chosen location. Remember that most writers work on a few drafts, changing around words and sentences to improve their text. Aim to improve your work by writing a couple of drafts.

Personal Writing

People choose to write about their own lives and experiences for many reasons. Perhaps they have witnessed a historical event first hand. Maybe they have led a long life and have seen interesting changes over time. Or, if they are well-known, they may be asked to write about themselves because people are interested in reading their story.

We already know that personal writing takes many forms. It can be a diary, a memoir, an autobiography or even a personal blog. What kind of personal writing have you done? Think about how often you update your Facebook status or Twitter account, or write a personal email, or a long text message. It's easy to see that we all have the urge to record our lives in some way, however small. Let's look at some features of good, descriptive personal writing.

Descriptive Writing

Descriptive writing is made up of creative words and sentences that help the reader to almost see, feel, taste, touch and hear what is being described.

Writers choose words very carefully – as carefully as you would choose what to wear when you want to impress someone or choose a gift for a friend.

Features of descriptive writing include:

- Appealing to the five senses (sight, sound, smell, taste and touch).
- Good use of verbs and adverbs.
- Good use of adjectives and nouns.
- Good use of similes, metaphors and personification.

Do you remember these features from last year?

Quick Revision

Verbs are action words (*dance, sing, sigh, skip*).

Adverbs modify verbs (dance *poorly*, sigh *contentedly*, skip *happily*), adjectives (a *very* funny laugh) or other adverbs (talked *quite* loudly).

Nouns are most of the things you see around you every day. A noun is a person, a place or a thing (nurse, cinema, car).

Adjectives describe nouns (*beautiful* day, *horrible* shirt, *cranky* child, *valiant* smile).

Similes are comparisons using 'like' or 'as'. For example, 'easy *as* Sunday morning'.

Metaphors are comparisons that do not use 'like' or 'as'. Metaphors say something is something else. For example, 'The moon is a golf ball and the frothy waves are lace decorating the shoreline.

Personification means giving human qualities to something. For example, 'The tree sighed', 'The sea roared'.

We will talk more about descriptive writing as we progress through *Great Expectations 2*. Let's read some samples of personal writing and think about the worlds the writers inhabit and why they have chosen to write about them.

Memoirs

You may remember memoirs from *Great Expectations 1*. We will now continue our study of these texts. Memoirs are a personal recollection of someone's memories and experiences, perhaps of their childhood, growing up, their career experiences or of high and low points in their life. What makes memoirs different from autobiographies is that they often focus on a single time or theme, rather than on an entire lifetime's worth of experiences.

 # Full On *by Ivan Yates*

Ivan Yates is an Irish radio broadcaster and a former business owner and politician. At one point in his career he owned a chain of betting shops. In this extract from his memoir, *Full On*, he talks about his early love of horse racing and betting.

One of my best friends at Aravon, Tim Bradford, who went regularly to race meetings, asked me one weekend if I'd like to go to Leopardstown with him and his father. Would I what! It was Fantasy Land: the beauty of the rippling equine muscles, the smell of the horses in the parade ring, the glorious colours of the racing silks worn by the jockeys, the tension of the grooms in the pre-parade ring saddling up, the roar of the crowd in the grandstand at the climax of the race, the thud of the horses jumping and landing at high speed, the buzz of the betting ring. I couldn't get enough of it. Mr Bradford wore a trilby, smoked a pipe and worked in Gallagher's large tobacco firm as company secretary. He heavily backed a winner at 5/4 that day and I was impressed to death.

At St Columba's College I befriended lads with racing connections. Captain Christy, the winner of the Cheltenham Gold Cup in 1974, was owned by the parents of a chap in my dormitory. I envied the fact that he was allowed out whenever the horse was running. I also got to know my classmate Paddy Cooper, whose father, Tom, was one of the top bloodstock agents and was buying the most expensive horses, with the best American pedigrees, for the legendary Vincent O'Brien and his various owners. I once asked Paddy which was the most exciting two-year-old his father had bought for them. 'My dad says watch out for The Minstrel' was the answer.

I backed this horse, with his chestnut coat and distinctive four white socks, every time he ran. He was beaten in the 2,000 Guineas but won both the Epsom Derby and the Irish Derby in 1977. My first visit to the Curragh coincided with The Minstrel running in the green and turquoise colours of Robert Sangster. During the summer months horses looked even better in their gleaming coats. Any horse carrying the rug with the initials MVO'B separated me from my cash, especially when Pat Eddery took over as stable jockey to Vincent O'Brien.

In later years I became an enthusiast for his horses, such as Roberto, Thatch, Lomond, Alleged, Artaius, Apalachee, Golden Fleece, Storm Bird and El Gran Señor. I backed quite a lot of bad ones as well.

Throughout my early adolescence, I was too young to be allowed into a betting shop, so I would engage assorted adults as runners to get down my bets. I got to know all the betting shops in Enniscorthy: Powers, Corcorans, Paddy Breen (a crafty old codger) and my idol Pete Lennon, who seemed to offer odds on everything that moved, displaying them on boards around the walls in bright marker colours. In the racetrack betting rings, I would seek out bookie Paddy 'Pro' Doyle from Enniscorthy. He wore a trilby and had a distinctive deep, husky voice. Instead of giving me a ticket to record my bet, he would say, 'Down to Ivan.' It made me feel like a trusted regular.

During the autumn and winter of 1973, I would bring my one-shilling pocket money each week to his shop to back Leeds United to win the Division One football championship. Under Don Revie, the club had been close to victory in the two previous seasons. At the weekends, I would check the results and marvel at the feats of Bremner, Clarke, Giles, Harvey and Hunter. They won the title that season. I duly collected a little bundle the following May. Another touch I pulled off, some years later, was in the Eurovision Song Contest. I recorded all the entries, and played them over and over again until I was sure that Bucks Fizz, representing the UK and singing 'Making Your Mind Up' was a certainty to win. I backed the group and collected a tidy sum.

I begged my mother during our holidays in Mayo to bring us to the races. I hadn't the patience for more rod fishing on the lake because I was catching damn-all. She kindly accompanied us to Tuam races on the Friday, after the three-day Galway race festival. The following year she brought us to the Galway races. It was a Thursday, the Galway Guinness Hurdle day. The crowds were so enormous that it was impossible to get a place in the stand. I backed a horse ridden by Ben de Haan in red colours. I was jumping up and down behind a throng of people to get a glimpse of the finish. He won. I was in seventh heaven. At twelve years of age, I vowed I would always come to this race meeting if I could. Annual repeat winners, like Spanner and Pinch Hitter, are still etched in my mind.

GLOSSARY

Trilby: A hat, made of soft felt, with a narrow brim and an indented crown.

Pedigree: The lineage or ancestry of a family; the descent of an animal, whether it is pure bred and of a good pedigree.

Distinctive: Something that stands out.

Throng: A crowd, mass, multitude or horde.

 # A. Reading

Rate this text for readability. Write the word/phrase of your choice into your copy.

VERY EASY ☐   **EASY** ☐   **OKAY** ☐   **HARD** ☐   **VERY HARD** ☐

 # B. Literacy Questions

1. Reread the writer's description of Leopardstown as 'Fantasy Land'. Identify and list three examples of good descriptive writing that help you to visualise the setting.

2. What impression do you get of the author as an adolescent boy? Support your points with quotations from the text.

3. List three pieces of information that inform the reader about life in Ireland in the 1970s.

 # C. Numeracy Question

The writer mentions his one shilling a week pocket money. Find out how much this would be worth in today's money.

 # D. Personal Writing – My Passion

It is obvious that, as a teenager, Ivan Yates was passionate about horse racing and enjoyed betting. What are you passionate about? On **page 7** of your **PORTFOLIO**, write one *descriptive* paragraph about your chosen topic. Try to be as descriptive and interesting as Ivan Yates is in the above text. You can look back at the features of descriptive writing on **page 4** if you need to.

 # E. Oral Language

Discuss the following question in pairs or groups.

Some people think that horse racing is a cruel sport. Do you agree or disagree? Why?

 # F. Reading – Self Assessment

Fill out the Self Assessment on **page 7** of your **PORTFOLIO**.

Salty Baby *by Orla Tinsley*

Orla Tinsley is a young Irish journalist. Her memoir, *Salty Baby*, talks about her life growing up with cystic fibrosis (CF). In this extract, she is in hospital at Christmas time.

1. There was just one thing all of us people with CF had in common: both of our parents were carriers of the gene, and it was just pure chance that they fell in love with each other and that they had a child with CF, something they didn't expect. And I felt guilty about that, that I couldn't be better for them, my parents. I wanted to be stronger, faster, more accomplished. Now, I was just a mess.

2. In order to combat the vomiting and weight loss, the doctors decided to feed me through a nasogastric (NG) tube because I wasn't keeping enough nutrients down. My concentration span became diluted from the continuous drugs and half-sleep. Thoughts jumped around my head, fighting for coherence, so I listened to music to drown them out – the Corrs, the *Heartbeat* soundtrack, Dusty Springfield, *Les Misérables*, anything by Andrew Lloyd Webber. At music summer camp when I was ten I had sung 'I Don't Know How to Love Him', from *Jesus Christ Superstar*, on stage. The words and the melody fused together like scent drifting from a fragrant candle. It moved me somewhere deep inside. I found songs that applied to what I was feeling, or an event that happened that day, or was going to happen later and I stuck myself inside the music, letting it seep through me and drag me into a subconscious plane. My eyes fell into a trance then, playing out scenarios and thinking and over-thinking. The best time to listen to music was at night. I used it to block out the feeling of the newly inserted NG feed plopping into my stomach through the tube in my nose.

3. When they took me out of the cubicle and sent me back to the ward, Marie was there for me again. I badly needed distraction from my own thoughts and feelings, and Marie could provide it. Neither of us wanted to be the one who went home first and left the other. Making the most of being in here was the fun part. Occasionally a nurse would come in and call 'Quiet Time' at us and make us separate and stay in our own beds for a few hours, but this particular night, we knew no one would be attempting to supervise our antics: it was the nurses' Christmas party. Once the day staff had trickled away, around 9pm, it was time for fun. Angela and Niamh were on duty that night, and Marie and I were going to have our Christmas 'Girlie Night' in with them. It was going to be better than the nurses' night out.

4. We started in the treatment room. The kitchen was tucked into a small space between it and the ward. I knew the combination to both. Someone had recorded two movies for the ward: *Clueless* and *My Girl*. We kept the tapes in Marie's room and watched them almost daily, fluctuating between the pain of losing Thomas J. to his bee allergy and the excitement and fear of high school. I wanted to be in both places, all at once: I wanted to be Vada and Cher and have both worlds. It would never be possible, I knew, but right here in our world it was. Here we could watch ourselves with the hopes, dreams and responsibilities of these roles and never have to play them. It was as though someone had built a house and trapped us in between the double-glazing. We understood what it was to be alive like no one else could, but life was not something we could touch.

5. That was why the make-over was such a good idea. That night Marie painted my nails perfectly with smooth strokes. When I painted hers I was less steady, but they turned out okay. Then we moved to our legs. Neither of us had ever waxed before and I can't remember how we came to the decision to do it. I think Marie's mother got the stuff for us. In the treatment room was a bed, covered in a crisp white blanket and pillow. It was the perfect beautician's bench. We filled two blue kidney bowls with water and set the wax strips alongside. After some poking and giggling, Marie started us on our rite of passage into adulthood. Like Cher and Dionne, I thought, in *Clueless*. But really it was more like the relationship between the main character, Cher, and the new girl, Tai. Cher showed Tai how to act, dress and exercise. She taught her how to be a girl.

6. Marie held the wax on as long as the instructions said, and then a little longer. We needed to make sure it would all come off. Marie yanked the strip and I wrinkled my nose, expecting my skin to rip off in one swoop. Ouccch! I called before looking up. From my knee down, the skin was perfectly smooth. My mother always said it didn't look like I had hair there anyway and I had believed her, but suddenly that 'invisible' hair was stuck all along the strip, bristly and bulging compared to smooth, panging red patch shining along my bone. I had to get more off. Marie went for it again, and I yelled more this time, but it was quicker and soon I was all done. I felt silky and smooth, as though I had slipped into new legs. It made me think of a scene from *Clueless* where Christian, a Billie Holiday-loving stud (played by Justin Walker), swings around to Cher in the classroom and picks up the pencil she had elbow-nudged over the desk. 'Nice stems,' he says. I acted out the scene for Marie and we giggled.

7. We bopped around the nurses' station, pleading with Angela to mark our coming-of-age with a Chinese takeaway. She finally relented and placed an order for us. We sat in the treatment room, marvelling at our legs and nails, waiting for our grub. Alma and Bernie's spare uniforms were hanging on hooks on the wall behind us. We looked at each other and, overcome by a wave of temporary insanity, we doubled over in laughter as we slipped the clothes off the hangers. I climbed into Alma's uniform and marvelled at how her trousers were too big for me – how could petite Alma be bigger than me? Marie had to hop into Bernie's because of her bad foot and we stood there, falling around with laughter until we were breathless. We walked to the kitchen and then dared each other – up the corridor then back? On tiptoes, biting our lips to stop the giggles, we remained calm and even smiled sweetly at a passing parent. As soon as the parent moved out of sight we burst into laughter and darted back to our den, ripping the clothes off as Angie called us for our food. She stuck her head round the door, 'What are you two up to?' She always knew when there was mischief afoot, and welcomed it. We stood in front of her with our pyjamas ruffled, red-faced. 'Best get plates!' I sang and skipped to the kitchen.

8. We ate our Chinese in the playroom. It was decorated with Winnie the Pooh and Tigger and had two large slide-up windows. You could sit on the sills watching the steam from the grey building downstairs rise outside and not have to breathe it in. There was swirling warmth in this room too – no other ward had that. We sat on the leather loungers, designed for parents to rest in. There was a small, grey TV and video combo sticking out of the wall high up in the corner, the sore thumb of the room. You could never tune RTÉ in on it properly and the only other option was to make Sonic the Hedgehog jump through hoops. We chatted in there and afterwards in my room, whispering so as not to wake the three other patients.

9. I lay in bed, Marie in the lounger beside me. We talked about people we knew in here. 'How's Eddie?' she asked. Eddie had had a tracheotomy tube since birth because he couldn't breathe properly or speak and he was in hospital a lot. He was about ten years old. My friend Matthew, who had CF too, had introduced me to him years earlier. Eddie was a lovely boy with light brown hair and piercing eyes. Eddie was dead.

'Eddie's dead, sorry,' I said, because it seemed like the only way to do it. Marie was like me, she didn't cry.

'The poor little mite, God rest him,' she said surprisingly fast and then she sat, mouth open, as though blowing an invisible bubble.

'Girls! Quiet. Time.' It was the other nurse, Niamh.

'Okay, just two minutes please, we've just— '

'No just. No buts. Bed!' I hated Niamh.

10. I lay in my bed, thinking about what I had told Marie and a shivering feeling throbbed in my chest. I felt it was my fault. I had said it wrong and I should have timed it better. I lay flat and felt a warm pool hover in my stomach, like a mini sea full of wrecked ships waiting to be fished out. I let them come up my oesophagus. Relief. I heaved the lumps into the blue bowl, brown against blue always showed up the contents starkly. Half-digested chicken curry. I had eaten the whole thing because I could, because there were no rules and there was no one to stop me.

GLOSSARY

Cystic fibrosis: A hereditary disorder affecting the exocrine glands. It results in thick mucus which may block glands and lead to infections.

Coherence: Logical, ordered, unified, coherent.

Fluctuating: To vary, differ, alter.

Accomplished: Highly skilled or trained.

Combat: To take action to prevent, or to engage in a fight against.

Nasogastric tube: A slim tube inserted through the nose to reach the stomach.

A. Reading

Rate this text for readability. Write the word/phrase of your choice into your copy.

VERY EASY ☐   **EASY** ☐   **OKAY** ☐   **HARD** ☐   **VERY HARD** ☐

 ## B. Literacy Questions

1. Why does Orla have cystic fibrosis?
2. How do songs and music help Orla to deal with her situation?
3. 'We understood what it was to be alive like no one else could, but life was not something we could touch.' What do you think Orla means by this statement? Read paragraph 4 again to figure this out.
4. Explain your response to Orla's memoir. How does it make you feel? You can use the list of questions below to help you with your answer.
5. List two examples of descriptive writing from the extract that appealed to you.

 ## C. Pairwork

Imagine that you have the opportunity to interview Orla Tinsley for your school magazine. With a partner, make a list of five questions that you might ask Orla.

 ## D. Writing

Paragraph 8 in Orla Tinsley's memoir describes the playroom very effectively. Read it again and describe a room of your choice. It can be any room you like. Try to do as Orla did and include objects, colours and smells.

  ## E. Reading – Self Assessment

Fill out the self assessment on **page 8** of your **PORTFOLIO**.

My Response to Texts

Having read two memoirs, think about how you responded to them. Consider the impact texts have on you. Fill out your responses on **page 8** of your **PORTFOLIO**.

Ask Yourself:

- What did you discover?
- What do you think about it? Can you explain/understand it?
- How do you feel about the text/topic/issue?
- What ideas do you have about the text/topic/issue?
- Did it inspire you?
- What did you already know about it?
- What have you learned that is new?

Capital Letters

Let's revise what we learned about capital letters in *Great Expectations 1*.

Capital letters are used for:

- **Names** of places (people, cities, towns, countries, rivers, mountains, continents, planets, oceans, seas, etc.) companies and products.
- **At the start of sentences**. For example, '**A** big, grey gander it was.'
- **Titles** of books, plays, poems, films and TV programmes.
- **Days** of the week and **months** of the year, but not for seasons.

A. Writing

Rewrite the following sentences, inserting capital letters where they belong.

1. Mico laughed out loud as he thought of peter lost in boston.
2. The volga river flows through moscow in russia.
3. Mark twain was born in missouri in November, 1835. his real name is samuel langhorne clemens.
4. Robert louis stevenson wrote the story of dr Jekyll and mr hyde in 1886.
5. Juan likes special k for breakfast but iga prefers shreddies and bob likes porridge.
6. The film *frozen* stars kristen bell, idina menzel, jonathan groff and josh gad.
7. Henry ford began making cars in the early 1900s and in 1908 made the famous model T car.
8. Petra kvitová won the wimbledon ladies' singles title in 2014.
9. Lidl, aldi, tesco, dunnes and supervalu are the main supermarkets in Ireland.
10. Man united play at old trafford and liverpool play at anfield.

B. Writing

Rewrite the following paragraph, inserting capital letters and full stops.

The first films, made in the early 1900s, were silent and were in black and white sound was developed after 1927 comedies starring charlie chaplin and buster keaton were popular famous silent comedians included laurel and hardy and the little rascals laurel and hardy and the three stooges were slapstick comedians this means they fell over, tripped up, hit each other and generally clowned about walt disney set up a cartoon studio in hollywood in 1923 and developed animation his most successful early films include *snow white and the seven dwarfs*, *pinocchio* and *bambi* post-1945 he had success with *alice in wonderland*, *peter pan* and *cinderella* in the late 1940s walt disney thought about building a theme park, disneyland disneyland opened on 17 July 1955 in los angeles.

C. Writing

Correct the mistakes in the following text. Rewrite it, putting in capital letters where they belong, removing them where they do not belong and correcting punctuation errors.

The gaa was Founded in hayes hotel, thurles in 1884 by Michael cusack and Maurice davin. archBishop Thomas William croke was the First Patron of the association. He Died in 1902 and the gaa decided to erect a Memorial in his honour. They fundraised and bought jones Road sports ground in 1913 which they Renamed crokeparK. The Tailteann games were held in croke park in 1924 and the government gave the gaa £10,000 to upgrade the park, they used this to build the Hogan stand. The first president of Ireland was douglas hyde, elected in 1937. He was also a patron of the gaa. He was removed as Patron of the Organisation in 1938 for disobeying the Rules about the 'exclusion of foreign games', when he attended (in an official capacity) an international soccer match in dalymount Park between Ireland and poland. When world war II broke out in 1939 restrictions on travel and fuel affected matches and training and reduced the number of events being held. In 1961 Telefís éireann (now RTÉ) was set up and began televising gaa matches. Nineteen eighty-four marked the Centenary of the gaa and the all Ireland hurling final was played in thurles that year. Sponsorship of jerseys was introduced in 1991 and in 1993 redevelopment of croke park began section by section. In 2003 when the work was completed it had a capacity of 82,300 and the world Special Olympics were held there.

Sentences

You need to put the words in a sentence in the correct order, so that the sentence sounds right and makes sense.

Rewrite the following sentences so that they make sense. As well as correcting the word order, you may have to change the tense of some words and make other corrections.

1. Zara her homework done quick then spent two hours on Facebook.
2. Ken could of lawn the mowed but was simply to lazy too.
3. The children ought to have healthy snacks ate rather than junk food.
4. Alice was wanting the cinema to go to after she done her homework.
5. It were raining so heavily that they could not see to where they were going.

Syntax means the order of words to form a sentence. Usually, the order is **subject**, **verb**, **object**.

- The dog ran across the road: *Dog* is the **subject**. *Ran* is the **verb**. *Road* is the **object**. *The* is the **definite article** and *across* is a **preposition**. Prepositions are the words that show the relationship between a noun and another word in the sentence.

The **subject** in a sentence is the main, central or important thing in the sentence. The **subject** is doing/saying something, or something is happening to them. So the **subject** is the word in a sentence which is most connected to the **verb** (action word).

- The children screamed: *The* is the **definite article** referring to the children. *Children* is the **noun** and is the **subject** in the sentence: the sentence is about children. *Screamed* is the **verb**.

To find the **subject**, look for the **verb** and ask 'what or who?'. The **subject** of a sentence is the 'do-er' of the action.

- The car sped away: *Car* is the **subject**. *Sped* is the **verb**.
- Lions roar when they are hungry: *Lions* is the **subject**. *Roar* is the **verb**.
- The cat purred: *Cat* is the **subject**. *Purred* is the **verb**.
- Thunder roared. Lightning flashed. Rain pelted down: *Thunder*, *lightning* and *rain* are the **subjects**. The **verbs** are *roared, flashed* and *pelted*.
- The birds chirped loudly in the early morning light: The **verb** is *chirped*.
- Ivana strolled aimlessly around Hyde Park: The **verb** is *strolled*.
- The children screamed happily as they whizzed down the water slide: *Happily* is an **adverb** describing how they screamed. *As* is a **preposition**. *They* is a **personal pronoun** used instead of repeating the **noun** *children*. *Whizzed* is a **verb**. *Down* is a **preposition**. *The* is the **definite article**. *Water* and *slide* are **nouns**.

Remember, you don't need to learn all of these things at once. You can refer back to this section when you are writing or redrafting your work.

A. Writing

Identify the subject and the verb in the following sentences. Write the answers into your copy.

Sentence	Subject	Verb
The witch cackled.		
Owls hoot at night.		
Waves dance in light breezes.		
Thomas gobbled the cake.		
Síne sang sweetly.		
Rotten eggs stink.		
Autumn leaves tumble down.		
The bells rang softly.		
Hermione defeated him again.		
The audience clapped enthusiastically.		

 ## B. Pairwork

A. In pairs, identify the subject in each of the following sentences.

1. Tom whistled as he worked.
2. The clowns were having as much fun as the children.
3. Rhona and Donal argued over the outcome of the match.
4. They weren't sure if they'd lost the mobile phone in the cinema or in the café.
5. The zookeeper wished that the animals weren't so restless.
6. The hungry dog barked incessantly outside the back door.
7. Grass grows quietly and stealthily.
8. Weeds insidiously strangle flowers.
9. She dolloped cream into the steaming coffee.
10. They thought deeply about what had occurred.

B. In pairs, write five sentences and underline the subject in each sentence.

 ## C. Visual Literacy

In pairs, chat about the images below and then make a list of interesting adjectives describing the nouns in the pictures. For example, the second picture depicts a small, cute, cosy, grey-and-white-striped kitten. See how creative and inventive you can be with your words.

Personal Blogs

A personal blog is like a diary. The writer records their thoughts on a regular basis. Sometimes they focus on a particular theme or simply reflect on their day-to-day life. They do this online, where readers can keep up with the blogger's life and sometimes comment on the posts or interact with the writer. In the following texts, you will see how bloggers can use stories and details from their lives to inform, entertain and make us think about the world around us.

Legless in Dublin *by Louise Bruton*

Louise Bruton is a young Irish journalist who uses a wheelchair. Her blog, Legless in Dublin, is about navigating the city in her chair. In this blog post, she talks about being fitted for a new chair.

Not a single day goes by where I don't realise that I am in a wheelchair. This is stating the bleedin' obvious. Hopping out of bed every morning and into the chair. Hoping my dog isn't sitting underneath the wheel when I move. Loading the chair into the passenger seat before I drive my car. These are the everyday things that I do with my chair that are a reminder but not an examination.

I am in the process of being measured and fitted for a new wheelchair and it is a draining experience. What tyres would you like? What brakes would you like? What angle do you want your spine tilted at? What colour do you want? Do you want mud guards? Do you want arm rests? How high do you want your knees raised? How long do you want the seat to be?

I am being measured in centimetres and inches. I am thoroughly being examined.

Every other day, I can brush off the fact that I am in a wheelchair but when you have to describe to the millimetre what you need, you're being asked to look at things that you normally try to brush past and forget. Or, if you don't know what you want, you are being told what other people have and it's suggested that you go with it.

I made the grave error in asking for an arm rest that's strong enough for me to sit on at concerts. Being at crotch level means that I need an extra bump to see the stage so this request makes sense to me. "You're not meant to be sitting on arm rests. They're not strong enough." Oh, Lord! If they saw me swinging out of the arm rests during Kelis's set at Electric Picnic this year or even sitting on them so I can reach the wine glasses on the top shelf in my kitchen, then they would know that they're doing the job.

The initial design of a wheelchair is never my actual intention. I have said so many times that there is no blueprint for disability. I am in no way delicate. I fling myself about. I climb, I roll and I tumble and I need a chair that can do all of that with me.

Getting fitted for a wheelchair is like being fitted for a permanent office chair. It's in a fixed position so what you order is what you will be sitting in for the majority of the day. In work. In the pub. Walking down the street. Going to your friend's house. Stumbling home at 6am. Your permanent office chair is there and you want it to be perfect. You don't want to feel restricted by your chair and in my case, when the chair is lying flat on its back on a beach and me roaring laughing, you don't want your chair to prevent whatever unplanned rolls and tumbles lie in your future.

Imagine being presented to a plastic surgeon and being told the options of what you could change about your body. Initially, you don't think that you have any body issues but when the list goes on and on... well, you definitely don't feel like a Kardashian by the end of it.

Unfortunately, so many people look in the mirror and do not like what they see. Sadly, today is one of those days where I have to stare at my reflection and examine every square inch of me and the chair. It's the grand admittance of having a chair. It's not just me anymore. I come with spokes, wheels and – rules be damned – soon I'll come with arm rests strong enough to sit me and whoever is sitting on my knee.

A. Reading

Rate this text for readability. Write the word/phrase of your choice into your copy.

VERY EASY ☐   **EASY** ☐   **OKAY** ☐   **HARD** ☐   **VERY HARD** ☐

B. Literacy Questions

1. What kinds of things does Louise have to think about that non-wheelchair users do not? You may refer to the text in your answer.

2. In what ways does Louise use her chair that you might not have expected?

C. Writing

Write a paragraph or more about your own experience of disability. Write about how you have experienced disability or about someone that you know. In your writing, consider the good and the bad times you have experienced.

D. Research

Have you seen the film *Inside I'm Dancing*? It's worth watching. It's funny and poignant and gets you thinking about the issues surrounding disabilities in society.

Starry, Starry Night *by Wil Wheaton*

Wil Wheaton is an American actor and writer. In the following post from his blog, wilwheaton.net, he is woken by his wife Anne to witness a meteor shower.

1. I stayed up until almost one this morning, reading comic books. I know, it's like I'm 12 all over again. And it's awesome.

    Around four, Anne woke me up.

    "What's wrong?" I said, while I was still waiting to clear immigration between Dreamland and Reality.

    "Nothing. I just couldn't sleep, so I got up and went outside to watch the meteor shower. It's really cool, and I knew you'd want to see it." I sat up, pushed the covers to one side, and ignored the grumbling protests of our dog, who had just lost his primary source of warmth and cuddling.

    "It's cold out, though, so put something warm on."

    I grabbed a hoodie and put on my totally-not-lame-but-always-make-me-feel-self-conscious-to-wear-them slippers. I walked through the dark house, past the quiet and strangely comforting hum of my aquarium's filter, and out onto our patio.

2. I know it's cliché, but the stars were brilliant jewels against a field of black velvet. Betelgeuse was a brilliant red. The Orion Nebula was bright and fuzzy. Sirius, in Canis Major, was such a bright bluish-white I couldn't look directly at it. To the North, Ursa Major dominated the sky, and I could even see Mizar without any effort. Back on Earth, a distant train's whistle sounded from far away, probably from the train yard near Commerce.

3. "You just missed a fireball," Anne said, quietly. She pointed to the Eastern sky and added, "and there have been tons of little flashes from over there, too."

    I wrapped my arms around myself to stay warm and let my eyes roam across the sky. I didn't see any fireballs, but I saw lots of meteors fly across the sky, greenish and yellowish trails flashing then fading behind them.

    Maybe it's because I wasn't entirely awake, or maybe it's because I'd been reading about mutants and other worlds before I went to sleep, but as I looked up into the sky, toward Castor and Pollux, I really felt, for the first time in my entire 38 years on this planet, the overwhelming vastness of the universe.

4. Where I have always felt awe, I felt small. Where I have always felt inspiration, I felt vulnerable. *"I'm on a planet, spinning on its axis, racing around a star, moving faster than my mind can comprehend, through that,"* I thought. *"And right now, that planet is flying through an ancient asteroid debris, bits of dust and rock smacking into its atmosphere like bugs against a windshield."* I felt a little freaked out.

5. I've quoted Carl Sagan's *Pale Blue Dot* so many times, I don't need to look it up anymore to get it right, but last night, looking up into the enormity of the universe, it was suddenly more than poetry and a reminder to take better care of each other.

I moved closer to Anne and put my arms around her. She leaned her head back against my chest and we looked up into the sky together, watching faint meteors streak across the sky every few seconds.

"I'm glad you woke me up," I whispered. "Thank you."

"I'm sorry you didn't get to see the fireballs," she said.

"Nah, it's okay. I didn't need to."

The train's whistle sounded again. This time, it didn't seem so far away.

We stood there and watched the sky for several minutes, until our hands and feet were numb with the cold, and went back inside. When I got back into bed, I pulled the covers up over my head, and tucked them around myself as tightly as I could. It took a long while for sleep to reclaim me.

 ## A. Reading

Rate this text for readability. Write the word/phrase of your choice into your copy.

VERY EASY ☐   **EASY** ☐   **OKAY** ☐   **HARD** ☐   **VERY HARD** ☐

 ## B. Literacy Questions

1. Why did the author stay up until 1am?
2. Why did Anne wake him up at 4am?
3. Identify and explain the metaphor about the stars.
4. What impression do you get of the relationship between the author and Anne? Use quotes to support your answer.
5. '… looking up into the enormity of the universe, it was suddenly more than poetry and a reminder to take better care of each other'.

   Try to explain the impact that looking at the stars at 4am had on the author.

 ## C. Writing

Think about a similar experience that you have had. Perhaps you were in awe of or were inspired by the stars, a glorious sunset, a beautiful dawn, a fabulous snow scene, or another breathtaking view or experience of nature. Write a short paragraph explaining what you saw and the impact it had on you.

 ## D. Research

For centuries people have been fascinated by astronomy. Why not research the stars named in the extract and write a brief sentence or two about each one?

The stars also feature repeatedly in literature in plays, novels and poems. For example:

William Shakespeare	*King Lear*	**Kent** 'It is the stars,/ The stars above us, govern our conditions'
Seán O'Casey	*Juno and the Paycock*	**Boyle** 'What is the stars, what is the stars?'

Do some research and find other examples where the stars feature as a symbol, motif or metaphor in drama, fiction or poetry.

A Week Without My Smartphone *by Laura Carland*

Laura Carland is an Irish blogger based in Belfast. When she accepted a challenge to live without her smartphone for one week, she wrote a daily blog recording life without the device. In the following extract she recounts the first three days of her challenge.

MONDAY

9:30
I have slept in. I check my alarm clock and realise I didn't set it properly. I am shockingly late for work and must run for the bus. Having left my iPhone at home to resist temptation, I have no method of contacting my boss about why I'm not sitting at my desk wearing my usual 'I wish I was dead' face.

9:50
The bus stop. Someone has ripped the timetable from the post and I have no idea when the bus is going to arrive.

10:00
I am genuinely at a loss to remember how I survived bus stops before I gave in to peer pressure and got a smartphone. These last ten minutes have been amongst the longest of my life. People are passing by, looking at me silently stare straight ahead with an emptiness in my eyes they cannot fathom.

11:10
I decide to not tell my boss *why* I have purposely left my iPhone at home because one doesn't need one's employer knowing that one is willing to carry over silly challenges from the weekend. I am told to try to use a payphone next time so they know I haven't tripped and fallen into a ravine or been eaten by badgers during the night. Given that everyone and their granny has a mobile now, I wonder if payphones still exist. This passes a few minutes and I make a mental note to think about payphones again next time I'm at a bus stop.

11:20–17:00
INTERNET. PRECIOUS, PRECIOUS INTERNET.

17:30
This bus timetable clearly hasn't been updated in years. I will be standing here until I am but a scorched mark upon the earth.

17:32   I think about payphones and realise that since mobiles have eroded my ability to remember telephone numbers, if I found a phone box, I wouldn't be able to call anyone anyway.

17:33   I AM SO BORED.

17:45   I make another mental note to bring a book tomorrow. It didn't occur to me how much time I have in between 'using my smartphone' and 'doing something where I cannot physically use my smartphone'. I think of the marvellous possibility of the week and what I can achieve without an attention-seeking blinking tablet in my hands. I could paint something. Think of the writing I could do! I could finally make a sizeable dent in that pile of books I've yet to read! Yes, t'would be a week of opportunity.

17:46   I WANT MY PHOOONE. Something could be happening on Twitter, something *exciting* and by the time I get home all the fuss will have passed and anything I say will be old news. This is horrible.

18:01   The bus is eerily quiet. It occurs to me that I am the only disconnected human being on this bus. Everyone else is locked to a screen or a device, cutting them off from the outside world. The weather is melancholic but beautiful and they don't even look up to appreciate it.

18:30–22:00   INTERNET. PRECIOUS, PRECIOUS INTERNET.

22:10   I find my phone and hold it to my cheek. *Only six days to go, my beloved. Only six days to go.*

TUESDAY

8:20   I have slept in. Again.

8:30   Against all my better judgment, I take my phone with me. I can't risk getting into a situation where I can't contact someone in an emergency. *Yes, an 'emergency'. You tell yourself that, Laura. You utter, utter failure.*

8:45   I text back some friends. It feels nice to use the little chap. I'm not cheating unless I launch an app or any other unique-to-a-smartphone novelty but the temptation is great. Apps. Oh how much you want them when you can't have them and when you can have them you don't want to use them because Temple Run is a stupid game anyway.

8:46   I really, really, really want to play Temple Run.

9:00–16:50   INTERNET. SWEET GIFT FROM THE GODS. INTERNET!

17:40   I have forgotten the book I made a mental note to remember yesterday. Is that ironic? I genuinely can't remember. Over the years, old knowledge has been pushed out of my brain to make way for necessary skills like 'thumb swiping' and 'How to connect my Apple products to my worn, wire-exposing cable I'm too cheap to replace, without being electrocuted'. I don't need to store knowledge in my brain anyway. That's what Safari is for on my phone. It's my source of knowledge. I think about 'irony' and that passes the time for a minute. I should have made a mental note to write it down in the notebook I also made a mental note to remember but forgot. My mental notes are *useless.*

17:41   God, writing in a notebook makes me look *so arty*. This feels *brilliant*. Ha! A stranger is looking at me. They probably assume I'm furiously scribbling the next great novel of my generation. Little do they know I'm drawing a rebellious pig on a skateboard.

17:45   Apparently, there is a new Frankie and Benny's opening in a street somewhere in Belfast. I find this out from a billboard. Most of my information these days comes from my Twitter app so this is refreshing. It's nice to decide when *I* want to see advertising rather than being bombarded by, and subsequently having to wade through, flashing, desperately needy pop-ups. I don't know the street the new restaurant is on. I go to look it up and then curse silently to myself.

17:47   I ask the person sitting next to me where in Belfast I would find the 'Hillsborough Road'. They tell me it's in Lisburn; a completely different town. Well that made me look stupid. Without my Google Maps app to stop me being lost and confused, I must remain lost and confused.

17:55   I am making an old woman feel uncomfortable because I have been staring blankly at her from my seat on the bus and didn't notice. If I had my iPhone, I'd be so distracted I wouldn't even know I was *on* a bus.

19:30   There is a light on in my bag. My iPhone has knocked against something inside and an app has popped up. I squint with one eye and don't look out of the other. It's… it's Angry Birds. Oh. My. God. I feel my fingers reach down to pick up the phone to play but I resist. Barely. The temptation is too great. Tomorrow, the phone has to stay at home.

WEDNESDAY

8:30   Slept in. Again. It seems that I have no idea how to use an alarm clock. The aforementioned alarm clock gets thrown against the wall.

10:00–16.50   Mercifully I am so busy drowning in spreadsheets I have no time to think about smartphones.

16:55   There is smoke on the horizon. A fire. A big fire indeed. There are helicopters circling the blaze. Helicopters are common in Belfast because we're always up to something but this was different. There were *many* helicopters. Something is happening. Something that requires the emergency services and I have absolutely no way of finding out what. I am very unsettled without my smartphone nearby. Being unable to use my smartphone is like having an itch I just can't scratch. It's like permanently walking around having forgotten to put on underwear. It's disconcerting just being unable to hold it. I'm *always* holding it, like an extension of myself, often gazing down at it making sure it hasn't been snatched from my grip by pixies.

17:50   I watch the news on TV to find out about the blaze. The fire was from rioting. The usual. Watching the news on TV is frustrating. I wonder what I did before I could receive only the information I was interested in. With my smartphone I've the ability to filter my news, which makes me realise just how little I subject myself to bad news, subconsciously protecting myself from the horrors of the world. This unfiltered news is very depressing.

18:00   Mmm my dinner is *delicious*. I want to Instagram it to remember it FOREVER (!!!) but I cannot. Part of my soul breaks. Why the hell would I want a photograph of my dinner anyway? What a pointless thing to take a picture of. 'Gather round, children, and I'll show you a photo of a bloody good steak I had one time that I artificially aged for artistic purposes.'

18:30–22:00   I sit down to properly catch up on some Social Networking via THE INTERNET, PRECIOUS, PRECIOUS INTERNET, and discover I haven't really missed much. You assume that by being disconnected you are missing *everything* – scandal, weddings, photos, controversial statements, a good debate – but nothing has really happened. When you dedicate time to social networking in one chunk rather than digesting it slowly in tidbits throughout the average day, there isn't really a lot of substance. Facebook is a landscape full of faces of people I barely know littering my timeline with photos of their babies; and Twitter, whilst great in slices, is just a long block of nothing blurring into one. Emails are also harder to answer in a block and I find myself closing the laptop and wondering what is happening outside.

23:00   I smile knowing that I have the rest of the week off. No need to set an alarm. No need to fret about missing out because I'd have the internet handy at home. Yes. This would be an easy challenge after all.

A. Reading

Rate this text for readability. Write the word/phrase of your choice into your copy.

VERY EASY ☐   **EASY** ☐   **OKAY** ☐   **HARD** ☐   **VERY HARD** ☐

 ## B. Literacy Questions

1. How many times did Laura sleep in during the challenge?

2. What city is Laura living in?

3. Identify one example of exaggeration (hyperbole) in the blog post. What effect does exaggeration have on a reader (i.e. how do you react to it)?

4. What kind of job does Laura have? What does she do at work? Support your answer with quotes.

5. Explain why Laura's 'mental notes are *useless*'.

6. Laura suggests that people who are using devices all the time are actually in another world. Find one example in the blog that proves this.

7. Laura wants the best of both worlds. Copy the following table, then find and list the positives and negatives that Laura identifies with smartphones.

Positive	Negative
filter the news on her phone	desperately needy pop-ups

 ## C. Writing

Do as Laura did! Survive without your smartphone for a week. Copy the format and style of Laura's blog to write your own daily blog. Use the template on **page 10** of your **PORTFOLIO**. Write a few drafts until you are happy with a final one.

Swap blogs, compare them and enjoy reading what others have written.

 ## D. Oral Language

'Facebook is a landscape full of faces of people I barely know littering my timeline with photos of their babies; and Twitter, whilst great in slices, is just a long block of nothing blurring into one.'

Do you agree with Laura's view of Facebook and Twitter? Have a debate about it. Find out more about how to debate on **page 238** of Chapter 4.

Descriptive Writing

The Five Senses

People and animals rely on their five senses to survive: the sense of sight, the sense of sound, the sense of smell, the sense of taste and the sense of touch. Imagine not having one or more of these senses. Some people do not have all five senses and it makes daily life far more challenging. When you are writing, try to make your text more real for your readers by appealing to the five senses. Help the readers to almost see, hear, smell, taste and touch what you are writing about. Read the following examples.

Sight

Then the schoolhouse chimney caught on fire. A fountain of sparks shot high into the night, writhing and sweeping on the wind, falling and dancing along the road. The chimney hissed like a firework, great rockets of flame came gushing forth, emptying the tiny house, so that I expected to see chairs and tables, knives and forks, radiant and burning, follow. The moss-tiles smouldered with sulphurous soot, yellow jets of smoke belched from cracks in the chimney. We stood in the rain and watched it entranced…

From **Cider With Rosie** by **Laurie Lee**

Sound

The Iban laughed. The river grew louder in the darkness. Something hooted. Something screamed in earnest further off. Something shuffled and snuffled around the discarded rice and fish bits flung in a bush from our plates.

From **Into the Heart of Borneo** by **Redmond O'Hanlon**

Smell

We came on the wind of the carnival. A warm wind for February, laden with the hot greasy scents of frying pancakes and sausages and powdery-sweet waffles cooked on the hotplate right there by the roadside…

From **Chocolat** by **Joanne Harris**

Taste

… one nibbled one's way like a rat through roots and leaves. Peas rolled under the tongue, fresh, cold, like solid water; teeth chewed green peel of apples, acid sharp, and the sweet white starch of swede… Slivers of raw pastry, moulded, warm, went down in the shapes of men and women…

From **Cider with Rosie** by **Laurie Lee**

Touch

The Beast was on the stairs. Buddy floated down to him. The Beast opened his mouth and something black flicked across his lips. Was his tongue black? It wasn't a tongue, it was the tip of a tail. A centipede's tail.

The Beast reached up and grabbed hold of it and it wriggled between his fingers. He started to pull and, inch by inch, the body started to come out, hundreds of legs writhing at the side. It was huge – as wide as a tie. The Beast was dragging it out of his mouth like a sailor pulling on a rope. Hand after hand. Yards of it. Black, scaly, shining with the juices from the Beast's throat. And at last, the head was there – its jaws pinched tight on something pink. It was the Beast's stomach. The centipede was fixed to it and if the Beast kept pulling he would turn himself inside out. Buddy screamed and the Beast let go. The centipede shot back down inside him.

From **Buddy** by **Nigel Hinton**

A. Writing

Can you find and list four examples of descriptive writing from the following extracts? Look for similes, metaphors, descriptive verbs, adjectives, personification and other examples of descriptive writing.

1.

The flickering lights of the trashed supermarket threw deep shadows from dark places, and Stephanie stepped through it all with one hand wrapped tightly round the golden Sceptre. Rows of shelves lay toppled against each other in a domino-sprawl of scattered food tins and ketchup bottles. She caught the scent of a small ocean of spilled vinegar and glanced to her right in time to catch a flash of pinstripe. Then she was alone again in this half-collapsed maze, the only sound the gentle hum from the freezers.

She edged into the darkness and out again into the light. Slow steps and quiet ones and once more the darkness swallowed her in its cold hunger. The maze opened before her. A man hovered there, a metre off the ground, as if he were lying on an invisible bed. His hands were clasped on his belly, and his eyes were closed.

Stephanie raised the Sceptre.

From *Skulduggery Pleasant: The Dying of the Light* by **Derek Landy**

2.

The fire behind me is burning bright as day and I can see that the girl's pyjamas don't have any holes in them at all. Not from ash or bullets. The only medical condition I can find is a big bruise on her forehead.

I grab a feather and hold it in front of her face, but I don't need to because when I crouch closer I can hear the snot rattling in her nose.

It's loud, but not as loud as the car engine noise I suddenly hear in the distance.

I peer over towards the road.

Coming along it fast are two black cars. They look just like the Nazi cars that came to the orphanage.

The Nazis must be coming back here to the scene of their crime to get rid of the evidence. I've read about this type of criminal behaviour in stories.

I haul the unconscious girl up onto my back and stagger through the smoke and sparks towards the fence. The hot wire burns my arm as I squeeze through, but I don't care. I just want to get me and this poor orphan safely hidden in the cabbages.

'What's your name?' I ask the girl for about the hundredth time as we trudge along the dark road.

Actually it's just me doing the trudging. She's still on my back, her arms round my neck.

As usual she doesn't reply. The only way I know she's awake and not unconscious is when I look over my shoulder at her and see the moonlight gleaming in her dark eyes.

From *Once* by **Morris Gleitzman**

B. Writing

1. Read the following text. In your copy, fill in the blanks, using the descriptive words below.

poisonous • darkest • new • sulphur • deepest • raspberry • secret • hot

I made myself a _____ milkshake and heated it up in the microwave and then went through to the living room to watch one of my *Blue Planet* videos about life in the _____ parts of the ocean.

The video was about the sea creatures who live around _____ chimneys, which are underwater volcanoes where gases are ejected from the earth's crust into the water. Scientists never expected there to be any living organisms there because it was so _____ and so _____, but there are whole ecosystems there.

I like this bit because it shows you that there is always something _____ that science can discover, and all the facts that you take for granted can be completely wrong. And I also like the fact that they are filming in a place which is harder to get to than the top of Mount Everest but is only a few miles away from sea-level. And it is one of the quietest and _____ and most _____ places on the surface of the earth. And I like imagining that I am there sometimes…

From ***The Curious Incident of the Dog in the Night-time*** by **Mark Haddon**

2. Think about your morning routine at home. Using as many of the senses as you can, try to describe it in five sentences or more. For example:

1. The swish and clank of curtain rails in my parents' room wakes me every morning.

2. I clamber groggily out of bed, hear a toilet flushing, a microwave droning, a press door slamming.

3. I shiver as my bare feet pad along the ice-cold kitchen tiles.

4. Weak sunlight illuminates the dining room.

5. I stare sleepily at the dew-drenched lawn and munch the soggy, sweet cornflakes, which I have doused liberally with sugar and warm milk.

6. Quickly dressing, I…

Nouns and Adjectives

A **noun** is the name given to a person, a place or a thing. There are four types of noun:

Common nouns	door, car, lamp, bag, apple, hose, sand, mouse, phone.
Collective nouns	a *swarm* of bees, a *pride* of lions, a *bouquet* of flowers.
Abstract nouns	beauty, love, friendship, jealousy, greed, hate, warmth.
Proper nouns	Canada, Tramore, Donegal, Sam, Ariel, Miranda.

Adjectives describe nouns. For example, the *freezing* snow, the *cool* breeze, the *hot* dinner, the *icy* glare.

Writing

A. Identify the nouns in the following sentences. List them in your copy.

1. Zoe packed her beachwear, sandals and towel, then slung the bag across her shoulder.
2. Rotten apples, wrinkly and oozing brown sludge, smeared the inside of the schoolbag.
3. Hot, spicy peppers, potatoes, chicken, mushrooms and onions sizzled in the enormous, black, heavy-duty wok.
4. The ski slopes gleamed in the dazzling sunlight, almost blinding her vision.
5. Ghosts, secrets, thieves, vampires and goblins made it a very exciting read.
6. Donal wore tattered robes and old sandals, dragging a brown bag behind him.
7. The log cabin in Austria looked warm and inviting, its light guiding them along.
8. Fish darted about nervously, gills pulsing wildly as the black net approached.
9. The library was old-fashioned, with faded carpets, worn desks and tatty books.
10. Simon counted three rabbits, a piglet, four hens, two kittens and four pups on the farm.

B. Adjectives describe nouns and make them interesting. For example: the *wizened* old witch, the *spooky* castle, the *tiger-skin* rug, the *magic* carpet, the *creepy* tunnel, the *delicious* ice-cream.

In your copy, fill in interesting adjectives for each of the following sentences.

1. He raced up the _____ stairs to the _____ tower and seized the _____ sword with which he smote the _____ dragon.
2. The cook chopped the _____ vegetables, sliced the _____ bread and stirred the saucepan of _____ rice.
3. A _____ breeze stirred the _____ evening. _____ stars began to peep from the _____ sky.
4. Slowly lifting the _____ oars, she rowed wearily to the _____ shore.
5. The _____ shoes were too tight, the _____ old ones were _____ and far more _____.
6. Sam flung the _____ sword at the half-dead _____ monster.
7. Their _____ wellies were much admired by the fashion experts.
8. Snarling and growling hungrily, the tiger pounced on the _____ bird.
9. _____fog obscured their view of the _____ harbour, yet they sailed on.
10. Waves danced merrily as the _____ children played happily in the sand.

Proofreading

Proofreading, or proofing, means reading back over your work in order to look for errors to correct. Use the following proofreading checklist each time you write.

I always aim to have:

- Capital letters at the start of sentences and for names of people, places, titles of books, poems and films, companies and brand names.
- Correct spelling by checking each word in my sentences.
- Correct grammar and syntax, which means I sometimes change my word order.
- Well-spaced letters and words so it's easier to read my text.
- Paragraphs.
- Correct punctuation.

Self Assessment

The best way to improve your work and do a better job next time is to assess yourself. These are the things you should think about and do after you've written a piece of work.

- Think about how I can improve it.
- Think about what my expectations are as a learner.
- Identify the Features of Quality or the good things in my work.
- Identify the things that I need to work on.
- Think about my next steps for further learning.

Paragraphing

Paragraphs separate parts of your writing. Text needs to be split into paragraphs so that it looks attractive and is easy to read. Most importantly, paragraphs help you to put your points in logical order.

Read the following examples. Notice that a new paragraph is made for each new point.

It's that time of year and the multiplexes are clogged up with noisy, spectacular big-budget blockbusters. *Maleficent*, *Godzilla*, *Edge of Tomorrow* and *X-Men: Days of Future Past* have already been released, and *Transformers 4*, *Dawn of the Planet of the Apes* and *How to Train Your Dragon 2* will appear over the next few weeks.

All of those films have budgets in excess of $150m (€110m), and none make excessive demands on the intellect. Instead, they rely on action, effects and simple stories of good versus evil to woo a largely teenage audience. This tried and tested summer blockbuster formula has been flogged to death so much in recent years that we've all grown tired of it, but it's worth remembering that once upon a time, these months were viewed as a fallow period by the studios.

Back in the 1960s and early 1970s, nothing much of note was released in June, July and August, when people abandoned darkened cinemas for the beaches, bars and restaurants. In America, the only summer dollars came from drive-in theatres, which by the 1970s were beginning to fall out of fashion, and quality movies with big budgets tended to get released in the winter.

'How iconic *Jaws* created the summer movie blockbuster' by **Paul Whitington**

GLOSSARY

Multiplexes: Large cinema complexes.

Blockbuster: Something powerful, such as a very successful film, book or show.

Excessive: More than is necessary, too much.

Woo: To try to gain the attention/affection/love of someone.

Flogged: In this context it means promoted; it can also mean beaten.

Fallow: Usually a field left unused so it can rest.

A. Writing

Separate the following text into paragraphs. There should be four in total.

The air is different. You notice it immediately. It's rarefied, finer, **invigorating**; it has a sense of the divine about it. Breathe and your **chakras** give a blissful little shudder. It's Nepal: home of the legendary **Gurkhas**, Everest and **Annapurna**, and birthplace of Buddha. The 6km journey from Tribhuvan International to the Soaltee Crowne Plaza gives a first glimpse into daily life. Rutted, potholed roads are flanked with masses of dangling wires, strung from **skewed** poles buckling under the weight of the cables they **endeavour** to support. Power outages are frequent; without warning, the entire Kathmandu valley can be pitched into blackness. The traffic is chaotic, with buses, cars, cows and motorbikes all **vying** for road space. The law requires only motorbike drivers to wear a helmet, so it's common to see bareheaded women and children riding pillion, sometimes five deep, amid the lunatic traffic. The Soaltee is an oasis of calm amid the craziness of Kathmandu. It has an outdoor swimming pool from which you can gaze up at the majestic Himalayas, and four restaurants, along with a bar and lounge. Once settled, our first stop was the Garden Terrace restaurant to sample some authentic Nepali cuisine and down a few Gorkhas. Daal bhat tarkari is a traditional dish – daal being a lentil soup; bhat, boiled grains and tarkari is essentially a vegetable curry. Momo, a type of stuffed dumpling, is **synonymous** with Nepal, and very moreish indeed! Desserts are also a delight, from gajar ko halwa (carrot pudding) to kheer (rice pudding) and, my favourite, sel roti (crispy rice doughnuts). Next morning, first stop was Swayambhunath, or Monkey Temple. The magnificent stupa (Buddhist shrine), **venerated** by Hindus and Buddhists, is set high on a hill that is reputed to have 'self-arisen' (swayambhu) from the waters of a lake that once covered the area. As you climb the 365 steps to the stupa, inquisitive monkeys clamber alongside, their babies clinging on for dear life.

From **'Nepal: Standing at the gates of heaven'** by Gemma Fullam

B. Dictionary

Use a dictionary to find the meaning of the words in **bold** in the above text.

Practise Paragraphing

A. Pairwork

Write one continuous block of text (a minimum of 10 sentences) about one of the following topics.

My favourite:

- sport
- television programme
- hobby

- band
- food
- season

- holiday
- film
- book.

Use imaginative, descriptive words.

Peer Assessment

Swap what you have written with the person beside you. Correct your partner's work and mark where the paragraphs should be in their text. Correct any errors using the proofreading checklist.

B. Oral Language Presentation

Let's use the topic you chose above to try an oral language presentation. First, you will need to do some research, then gather together your presentation and speak in front of your class. There are lots of tips on the following pages to help you with this.

When you have done your research, plan your presentation on **page 12** of your **PORTFOLIO**.

How to Research

Research is about:

- Finding information.
- Assessing and evaluating information.
- Synthesising and organising information.
- Presenting information.

Finding Information: What Are Your Sources?

- The internet
- Libraries
- Family/friends
- Organisations/companies
- Print media
- Broadcast media
- Other

The Internet

- Choose your online sources carefully. Avoid clicking on the first few sources shown in search engine results: often these are advertising-based and will waste your time.
- Scroll down and read the preview information that is shown in each search result. Choose wisely before you click on a source.
- Spend time reading and scanning online text.
- Do not expect instant, perfect, 'one size fits all' material. Copy and paste relevant text, making sure to record the author and where it was taken from.
- Save your material in folders on your device.
- Label your folders correctly.
- Save the reference details correctly, such as the date of download and the URL details.

Libraries

Use the search facility on the library computer to find information quickly. Type in a keyword or person's name and write down the details that appear. The Dewey Decimal Classification number assigned to each book will lead you to the shelf where the book is stored, or to other details about your topic. Ask a librarian for help if necessary.

A local library usually stores:

- Autobiographies
- Biographies
- Diaries
- Local history books, journals, historical magazines and similar publications
- Local newspapers (paper copies and copies on microfiche or microfilm, which you can access on request)
- Books on a wide range of topics, from sport to travel to almost everything in between.

Explore your local or school library for ideas and inspiration! Remember to make careful note of details such as book title and author.

Family/Friends

An oral source is good because you hear information from 'the horse's mouth'. You might wish to interview a person who knows a lot about your topic.

- Prepare your questions in advance.
- Consider recording the interview so that you have a record of the responses.

Surveys are also an important source of information. You may wish to find out about attitudes to a particular issue. To do this, you can draw up your questions and survey your target group (for example, classmates, teammates, teachers, parents, neighbours or relations).

You can email your survey using an online questionnaire provider such as SurveyMonkey, or distribute paper copies. Look back at page 152 of *Great Expectations 1* for details on analysing survey results.

Organisations/Companies

You might write a letter or send an email to an organisation or a company if you require specific information from them on your topic. See Chapter 4 (page 253) for information on writing formal letters.

Print Media

You may find articles, reports and interviews in print media that could contribute to your research topic. Keep a record of all the sources that you use.

- Newspapers: national, local and international.
- Magazines: there is a magazine available about almost every topic.
- Journals: these are like magazines but focus on more serious topics and are available in libraries.

Broadcast Media (Television, Radio and Internet)

There may be a podcast, documentary or programme that can give you information about your topic and provide you with an interesting informative source.

Assessing and Evaluating Information

Often, you will find too much information and the difficulty will lie in trying to decide what to keep and what to discard.

- Ask yourself if the information focuses on your research topic. Consider questions like, 'Is this relevant to my main aim/objective, my main question/thesis, my main point/topic?' Discard information if it is not relevant. Decide what to include based on what point it is making or how good it is. Retain any information that focuses on the topic.
- Keep in mind the length of the research topic and the time you will be allowed to present it (for example, 3 minutes). Providing too much information can often bore the audience.
- Choose interesting details. Remember that you control what you present to the listener. Form your own opinion based on what you find.

Consider categorising the information as follows:

A – what is essential and central and must be included.

B – what is interesting and worth saying if time allows.

C – what is interesting, but too detailed and wandering away from the main topic.

D – not at all relevant to the main topic.

Cross-reference Your Information

If you use more than one source, you may be able to compare information and check that any facts included are accurate. You may also be able to consider different opinions on a topic. This is called cross-referencing. One source may contradict or support another source.

Synthesising and Organising Information

This is the order and sequence of your information. How will you bring it all together? What order will you put your information in?

Organise the information in a logical sequence. For most topics, an easy way to present information is to start from the beginning of its history. However, you might like to dive into the middle and begin with a startling fact, a surprising statistic or an interesting point.

General Guidelines

- State your topic, using one sentence. For example, 'My research topic is…' or 'I have chosen to research…'
- Explain why you chose to research this topic: 'I chose this topic because…'
- Give a date, definition or starting point to introduce your topic. For example, 'Ronaldo was born in…' or 'The origins of cricket go back to…'
- Follow on from your introduction using a logical next-step sequence.
- Have perhaps three, four or five points, paragraphs or slides.

Your conclusion should be strong:
- Choose an interesting point, fact or statistic to end on.
- Give a one- or two-sentence summary.
- Conclude with confidence and have an impact on the listener.
- Do not rush the conclusion or let your voice trail off.

Presenting Information

Choose a medium to present your information. You might consider using:

- Notes
- PowerPoint
- Slideshow
- Whiteboard
- Flipchart
- Audio/visual clip/performance

Confidence is important. Rehearse your presentation, talk or performance and focus on communicating your research effectively to your audience.

Keep a good record of the sources of your information. You must acknowledge where you got the information from. You may also be asked to assess or critique the information you have gathered. What was good about a source? What was poor?

Student Reflection Note

When you do your oral language task and your written pieces for assessment, you are required to write a note about your research experience. It should include:

- A title.
- A brief account of the material or sources you accessed.
- An account of the part you played in the preparation and communication.
- A brief personal reflection where you comment on:
  - One important thing that I learned.
  - Things I would change or improve on.

Biographies

You may remember from last year that a biography is a book about a person's life, written by someone else. It usually discusses where the subject of the book was born and offers lots of different facts about their life. Biographies almost always feature a significant talent, story or event that has made a person noteworthy and of interest to others. While sentences in memoirs and autobiographies often include the words 'I' and 'me', biographies are written in the third person. This means that the sentences in a biography often include the words 'she' or 'he'. See what other features of biographies you notice as you read the following text.

Maeve Binchy: The Biography *by Piers Dudgeon*

The writer Maeve Binchy grew up in Dalkey, a seaside suburb of Dublin, which she found beautiful and enjoyable as a child but boring when she became a teenager. In the following extract from Piers Dudgeon's biography of Binchy's life, she is awaiting examination results and is on the cusp of a new stage in her life.

She no longer had a particular ambition. She was down to read Law at university, but had no desire to be a lawyer. She didn't at this point want to be a writer nor was she thinking about becoming a teacher. She wanted to enjoy life and with the results hanging over her she had been uncharacteristically moody and difficult at home, flaring up on any subject. Maureen realised that she was worried about her results and wondered if, like herself, Maeve would be more successful in work where no great further study was required.

At the same time, Maeve had not forgotten what had been sacrificed to get her this far. She was aware of her father's expectations of all the children to pass their exams, and remembered his warning that money might not always be there. As the eldest child she felt a duty to prove that they, the children of 'these great people', as she referred to her parents, were indeed swans and not ducks.

Dalkey was such a small town and however familiar and friendly on the surface, it was, like every other small town, full of small-town gossips. Everyone knew where everyone was and what you were doing all day and night. It was like being in a goldfish bowl. It was even suspected that telephone calls – all of which were routed through the local telephone exchange in those days – were listened into by the local postmistress. Imagine the buzz if she failed!

Well, whatever happened, there was at least change in the air. Whether or not she got the results she needed for university, nothing would be the same any more. She was about to make a break with the past, and about time!

Even at twelve, when she first came to live in Dalkey, she sensed she was in the wrong place. Everything seemed to point in the opposite direction, to the bright lights of Dún Laoghaire and the very bright lights of Dublin – the city in striking distance and yet off the map for her. She was never allowed to go there, except with her mother to shop.

Now that Maeve was seventeen, Dalkey seemed just about the dullest place on earth. Walking with Philippa past the pitch of Dalkey United they could appreciate the leggy fellows playing football, but they'd never get to know them. There was no cinema, no place for young people to dance, or even to meet. On Castle Street, the main street, there was the Queen's bar, the St Laurence Club at No. 17 – neither of which they could possibly go into, or would want to.

They went to McKenna's or Hill Stores for sweets, and there were a couple of cafés, one called The Matassa, but that was it. Most of the shops would close for lunch and everywhere was shut by 6 p.m. Apart from a sortie for fish and chips there was nothing for Maeve and her friends to do. The feeling of being trapped here had been gradual, but Maeve had become acutely aware of it after an exchange trip to France. A letter from a family in Compiègne, in northern France, had been passed to the Binchys by a friend. They were looking, they said, for an Irish family of a certain social status to take their daughter, Odile, for a few weeks in exchange for a child from England. The Binchys assumed that the snobbish element of the letter had been down to the family's poor understanding of the English language, but it transpired that this was not the case at all.

When Maeve arrived in Compiègne she was dreadfully nervous – she had never been out of Ireland before. She said '*très bien*' to everything, committing herself to she knew not what. The mother turned out to be a religious maniac. An impossibly rich aunt stamped around prodding people with her walking stick. The father took delight in penalising Maeve for her poor pronunciation of French by refusing to allow her to eat anything until she had got it right. This was a master stroke – Maeve learned good French very quickly after that.

When Odile's letters started arriving from Ireland, however, things changed for the better. Odile was able to report that although the Binchys didn't appear to be very wealthy they actually had two homes, one in the town close to Dublin and another on the far west coast by the sea at a place called Ballybunion. She had mistaken the house on Sandhill Road for a second home! More important, Odile let slip that the Binchys had paid for everything, even her ice creams.

This had an immediate effect on the French household. A quick calculation showed that they owed Maeve more than £30 in hospitality and suddenly she was being taken to Chartres, to châteaux in the Loire, even to Brussels. The trip was completely transformed. They taught her to ride a horse and to hunt and insisted that she kept a diary of everything they had paid for her to do.

Maeve had got the travel bug; she enjoyed observing the doings and habits of people outside her little bubble of Dalkey.

Before Compiègne she had had no inkling that anyone thought at all differently to the way she had been brought up to think. She was so completely *of* Dalkey, and had so little experience *beyond* Dalkey, that she had no reason to think that her home *in* Dalkey was singular in any way at all. It was while she was in France that she became determined to see more of the wider world.

And now that was once more at the forefront of her mind. What did it matter that no boy wanted to dance with her? She had decided that she was going to see the world before she'd let herself fall for any of them.

But first things first, she did not want to suffer the indignity of failing to matriculate. Today she had decided not to go to school with everyone else to get their results, but to cycle down to the Church of the Assumption – her church – and envelop herself in its comforting silence instead.

Maeve fell to her knees, praying that she would get the exam, telling God that she would be good for the rest of her life if she passed. Like Niamh in *Light a Penny Candle* – the first of the O'Connor siblings to go to university – if she had prayed any harder she would have 'prayed herself into a near coma'.

Fortunately, rescue was at hand.

When Maeve's sister heard the news for which Maeve was waiting, she mounted her bicycle and flew through the town to tell her. When she appeared through the doors at the west end of the church and shouted the good news, there was great satisfaction, not just that Maeve had got the 'Matric', but that all four children were now on their way.

GLOSSARY

Acutely: Extremely, very.

Sortie: In this context it means an outing; in military terms it was an attack by troops coming out of a defence position.

Transpired: Became apparent.

Matriculate: In addition to the Leaving Certificate, students could also choose to sit the Matriculation exams in order to secure entry to university.

A. Reading

Rate this text for readability. Write the word/phrase of your choice into your copy.

VERY EASY ☐   **EASY** ☐   **OKAY** ☐   **HARD** ☐   **VERY HARD** ☐

B. Literacy Questions

Work in pairs or small groups to figure out the answers to the following questions. Then write your own answer to each question into your copy.

1. What career options are mentioned for Maeve in the first paragraph?
2. Explain two benefits that the exchange trip to France brought to Maeve.
3. Describe the mother, the aunt and the father in the French family.
4. Find two pieces of evidence in the extract that prove Maeve was nervous about her exam results.

C. Writing

It is clear from this extract that Maeve Binchy's biographer has spent a lot of time finding out about her hometown, the details of significant moments in her life, the people she was surrounded by and how she felt about things.

On **page 14** of your **PORTFOLIO**, write about one memorable event in your life and include details about where you live, your family and your community.

Group Work – How to Work with Others

Benefits of Group Work

Group work can help you to:

- Break down difficult tasks into parts or steps.
- Plan and manage time.
- Understand things better by discussing them with your group.
- Tackle complex problems together.
- Explain your ideas to others.
- Listen to alternative ideas and points of view.
- Reach decisions that everyone agrees on.
- Develop your own voice and opinions.

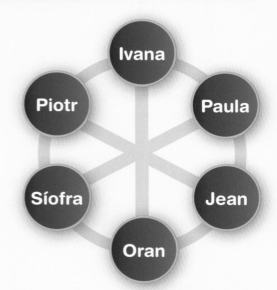

Tips for Good Group Work

Each member of the group should:

- Take their turn to speak.
- Listen to others and respect their views.
- Stick to deadlines/time limits.
- Have a task and be responsible for this task.
- Remember to criticise the ideas, not the person.
- Take into account that even though you are working in a group, each individual performance may be graded.
- Take their turn giving feedback.
- Be aware that the group will be graded or assessed.

Keeping Track of Your Group Work

Even though you are part of a group, it is important to reflect on your own work and how you are getting on as part of the group. Here are some of the ways that you can do this:

- Write a daily journal, diary or reflection on the progress of the task.
- Write a summary of what the group has achieved.
- Talk about any problems the group encountered.
- Describe how you contributed to the group.
- Explain how decisions were made. Did everyone work together?
- Summarise what you have learned by doing group work.

Each time you do a group project, you should fill in a group work assessment table like the one below in your **PORTFOLIO** to see how you're getting on.

Group Work Self Assessment

Traits	Yes	No	Sometimes	My Comment
I speak with confidence				
I avoid speaking				
I am indecisive				
I like to offer my opinion/ideas				
I enjoy group work				
I'm lazy and prefer to do very little				
I'm too shy to offer my opinion/ideas				
I prefer working on my own				
I dominate the group				
I like being a leader				
I like the challenge of group work				
I'm afraid of saying the wrong thing				

Group Work Peer Assessment

Name:	Good	Fair	Could Improve	Comment
Task:				
Contribution to doing the task				
Speaking skills				
Listening skills				
Persuasion skills				
Time-management skills				
Effort put into the task				
Ability to work well in a group				

Personal Writing

Personal writing means writing about yourself, using 'I' and 'my' and writing about your experiences, memories, feelings, thoughts, hopes, opinions and fears. Only you can write about how you truly feel, what you really think, what you like or dislike, admire or loathe. Only you can write your own unique, genuine, sincere, personal essay.

Think about the things you relate to when you:
- read an essay or a novel
- watch a film or TV show
- listen to someone's experience.

Sometimes you feel the same way as the character or the person you are reading about, watching or listening to. You may agree with their viewpoint, or have felt the same way they feel about something.

For example, see if you can relate to the narrator of the following poem.

Prize Night Envy

It takes two hours to honour those smarter than us
And watch them parade across the polished stage
To receive award
     after award.

Mama sits with the other parents.
She looks puzzled because I'm not called
Forward for a medal or a trophy.
I don't even get a certificate she can
Stick to the fridge.

Clair is sitting next to me
Defacing the programme.
She sneers when other people win
And groans instead of clapping.

There are sports awards.
William wins a swimming medal – gold –
    And when he sits
Back down he passes the medal
Along our row so I can touch it.

Stabbing jealousy makes my head spin,
And then there's guilt in my gut
Because William looks so proud,
And he has been so nice;
He deserves this medal.

I pass it back along the row
And Clair turns to me and says,
'You're friends with Will?'
And I shrug;
    I don't think we are friends
    Exactly.

For the finale we stand in our rows
Like dishevelled soldiers
And sing 'God Save the Queen'.

I don't know the words.
I just open and close my
Mouth and look straight ahead
Hoping no one will notice
The treason.

From *The Weight of Water* by **Sarah Crossan**

Oral Language

Think about films, books, songs and TV advertisements that have had an impact on you. How did you react to them? You may have related to how a character felt.

Discuss your experiences in pairs, groups or as a class.

When you identify your feelings and think about the impact that something has on you, you have material for personal writing.

How to Write a Personal Essay

You may be required to write a personal essay in your final assessment for JCSA. The following steps will help you:

Step 1: Remember the ACE strategy from *Great Expectations 1*. **Analyse** what you are being asked to do. Brainstorm ideas based on the title that you are given or come up with your own idea.

Step 2: Create. Use RAFT (Role, Audience, Format, Topic) to decide what your job is, who you are writing for, how you are going to write it and what you are writing about. Write your first draft.

Step 3: Prioritise your points into paragraphs.

Step 4: Write the essay in a logical way. Link each paragraph.

Step 5: Edit the essay and improve it. Use your proofreading steps from **page 32**.

Step 6: Redraft the essay.

Choose the most interesting or dramatic aspect of your experience. For example, if asked to write about 'My Summer Holidays', begin with the incident about how you nearly missed the flight, or the moment when you fell in love. Avoid the boring details like waiting in the baggage queue!

Sample Personal Essay: 'Things That Make Me Smile'

Step 1: Brainstorm the title.
Jot down the things that make you smile, make you laugh or make you happy.

Fill in the brainstorm cloud on **page 17** of your **PORTFOLIO**.

Step 2: Number the most interesting ones in order of importance: 1, 2, 3, 4. Number 1 must be the funniest, weirdest or quirkiest, in order to grab the attention of the reader. Number 2 is the next most interesting, and so on.

Step 3: Your first sentence should be unusual and attention-grabbing. Perhaps start with one word all by itself, or with a short dramatic sentence or piece of dialogue.

Step 4: Use paragraphs for new points. This will help to create order and coherence, which will improve your essay's structure and logic.

Step 5: Polish and perfect your work. Reread and rewrite the sentences in order to improve them. Work on your adjectives, verbs and adverbs. Think about using interesting comparisons, similes or metaphors. Choose your words as carefully as you would choose something delicious to eat from a menu. Don't just settle for any old word when there are millions to choose from. Use a thesaurus for inspiration.

Step 6: Proofread what you have written and correct any errors. Ask a friend to check it as well and consider their advice.

Sample Brainstorm

'Things that make me smile'

Use the **RAFT** strategy to decide on your structure:

R Role   A student writing an essay
A Audience   My teacher and my class
F Format   Essay form in paragraphs
T Topic   Things that make me smile

Use brainstorm clouds to record all the ideas you have for your essay:

A

> Dimples
> Jokes
> Cute chubby cheeks
> Finding money
> Scoring a goal

B

> An unexpected half-day
> Free classes
> Snow days
> Random acts of kindness

C

> Amusing misunderstandings
> Sunny days
> Music
> Images of cute animals

D

> Funny ads on TV
> Funny clips on YouTube
> Happy-ever-after endings
> Candlelight
> People who smile at me

Sample Opening Paragraphs: Things That Make Me Smile

1. Gleaming up at me it was, glinting in the hot afternoon sun: a gorgeous €2 coin, no doubt lost in the park by some other child. I snatched it up gleefully and two minutes later was happily licking a cool, sweet 99 cone. And I even had change! Don't you just love finding money? The unexpected surprise of it, the freedom it offers is totally pain-free. Like an unexpected gift, you relish the power it gives you. Of course, when you lose money you're glum, but *c'est la vie*! The ups and downs in life hopefully balance, so that what you lose on the swings you gain on the roundabouts.

2. As usual on those bitter, cold, winter mornings, I reluctantly swish open the curtains and groggily draw up the blinds. Suddenly I'm dazzled; then, a deep intake of breath, followed by 'Ooooh! It's snowing, look! Look!' Then, whooping and yelling, I wake the entire house. At least five inches of snow is blanketing the roads, paths and cars. Everything outside is totally white, meaning YIPPEE! A day off school! The sheer joy, bliss and excitement of this is indescribable. A day to play in the snow! Wow! What will I wear, apart from an ear-to-ear grin all day?

3. Tiny. Gorgeous. Soft. Cute. Adorable. My new puppy. My first ever puppy. Only six weeks old. Floppy, silly and warm, totally helpless and dependent on the kindness of someone else to feed and care for him. Smooth, silky, shiny new coat. Glistening, bright, inquisitive eyes that would melt your heart. We will become the best of friends. Inseparable.

4. Ha ha ha! Hilarious, so silly and ridiculous, the scrapes that people get into and the bizarre things they post on YouTube! It's not so funny that I've lost two hours instead of the ten-minute break I intended to take from doing boring homework. YouTube is simply addictive. Ah well… I yawn and my eyes are closing. There's no point in struggling through algebra or French verbs; I'll just have to set the alarm for 6am to get them done, or else face the wrath of the teachers. That in itself would make an interesting YouTube clip!

Peer Composition

As a group, write a shared personal essay. It can be hard to write a one-to-two page essay all by yourself so why not share ideas and make the task easier? Each group member writes one paragraph on their own idea. The paragraphs are then joined to form one group essay. You benefit from seeing each other's ideas and you get a better understanding of how to write an essay all by yourself once you have shared the task first. Here are some topics you can choose from.

1. My treasures
2. I remember one Christmas when I…
3. Sundays in my house
4. Technology in my life
5. Music and me

Step 1: The group discusses the titles and decides on one.
Step 2: The group brainstorms the title and jots down ideas.
Step 3: Each member chooses one idea or topic on which to write a paragraph.
Step 4: Each person writes their paragraph.
Step 5: The group reads each other's work and numbers the order of the paragraphs, beginning with the most interesting first.
Step 6: The group identifies the best elements of a personal essay, use of 'I', anecdotes, humour, descriptive language and so on.
Step 7: The group proofreads and improves the essay.
Step 8: Each person reads a paragraph of the essay aloud to the class.

Don't forget to fill in your Group Work Self Assessment and Peer Assessment on **page 18** of your **PORTFOLIO**.

Writing – Personal Essay

You have read many different types of personal writing in this chapter. Now it's time to create your own essay.

Choose one of the topics below, then brainstorm, write and redraft your essay on **page 19** of your **PORTFOLIO**.

- 'It was tough, but it was worth it in the end.'
- S/he is my hero/ine.
- My favourite photograph.

Diaries

In *Great Expectations 1* we learned that a diary is a personal record of events, experiences or thoughts. Like other types of personal writing such as blogs and memoirs, reading diaries can give us a greater understanding of other places and times.

The Diary of Mary Berg: Growing Up in the Warsaw Ghetto *by Susan Lee Pentlin*

World War II lasted from 1939 to 1945. In Warsaw, Poland, 15-year-old Mary Berg kept a diary as the German army poured into Poland. In this extract, it is nearing Christmas in the ghetto. (A ghetto is a part of a city occupied by a minority group.)

NOVEMBER 22, 1940

1. The ghetto has been isolated for a whole week. The red-brick walls at the end of the ghetto streets have grown considerably higher. Our miserable settlement hums like a beehive. In the homes and in the courtyards, wherever the ears of the Gestapo do not reach, people nervously discuss the Nazis' real aims in isolating the Jewish quarter. How shall we get provisions? Who will maintain order? Perhaps it will really be better, and perhaps we will be left in peace? This afternoon all the members of our LZA group gathered at my home. We sat in a stupor and did not know what to undertake. Now all our efforts are useless. Who cares for the theatre these days? Everyone is brooding over one thing and one thing only: the ghetto.

DECEMBER 15, 1940

2. Life goes on. My mother, as an American, is still allowed to leave the gates of the ghetto. As she leaves, she shows her passport, and the Nazi guard salutes her with great respect as he returns this American document. Recently my mother has made several such trips to do all sorts of errands for her friends. They are particularly appreciative when she can send letters abroad for them, because the post offices in the ghetto refuse such letters. As an American citizen, she can send out letters from the German post office without any special difficulty. Her passport is checked at the window—the name of the sender of the letter must be the same as that on the passport. I can imagine the surprise of people abroad when they see that letters from their closest relatives bear a stranger's name as the sender.

3. The relief office of the American colony in Warsaw is situated at 14 Mokotowska Street. Once a month, all American citizens receive a large package of foodstuffs for the sum of eleven zlotys—but its real value is three hundred, and it often contains articles that are unobtainable elsewhere at any price whatsoever.

GREAT EXPECTATIONS 2

The question of obtaining food is becoming ever more pressing. The official ration cards entitle one to a quarter of a pound of bread a day, one egg a month, and two pounds of vegetable jam (sweetened with saccharine) a month. A pound of potatoes costs one zloty. We have forgotten even the taste of fresh fruit. Nothing can be imported from the Aryan districts, although there is an abundance of everything there.

4. But hunger and the desire for profit are stronger than all the penalties threatening smugglers, and smuggling is now gradually becoming an important industry. Sienna Street, which forms one of the boundaries of the ghetto, is separated by walls only from the streets that cross it; the houses whose courtyards give on Zlota Street (Zlota is parallel to Sienna), the so-called "other side," are temporarily separated from the outer world by barbed wire. Most of the smuggling takes place here. Our windows face such a courtyard.

5. All night long there is a commotion there, and by morning, carts with vegetables appear in the streets and the stores are filled with bread. There is even sugar, butter, cheese—of course for high prices, for people have risked their lives to get these things. Sometimes a German sentry is bribed and a whole wagon full of all kinds of merchandise manages to get through the gates. The Germans have demanded that the Jewish community administration take steps to stop the smuggling. They have also ordered that a Jewish militia be formed to help the Polish police in maintaining order in the ghetto. The community is trying to recruit two thousand able-bodied men between the ages of twenty-one and thirty-five. War veterans are given preference. A high educational standard is also required: a certificate from a school is the minimum.

DECEMBER 22, 1940

6. The Jewish police is an accomplished fact. More candidates presented themselves than were needed. A special committee chose them, and "pull" played an important part in their choice. At the very end, when only a few posts were available, money helped, too... Even in Heaven not everyone is a saint... Their uniform consists of a dark blue police cap and a military belt to which a rubber club is attached. Over the visor of the cap there is a metal badge bearing the Star of David and the inscription *Jüdischer Ordnungsdienst* (Jewish Order Service)... Just like all the other Jews, the Jewish policemen must wear a white armband with the blue Star of David, but in addition, they wear a yellow armband with the inscription *Jüdischer Ordnungsdienst*. They also wear metallic badges with their numbers on their chests.

7. Among the duties of these new Jewish policemen are guarding the gates of the ghetto together with German gendarmes and Polish policemen, directing traffic in the ghetto streets, guarding post offices, kitchens and the community administration, and detecting and suppressing smugglers. The most difficult task of the Jewish police is the curbing of beggars—this actually consists in driving them from one street to another, because there is nothing else to do with them, especially as their number is growing from hour to hour.

8. I experience a strange and utterly illogical feeling of satisfaction when I see a Jewish policeman at a crossing—such policemen were completely unknown in pre-war Poland. They proudly direct the traffic—which hardly needs to be directed, for it consists only of rare horse-driven carts, a few cabs and hearses—the latter are the most frequent vehicles. From time to time Gestapo cars rush by, paying no attention whatsoever to the Jewish policemen's directions, and perfectly indifferent as to whether they run people over or not.

DECEMBER 24, 1940

9. Our second war Christmas. From my window, which faces the Aryan side, I can see Christmas trees lit up. But little pine trees were also sold in the ghetto this morning at exorbitant prices. They were smuggled in yesterday. I saw shivering people hurrying home with the little trees pressed to their chests. These were converts or first-generation Christians whom the Nazis regard as Jews, and whom they have confined in the ghetto.

GLOSSARY

Gestapo: The secret Nazi police force.
LZA: Lodz Artistic Group. A club Mary and her friends set up to raise relief funds.
Zloty: The basic monetary unit of Poland.
Sentry: A guard on watch duty.
Militia: An army created from the civilian community to supplement the main army.
War veterans: People who have long experience of war.
Aryan: In Nazi ideology, a person of the Caucasian race, not of Jewish descent.

A. Reading

Rate this text for readability. Write the word/phrase of your choice into your copy.

VERY EASY ☐   **EASY** ☐   **OKAY** ☐   **HARD** ☐   **VERY HARD** ☐

B. Literacy Questions

1. Why do you think that Mary and her family and friends have been forced to live in the ghetto?
2. Identify two problems that the Jewish community have living in the ghetto.
3. What advantages does Mary's mother have that the others do not have?
4. What quantities of food are available with the ration card?
5. How does Mary feel about the Jewish police? Support your answer with quotes from the extract.
6. Draw some of the scenes described above. Include the ghetto, main streets, houses and courtyards, barbed wire, red-brick walls, sentry guards and so on.

C. Oral Language

In pairs, discuss your existing knowledge of World War II, the Nazis, the Jewish people and Germany. On **page 24** of your **PORTFOLIO**, make a list of things you would like to find out.

D. Research

Narrow down your research on World War II by choosing one particular topic that you would like to find out more about. It could be the invasion of Poland, the yellow Star of David or another theme that interests you.

Research this topic in order to fill in gaps in your knowledge. Refer back to the information on How to Research on page 36 if you need to.

Present your findings to the class.

Memoirs, Personal Blogs and Diaries: Key Features

Memoirs

- Personal, subjective style; personal pronoun 'I' is used.
- Reflective tone, looking back on past experiences.
- Nostalgic tone at times, perhaps sentimentalising the past.
- Use of anecdotes.

Personal Blogs

- Personal, subjective style; personal pronoun 'I' is used.
- Personal response and reaction given to topics/events.
- Personal opinion stated, feelings expressed.

Diaries

- Personal, subjective style; personal pronoun 'I' is used.
- Reaction to events noted in a sequential way, daily/weekly.
- Personal feelings and opinions are expressed.

Read and Enjoy

In *Great Expectations 1*, we learned that fiction describes imaginary events and people. We also read a variety of extracts showing different styles of writing, genres and points of view.

Even though fiction presents us with characters and situations that are invented, good writers are often able to make their settings, events and characters so authentic that we react to them as if they are real. We think about what will happen next. We develop feelings about their world. We like and dislike characters. In this way, we can discover our own opinions about topics and scenarios that we have not yet or might never encounter in our lives. When we read fiction, it allows us to explore other people's lives and worlds and it also helps us to understand our own world.

In Chapter 2 we will begin to analyse some fiction extracts. Here is a taster of the kinds of stories we will read and enjoy.

The Hobbit *by J. R. R. Tolkien*

The Hobbit is a fantasy novel by J. R. R. Tolkien. It was published in 1937 and was an instant success. It is a prize-winning book that has long been regarded as a classic of children's literature. It tells the story of the hobbit Bilbo Baggins and his quest to find treasure, which is guarded by the dragon Smaug. The following extract describes Bilbo and his friends' horrific experience at the hands of the goblins.

Gandalf knew that something unexpected might happen, and he hardly dared to hope that they would pass without fearful adventure over those great tall mountains with lonely peaks and valleys where no king ruled. They did not. All was well, until one day they met a thunderstorm – more than a thunderstorm, a thunderbattle. You know how terrific a really big thunderstorm can be down in the land and in a river-valley; especially at times when two great thunderstorms meet and clash. More terrible still are thunder and lightning in the mountains at night, when storms come up from East and West and make war. The lightning splinters on the peaks, and rocks shiver, and great crashes split the air and go rolling and tumbling into every cave and hollow; and the darkness is filled with overwhelming noise and sudden light.

Bilbo had never seen or imagined anything of the kind. They were high up in a narrow place, with a dreadful fall into a dim valley at one side of them. There they were sheltering under a hanging rock for the night, and he lay beneath a blanket and shook from head to toe. When he peeped out in the lightning-flashes, he saw that across the valley the stone-giants were out, and were hurling rocks at one another for a game, and catching them, and tossing them down into the darkness where they smashed among the trees far below, or splintered into little bits with a bang.

Then came a wind and a rain, and the wind whipped the rain and the hail about in every direction, so that an overhanging rock was no protection at all. Soon they were getting drenched and their ponies were standing with their heads down and their tails between their legs, and some of them were whinnying with fright. They could hear the giants guffawing and shouting all over the mountainsides.

"This won't do at all!" said Thorin. "If we don't get blown off, or drowned, or struck by lightning, we shall be picked up by some giant and kicked sky-high for a football."

"Well, if you know of anywhere better, take us there!" said Gandalf, who was feeling very grumpy, and was far from happy about the giants himself.

The end of their argument was that they sent Fili and Kili to look for a better shelter. They had very sharp eyes, and being the youngest of the dwarves by some fifty years they usually got these sorts of jobs (when everybody could see that it was absolutely no use sending Bilbo). There is nothing like looking, if you want to find something (or so Thorin said to the young dwarves). You certainly usually find something, if you look, but it is not always quite the something you were after. So it proved on this occasion.

Soon Fili and Kili came crawling back, holding on to the rocks in the wind. "We have found a dry cave," they said, "not far round the next corner; and ponies and all could get inside."

"Have you *thoroughly* explored it?" said the wizard, who knew that caves up in the mountains were seldom unoccupied.

"Yes, yes!" they said, though everybody knew they could not have been long about it; they had come back too quick. "It isn't all that big, and it does not go far back."

That, of course, is the dangerous part about caves: you don't know how far they go back, sometimes, or where a passage behind may lead to, or what is waiting for you inside. But now Fili and Kili's news seemed good enough. So they all got up and prepared to move. The wind was howling and the thunder still growling, and they had a business getting themselves and their ponies along. Still it was not very far to go, and before long they came to a big rock standing out into the path. If you stepped behind, you found a low arch in the side of the mountain. There was just room to get the ponies through with a squeeze, when they had been unpacked and unsaddled. As they passed under the arch, it was good to hear the wind and the rain outside instead of all about them, and to feel safe from the giants and their rocks. But the wizard was taking no risks. He lit up his wand – as he did that day in Bilbo's dining-room that seemed so long ago, if you remember – and by its light they explored the cave from end to end.

It seemed quite a fair size, but not too large and mysterious. It had a dry floor and some comfortable nooks. At one end there was room for the ponies; and there they stood (mighty glad of the change) steaming, and champing in their nosebags. Oin and Gloin wanted to light a fire at the door to dry their clothes, but Gandalf would not hear of it. So they spread out their wet things on the floor, and got dry ones out of their bundles; then they made their blankets comfortable, got out their pipes and blew smoke rings, which Gandalf turned into different colours and set dancing up by the roof to amuse them. They talked and talked, and forgot about the storm, and discussed what each would do with his share of the treasure (when they got it, which at the moment did not seem so impossible); and so they dropped off to sleep one by one. And that was the last time that they used the ponies, packages, baggages, tools and paraphernalia that they had brought with them.

It turned out a good thing that night that they had brought little Bilbo with them, after all. For, somehow, he could not go to sleep for a long while; and when he did sleep, he had very nasty dreams. He dreamed that a crack in the wall at the back of the cave got bigger and bigger, and opened wider and wider, and he was very afraid but could not call out or do anything but lie and look. Then he dreamed that the floor of the cave was giving way and he was slipping – beginning to fall down, down, goodness knows where to.

At that, he woke up with a horrible start, and found that part of his dream was true. A crack had opened at the back of the cave, and was already a wide passage. He was just in time to see the last of the ponies' tails disappearing into it. Of course he gave a very loud yell, as loud a yell as a hobbit can give, which is surprising for their size.

Out jumped the goblins, big goblins, great ugly-looking goblins, lots of goblins, before you could say *rocks and blocks*. There were six to each dwarf, at least, and two even for Bilbo; and they were all grabbed and carried through the crack, before you could say *tinder and flint*. But not Gandalf. Bilbo's yell had done that much good. It had wakened him up wide in a splintered second, and when goblins came to grab him, there was a terrific flash like lightning in the cave, a smell like gunpowder, and several of them fell dead.

The crack closed with a snap, and Bilbo and the dwarves were on the wrong side of it! Where was Gandalf? Of that neither they nor the goblins had any idea, and the goblins did not wait to find out. They seized Bilbo and the dwarves and hurried them along. It was deep, deep, dark, such as only goblins that have taken to living in the heart of the mountains can see through. The passages there were crossed and tangled in all directions, but the goblins knew their way, as well as you do to the nearest post-office; and the way went down and down, and it was most horribly stuffy. The goblins were very rough, and pinched unmercifully, and chuckled and laughed in their horrible stony voices; and Bilbo was more unhappy even than when the troll had picked him up by his toes. He wished again and again for his nice bright hobbit-hole. Not for the last time.

Now there came a glimmer of a red light before them. The goblins began to sing, or croak, keeping time with the flap of their flat feet on the stone, and shaking their prisoners as well.

Clap! Snap! the black crack!
Grip, grab! Pinch, nab!
And down down to Goblin-town
 You go, my lad!

Clash, crash! Crush, smash!
Hammer and tongs! Knocker and gongs!
Pound, pound, far underground!
 Ho, ho! my lad!

Swish, smack! Whip crack!
Batter and beat! Yammer and bleat!
Work, work! Nor dare to shirk,
While Goblins quaff, and Goblins laugh,
Round and round far underground
Below, my lad!

It sounded truly terrifying. The walls echoed to the *clap, snap!* and the *crush, smash!* and to the ugly laughter of their *ho, ho! my lad!* The general meaning of the song was only too plain; for now the goblins took out whips and whipped them with a *swish, smack!*, and set them running as fast as they could in front of them; and more than one of the dwarves were already yammering and bleating like anything, when they stumbled into a big cavern.

It was lit by a great red fire in the middle, and by torches along the walls, and it was full of goblins. They all laughed and stamped and clapped their hands, when the dwarves (with poor little Bilbo at the back and nearest to the whips) came running in, while the goblin-drivers whooped and cracked their whips behind. The ponies were already there huddled in a corner; and there were all the baggages and packages lying broken open, and being rummaged by goblins, and smelt by goblins, and fingered by goblins, and quarrelled over by goblins.

I am afraid that was the last they ever saw of those excellent little ponies, including a jolly sturdy little white fellow that Elrond had lent to Gandalf, since his horse was not suitable for the mountain paths. For goblins eat horses and ponies and donkeys (and other much more dreadful things), and they are always hungry. Just now however the prisoners were thinking only of themselves. The goblins chained their hands behind their backs and linked them all together in a line, and dragged them to the far end of the cavern with little Bilbo tugging at the end of the row.

There in the shadows on a large flat stone sat a tremendous goblin with a huge head, and armed goblins were standing round him carrying the axes and the bent swords that they use. Now goblins are cruel, wicked, and bad-hearted. They make no beautiful things, but they make many clever ones. They can tunnel and mine as well as any but the most skilled dwarves, when they take the trouble, though they are usually untidy and dirty. Hammers, axes, swords, daggers, pick-axes, tongs, and also instruments of torture, they make very well, or get other people to make to their design, prisoners and slaves that have to work till they die for want of air and light. It is not unlikely that they invented some of the machines that have since troubled the world, especially the ingenious devices for killing large numbers of people at once, for wheels and explosions always delighted them, and also not working with their own hands more than they could help; but in those days and those wild parts they had not advanced (as it is called) so far. They did not hate dwarves especially, no more than they hated everybody and everything, and particularly the orderly and prosperous; in some parts wicked dwarves had even made alliances with them. But they had a special grudge against Thorin's people, because of the war which you have heard mentioned, but which does not come into this tale; and anyway goblins don't care who they catch, as long as it is done smart and secret, and the prisoners are not able to defend themselves.

"Who are these miserable persons?" said the Great Goblin.

"Dwarves, and this!" said one of the drivers, pulling at Bilbo's chain so that he fell forward onto his knees. "We found them sheltering in our Front Porch."

"What do you mean by it?" said the Great Goblin turning to Thorin. "Up to no good, I'll warrant! Spying on the private business of my people, I guess! Thieves, I shouldn't be surprised to learn! Murderers and friends of Elves, not likely! Come! What have you got to say?"

"Thorin the dwarf at your service!" he replied – it was merely a polite nothing. "Of the things which you suspect and imagine we had no idea at all. We sheltered from a storm in what seemed a convenient cave and unused; nothing was further from our thoughts than inconveniencing goblins in any way whatever." That was true enough!

"Um!" said the Great Goblin. "So you say! Might I ask what you were doing up in the mountains at all, and where you were coming from, and where you were going to? In fact I should like to know all about you. Not that it will do you much good, Thorin Oakenshield, I know too much about your folk already; but let's have the truth, or I will prepare something particularly uncomfortable for you!"

"We were on a journey to visit our relatives, our nephews and nieces, and first, second, and third cousins, and the other descendants of our grandfathers; who live on the East side of these truly hospitable mountains," said Thorin, not quite knowing what to say all at once in a moment, when obviously the exact truth would not do at all.

"He is a liar, O truly tremendous one!" said one of the drivers. "Several of our people were struck by lightning in the cave, when we invited these creatures to come below; and they are as dead as stones. Also he has not explained this!" He held out the sword which Thorin had worn, the sword which came from the Trolls' lair.

The Great Goblin gave a truly awful howl of rage when he looked at it, and all his soldiers gnashed their teeth, clashed their shields, and stamped. They knew the sword at once. It had killed hundreds of goblins in its time, when the fair elves of Gondolin hunted them in the hills or did battle before their walls. They had called it Orcrist, Goblin-cleaver, but the goblins called it simply Biter. They hated it and hated worse any one that carried it.

"Murderers and elf-friends!" the Great Goblin shouted. "Slash them! Beat them! Bite them! Gnash them! Take them away to dark holes full of snakes, and never let them see the light again!" He was in such a rage that he jumped off his seat and himself rushed at Thorin with his mouth open.

Just at that moment all the lights in the cavern went out, and the great fire went off poof! into a tower of blue glowing smoke, right up to the roof, that scattered piercing white sparks all among the goblins.

The yells and yammering, croaking, jibbering and jabbering; howls, growls and curses; shrieking and skriking, that followed were beyond description. Several hundred wild cats and wolves being roasted slowly alive together would not have compared with it. The sparks were burning holes in the goblins, and the smoke that now fell from the roof made the air too thick for even their eyes to see through. Soon they were falling over one another and rolling in heaps on the floor, biting and kicking and fighting as if they had all gone mad.

Suddenly a sword flashed in its own light. Bilbo saw it go right through the Great Goblin as he stood dumbfounded in the middle of his rage. He fell dead, and the goblin soldiers fled before the sword shrieking into the darkness.

The sword went back into its sheath. "Follow me quick!" said a voice fierce and quiet; and before Bilbo understood what had happened he was trotting along again as fast as he could trot, at the end of the line, down more dark passages with the yells of the goblin-hall growing fainter behind him. A pale light was leading them on.

"Quicker, quicker!" said the voice. "The torches will soon be relit."

"Half a minute!" said Dori, who was at the back next to Bilbo, and a decent fellow. He made the hobbit scramble on his shoulders as best he could with his tied hands, and then off they all went at a run, with a clink-clink of chains, and many a stumble, since they had no hands to steady themselves with. Not for a long while did they stop, and by that time they must have been right down in the very mountain's heart.

Then Gandalf lit up his wand. Of course it was Gandalf; but just then they were too busy to ask how he got there. He took out his sword again, and again it flashed in the dark by itself. It burned with a rage that made it gleam if goblins were about; now it was bright as blue flame for delight in the killing of the great lord of the cave. It made no trouble whatever of cutting through the goblin-chains and setting all the prisoners free as quickly as possible. This sword's name was Glamdring the Foe-hammer, if you remember. The goblins just called it Beater, and hated it worse than Biter if possible. Orcrist, too, had been saved; for Gandalf had brought it along as well, snatching it from one of the terrified guards. Gandalf thought of most things; and though he could not do everything, he could do a great deal for friends in a tight corner.

"Are we all here?" said he, handing his sword back to Thorin with a bow. "Let me see: one – that's Thorin; two, three, four, five, six, seven, eight, nine, ten, eleven; where are Fili and Kili? Here they are! twelve, thirteen – and here's Mr Baggins: fourteen! Well, well! it might be worse, and then again it might be a good deal better. No ponies, and no food, and no knowing quite where we are, and hordes of angry goblins just behind! On we go!"

On they went. Gandalf was quite right: they began to hear goblin noises and horrible cries far behind in the passages they had come through. That sent them on faster than ever, and as poor Bilbo could not possibly go half as fast – for dwarves can roll along at a tremendous pace, I can tell you, when they have to – they took it in turn to carry him on their backs.

Still goblins go faster than dwarves, and these goblins knew the way better (they had made the paths themselves), and were madly angry; so that do what they could the dwarves heard the cries and howls getting closer and closer. Soon they could hear even the flap of the goblin feet, many many feet which seemed only just round the last corner. The blink of red torches could be seen behind them in the tunnel they were following; and they were getting deadly tired.

"Why, O why did I ever leave my hobbit-hole!" said poor Mr Baggins bumping up and down on Bombur's back. "Why, O why did I ever bring a wretched little hobbit on a treasure hunt!" said poor Bombur, who was fat, and staggered along with the sweat dripping down his nose in his heat and terror.

At this point Gandalf fell behind, and Thorin with him. They turned a sharp corner. "About turn!" he shouted. "Draw your sword Thorin!"

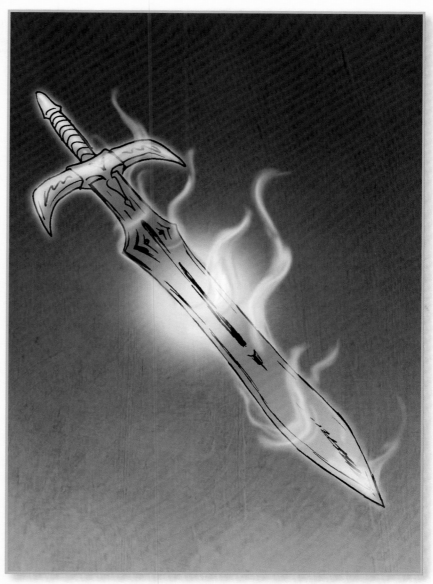

There was nothing else to be done; and the goblins did not like it. They came scurrying round the corner in full cry, and found Goblin-cleaver, and Foe-hammer shining cold and bright right in their astonished eyes. The ones in front dropped their torches and gave one yell before they were killed. The ones behind yelled still more, and leaped back knocking over those that were running after them. "Biter and Beater!" they shrieked; and soon they were all in confusion, and most of them were hustling back the way they had come.

It was quite a long while before any of them dared to turn that corner. By that time the dwarves had gone on again, a long, long, way on into the dark tunnels of the goblins' realm. When the goblins discovered that, they put out their torches and they slipped on soft shoes, and they chose out their very quickest runners with the sharpest ears and eyes. These ran forward, as swift as weasels in the dark, and with hardly any more noise than bats.

That is why neither Bilbo, nor the dwarves, nor even Gandalf heard them coming. Nor did they see them. But they were seen by the goblins that ran silently up behind, for Gandalf was letting his wand give out a faint light to help the dwarves as they went along.

Quite suddenly Dori, now at the back again carrying Bilbo, was grabbed from behind in the dark. He shouted and fell; and the hobbit rolled off his shoulders into the blackness, bumped his head on hard rock, and remembered nothing more.

ASSESSMENT

Complete this assessment on **page 25** of your **PORTFOLIO**.

 ## Written Assessment

A. Capital Letters

Circle the words that should begin with a capital letter in the following text. This is the final paragraph from the short story 'The Dead', by **James Joyce**.

a few light taps on the pane made him turn to the window. it had begun to snow again. he watched sleepily the flakes, silver and dark, falling obliquely against the lamplight. the time had come for him to set out on his journey westward. yes, the newspapers were right: snow was general all over ireland. it was falling on every part of the dark central plain on the treeless hills, falling softly upon the bog of allen and, farther westward, softly falling into the dark mutinous shannon waves. it was falling, too, upon every part of the lonely churchyard on the hill where michael furey lay buried. it lay thickly drifted on the crooked crosses and headstones, on the spears of the little gate, on the barren thorns. his soul swooned slowly as he heard the snow falling faintly through the universe and faintly falling, like the descent of their last end, upon all the living and the dead.

 ## Peer Assessment
Count your circled words and compare results.

B. Descriptive Writing: The Five Senses

Write two descriptive sentences for each of the five senses.

Sight _____

Sound _____

Smell _____

Taste _____

Touch _____

(10 marks)

ASSESSMENT

C. Cloze Test

Fill in the blanks, using the adjectives below.

small • luxuriant • hottest • hard • heavy-eared • golden
• normal • sweltering • low • unbearable

The wheat was high that year. In late spring it had rained a lot, and by mid-June the stalks were higher and more _____ than ever. They grew densely packed, _____ ready to be harvested.

Everything was covered in wheat. The _____ hills rolled away like the waves of a _____ ocean. As far as the horizon nothing but wheat, sky, crickets, sun and heat.

I had no idea how hot it was, degrees centigrade don't mean much to a nine-year-old, but I knew it wasn't _____.

That damned summer of 1978 had gone down in history as one of the _____ of the century. The heat got into the stones, crumbled the earth, scorched the plants and killed the livestock, made the houses _____. When you picked the tomatoes in the vegetable garden they had no juice and the zucchini were _____ and _____. The sun took away your breath, your strength, your desire to play, everything. And it was just as _____ at night.

From ***I'm Not Scared*** by **Niccolò Ammaniti**   (10 marks)

ASSESSMENT

D. Match Up

Match up the adjectives with the nouns.

Adjectives	Nouns	Adjectives	Nouns
cross	bread	rusty	door
happy	jellies	worn	pages
cold	teacher	cracked	dress
fresh	child	beautiful	cup
sour	wind	crisp	nail

Adjectives	Nouns	Adjectives	Nouns
cross	teacher		

(10 marks)

E. Subject and Verb in a Sentence

The subject is the 'do-er' and the verb is the action word. List the subject and verb in the following sentences.

Sentence	Subject	Verb
Mice eat cheese.	mice	eat
Molly loves skipping.		
They all ran the marathon.		
The trees are in full bloom.		
Toothache gnaws at you.		
Clouds gather and the sky darkens in winter.		
If she had checked first, she'd have seen him there.		
Swallows twitter in the sky.		
The flight attendants were exhausted.		
Time waits for no man.		

(20 marks)

ASSESSMENT

F. Paragraphs

Rewrite the following text using paragraphs and correct any errors in spelling, capital letters and punctuation. You should have four paragraphs.

half of the world's wild animals have been lost in the past 40 years because of habitat destruction, hunnting and deforestation, ackording to a report by the world wide Fund (WWF) for nature. The living Planet report found that populations of mammals, birds, reptiles, amphibians and fishes have fallen on average by 52 per cent since 1970. the wwf looked at 10,380 species across the world. the situation is worst in low-income countries, where wildlife popilations declined on average by 58 per cent between 1970 and 2010. latin america has had the bigest loses, with a drop of 83 per cent, but Europeen speceis have also sufered, including the turtle dove, red squirels and white seals. The decline can almost entirely be attributed to humen activity, through habitat loss, deforestation, climate change, overfishing and hunting, the report said.

Peer Assessment

Compare your paragraphs and corrections with your partner.

G. Spelling

Give the correct spelling for these commonly misspelled words.

Accommadation	Excelant
Acident	Febuary
Awkard	Goverment
Arguement	Grammer
Buisness	Garantee
Beggining	Imediately
Beleive	Independant
Comittee	Recieve
Consience	Rythm
Definitley	Seperate
Desside	Truely
Embaras	Villian

(24 marks)

Writing Fiction

How do writers write books? Many writers are avid readers who have good imaginations and like to work with words. They may spend a long time crafting the plot or story, developing the characters, creating atmosphere and redrafting their sentences hundreds of times. In this chapter, you will learn about the elements required to write a story and you will have opportunities to work and experiment with these elements.

By reading regularly, you will gain ideas and inspiration for your own writing. The more you read, the more ideas you get and the more your vocabulary grows. The more words you come across from regular reading, the better you will become at understanding text, answering comprehension questions and writing pieces of text yourself.

Checklist for Story Writing

Does the story have a good narrative shape or structure? Look for:

- A beginning/introduction.
- A middle with a problem or conflict.
- A resolution of the problem and an end.
- Compelling action.
- Paragraphs.
- Descriptive verbs, adverbs and adjectives.
- Good flow or continuity.
- A mix of short and long sentences.
- Punctuation (commas, exclamation marks, etc.) for pause and effect.
- Atmosphere – mystery, excitement, tension, suspense.
- A twist at the end.
- Similes/metaphors.

Oral Language

'I couldn't put it down, it was a real page-turner.'

'It was gripping'.

'You just have to read it'.

'The ending was incredible; I'd never have guessed it'.

In pairs, think about books that you liked so much that you couldn't put them down.
Chat about what it is that makes you want to continue reading a book or story.
How do writers grab and maintain the attention and interest of the reader?

Ingredients in a Story

Let's work through some of the key features of a good story. Remember, not everything on the list will feature in every story. You can refer back to it as you read the examples of fiction later in the chapter or when you are doing your own writing.

Plot: This is the series of events that take place in the story. There may be a main plot and a few subplots. The main plot might be the serious plot and the subplot might be lighter, with humour or comedy.

Subplot: This is another story within the main story. For example, in Shakespeare's *The Merchant of Venice*, the main plot is the conflict between Antonio and Shylock and the subplot is the romances between Bassanio and Portia, Nerissa and Gratiano and Lorenzo and Jessica. In *The Lord of the Rings* the main plot is Frodo's quest but the subplot is Pippin and Merry's escape from the Orcs.

Action: This is the development of events in a story. It is what characters do, what causes them to do these things and what the consequences of their actions are. Most stories have problems and conflict. If there are a number of crisis points, they add to the excitement. When the conflict reaches a moment of great crisis or interest, this is the climax of the story. It is the turning point. The reader then wonders what will happen next, how the story will proceed and how it will end.

BOOKS ARE A **UNIQUELY** PORTABLE **MAGIC**

- Stephen King

Setting: This is the place or location and the time in which the story happens; for example, India in the 1990s, a farm in Wales in 2010, New York in 1832 and so on.

Characters: These are the people in the story. For example, the main character, their best friend and a third party are often central in a story.

Dialogue: This is the conversations that occur in the story.

Narration: The person who tells the story is the narrator. You may remember from *Great Expectations 1* that stories are told using 'I' (first person) or 'he/she' (third person) narration. The narrator's view affects the story. The same story can be told differently by characters who have different viewpoints or perspectives.

If a story is told using 'I', you get an insight into how the narrator feels and how the narrator views other characters and events. 'I' is direct, almost from 'the horse's mouth'.

If a story is told using 'he/she', it's less direct. You get the story from the viewpoint of one character. Rather than saying 'My name is Martha. I am fifteen years old', the writer narrates the story from one character's point of view and might say instead 'Martha was fifteen years old. She...'

Another type of third person narrator is an omniscient narrator who knows everything and relates the entire story about all characters and events. The omniscient narrator is not a character in the story; instead they are able to talk about the feelings and points of view of everyone in the story. It is almost as if they are looking down on events as they happen.

First person	Second person	Third person
I	You	He/she or omnicient narrator
Personal, intimate, direct	Rare. Hard to narrate using 'you'	More distant, less personal, less direct than 'I'

Description/imagery: What can you imagine or see when you read a story? Good descriptive words help you to visualise or almost experience the five senses (sight, sound, smell, touch, taste).

Studying Fiction

Whether you are exploring a novel from the prescribed list or simply reading for pleasure, you will learn about how a story is created. If you think about how the writer has crafted their narrative, it may help you to craft your own stories. You may become more conscious of how to write an interesting introduction, how to be more descriptive, how to put a twist into your stories, etc. Examining the structure of a novel is like peering behind the scenes to see how it works and how it all fits together.

Narration, characters, setting, plot and language are just some of the things you should think about when studying a story or a novel.

A writer structures the story by arranging the order of events in a particular way. A good story will have all the elements – plot, action, characterisation, atmosphere, dialogue and descriptive language – knitted together well.

In this chapter, we will examine a number of extracts that show us different aspects and features of storytelling and help us to develop our own writing skills.

Characterisation

Divergent *by Veronica Roth*

Read the following extract from *Divergent* by Veronica Roth and focus on the characters. Think about how they are described and what kinds of people they are.

Roth was born in New York but raised in Illinois. She studied creative writing in college and published the *Divergent* trilogy to great acclaim, winning numerous awards. Book two in the trilogy is *Insurgent*, followed by *Allegiant*.

In the following extract, Tris, the narrator, who belongs to the Abnegation faction (group), is facing an important aptitude test in school, which will be followed by a Choosing Ceremony.

There is one mirror in my house. It is behind a sliding panel in the hallway upstairs. Our faction allows me to stand in front of it on the second day of every third month, the day my mother cuts my hair.

I sit on the stool and my mother stands behind me with the scissors, trimming. The strands fall on the floor in a dull, blond ring.

When she finishes, she pulls my hair away from my face and twists it into a knot. I note how calm she looks and how focused she is. She is well-practiced in the art of losing herself. I can't say the same of myself.

I sneak a look at my reflection when she isn't paying attention—not for the sake of vanity, but out of curiosity. A lot can happen to a person's appearance in three months.

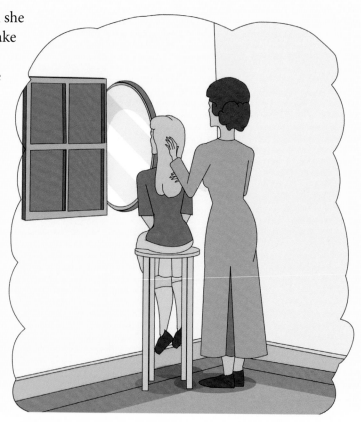

In my reflection, I see a narrow face, wide, round eyes, and a long, thin nose—I still look like a little girl, though sometime in the last few months I turned sixteen. The other factions celebrate birthdays, but we don't. It would be self-indulgent.

"There," she says when she pins the knot in place. Her eyes catch mine in the mirror. It is too late to look away, but instead of scolding me, she smiles at our reflection. I frown a little. Why doesn't she reprimand me for staring at myself?

"So today is the day," she says.

"Yes," I reply.

"Are you nervous?"

I stare into my own eyes for a moment. Today is the day of the aptitude test that will show me which of the five factions I belong in. And tomorrow, at the Choosing Ceremony, I will decide on a faction; I will decide the rest of my life; I will decide to stay with my family or abandon them.

"No," I say. "The tests don't have to change our choices."

"Right." She smiles. "Let's go eat breakfast."

"Thank you. For cutting my hair."

She kisses my cheek and slides the panel over the mirror. I think my mother could he beautiful, in a different world. Her body is thin beneath the gray robe. She has high cheekbones and long eyelashes, and when she lets her hair down at night, it hangs in waves over her shoulders. But she must hide that beauty in Abnegation.

We walk together to the kitchen. On these mornings when my brother makes breakfast, and my father's hand skims my hair as he reads the newspaper, and my mother hums as she clears the table—it is on these mornings that I feel guiltiest for wanting to leave them.

*****

The bus stinks of exhaust. Every time it hits a patch of uneven pavement, it jostles me from side to side, even though I'm gripping the seat to keep myself still.

My older brother, Caleb, stands in the aisle, holding a railing above his head to keep himself steady. We don't look alike. He has my father's dark hair and hooked nose and my mother's green eyes and dimpled cheeks. When he was younger, that collection of features looked strange, but now it suits him. If he wasn't Abnegation, I'm sure the girls at school would stare at him.

He also inherited my mother's talent for selflessness. He gave his seat to a surly Candor man on the bus without a second thought.

The Candor man wears a black suit with a white tie—Candor standard uniform. Their faction values honesty and sees the truth as black and white, so that is what they wear.

The gaps between the buildings narrow and the roads are smoother as we near the heart of the city. The building that was once called the Sears Tower—we call it the Hub—emerges from the fog, a black pillar in the skyline. The bus passes under the elevated tracks. I have never been on a train, though they never stop running and there are tracks everywhere. Only the Dauntless ride them.

Five years ago, volunteer construction workers from Abnegation repaved some of the roads. They started in the middle of the city and worked their way outward until they ran out of materials. The roads where I live are still cracked and patchy, and it's not safe to drive on them. We don't have a car anyway.

Caleb's expression is placid as the bus sways and jolts on the road. The gray robe falls from his arm as he clutches a pole for balance. I can tell by the constant shift of his eyes that he is watching the people around us — striving to see only them and to forget himself. Candor values honesty, but our faction, Abnegation, values selflessness.

The bus stops in front of the school and I get up, scooting past the Candor man. I grab Caleb's arm as I stumble over the man's shoes. My slacks are too long, and I've never been that graceful.

The Upper Levels building is the oldest of the three schools in the city: Lower Levels, Mid-Levels, and Upper Levels. Like all the other buildings around it, it is made of glass and steel. In front of it is a large metal sculpture that the Dauntless climb after school, daring each other to go higher and higher. Last year I watched one of them fall and break her leg. I was the one who ran to get the nurse.

"Aptitude tests today," I say. Caleb is not quite a year older than I am, so we are in the same year at school.

He nods as we pass through the front doors. My muscles tighten the second we walk in. The atmosphere feels hungry, like every sixteen-year-old is trying to devour as much as he can get of this last day. It is likely that we will not walk these halls again after the Choosing Ceremony—once we choose, our new factions will be responsible for finishing our education.

Our classes are cut in half today, so we will attend all of them before the aptitude tests, which take place after lunch. My heart rate is already elevated.

"You aren't at all worried about what they'll tell you?" I ask Caleb.

We pause at the split in the hallway where he will go one way, toward Advanced Math, and I will go the other, toward Faction History.

He raises an eyebrow at me. "Are you?"

I could tell him I've been worried for weeks about what the aptitude test will tell me—Abnegation, Candor, Erudite, Amity, or Dauntless?

Instead I smile and say, "Not really."

He smiles back. "Well... have a good day."

I walk toward Faction History, chewing on my lower lip. He never answered my question.

The hallways are cramped, though the light coming through the windows creates the illusion of space; they are one of the only places where the factions mix, at our age. Today the crowd has a new kind of energy, a last day mania.

A girl with long curly hair shouts "Hey!" next to my ear, waving at a distant friend. A jacket sleeve smacks me on the cheek.

Then an Erudite boy in a blue sweater shoves me. I lose my balance and fall hard on the ground.

"Out of my way, Stiff," he snaps, and continues down the hallway.

My cheeks warm. I get up and dust myself off. A few people stopped when I fell, but none of them offered to help me. Their eyes follow me to the edge of the hallway. This sort of thing has been happening to others in my faction for months now—the Erudite have been releasing antagonistic reports about Abnegation, and it has begun to affect the way we relate at school. The gray clothes, the plain hairstyle, and the unassuming demeanor of my faction are supposed to make it easier for me to forget myself, and easier for everyone else to forget me too. But now they make me a target.

GLOSSARY

Factions: Smaller groups who disagree, within one large group.
Self-indulgent: Doing whatever you please.
Elevated: Situated higher than everything else.
Illusion: A deceptive appearance, giving an untrue idea of something else.

A. Reading

Rate this text for readability. Write the word/phrase of your choice into your copy.

VERY EASY ☐   **EASY** ☐   **OKAY** ☐   **HARD** ☐   **VERY HARD** ☐

B. Literacy Questions

1. Is the extract told in first or third person? Support your answer with quotes.
2. What important event is the narrator facing?
3. How would you describe the narrator? What kind of person is she?
4. The characters in *Divergent* are divided into factions. Describe the main groups discussed here: Candor, Abnegation and Dauntless. What do they value and how do they differ?
5. Would you like to continue reading this story? Why? Discuss this with the person beside you.

C. Drawing

The bus journey and the roads are described in detail. Read this part again. Draw the scene as you imagine it to be.

D. Oral Language

'There is one mirror in my house.'

Imagine your house with only one mirror. Imagine that you can look at your reflection only once every three months. Discuss the following questions with a partner.

1. Would it be difficult to live without mirrors?
2. Do we have too many mirrors in our homes?
3. Do we worry too much about our appearance? Are we too vain? Are we insecure?

Focus on Characters

Most books will have one or more major characters and a number of minor characters. There are a number of different names for the types of character we encounter in books.

Good	Bad	Ambiguous
Hero/heroine Protagonist	Villain Antagonist	Anti-hero

Usually there is a main character (protagonist) who is a good character. He/she encounters problems, challenges or conflicts often caused by the bad character, the antagonist or villain.

The good character usually defeats the bad character. Here are some examples of good characters defeating bad characters:

- *The Three Little Pigs* – Three good pigs, one bad wolf. The third pig outsmarts the wolf.
- *Harry Potter* – Harry the good, heroic character defeats Voldemort.
- *Percy Jackson & the Olympians* – Percy Jackson defeats Kronos.

Just like the people we encounter in the real world, fictional characters are very rarely 100 per cent good or bad. When we encounter a character who is a reluctant hero or someone who has flaws such as meanness or selfishness but who is still ultimately good, we refer to them as an 'anti-hero'.

Well-written and developed characters hook the reader. If we care about the good characters, we will cry if they die or suffer, we will hope that they survive all challenges and injustices and win in the end.

However, sometimes the good characters lose, suffer an injustice or are powerless or unlucky. For example:

The Boy in the Striped Pyjamas – Bruno dies.
The Fault in Our Stars – Augustus dies of cancer.

Usually the reader identifies with a character. The strengths and weaknesses of characters are revealed and the reader empathises with emotions such as fear, love, guilt, anxiety, indecision and loneliness. The actions of characters often teach the reader something about life.

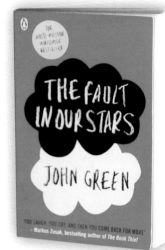

Oral Language

In pairs, chat about your favourite heroes and villains. For example, Thomas in *The Maze Runner* or Frodo in *The Lord of the Rings*. Talk about why you liked/disliked them and make a list of their heroic or villainous qualities.

Characters and Action

Stories typically involve a third important character. This character sparks the conflict and the twists and turns. For example, in *The Fault in Our Stars*, Hazel writes to Peter Van Houten in Amsterdam, which leads her and Augustus on their journey to visit him.

Often in romance stories, there is a love triangle involving a third character. In Shakespeare's *Romeo and Juliet*, Romeo and Juliet are tormented by Paris. In *Private Peaceful*, both Tommo and Charlie fall in love with Molly.

There wouldn't be action if there was only the protagonist and antagonist, the good and the bad. There has to be someone and something to cause waves, otherwise it would be a boring story!

Change is vital in any story. The hero or heroine has to get into situations that challenge him/her. If the central character fails a challenge, the reader feels sympathy. If they misbehave or do something the reader doesn't expect or like, the reader is engaged. A protagonist must make choices, so that we want to see what will happen as a result.

Group Work

In groups, think about two or three different scenarios for the following plot: a love triangle between James, Lauren and Tom. Then jot them down on **page 32** of your **PORTFOLIO**.

For example:

The scene is set at a disco. The good character is James, who fancies Lauren. James plucks up the courage to chat up Lauren and dance with her. This would be a boring story if they danced, fell in love and dated and nothing else happened.

However, at the disco, Tom suddenly storms over, taps James on the shoulder and says aggressively, 'Who the hell are you, what's going on?'

If it's the old story of two men fighting over the same woman, the good guy usually wins and the bad guy loses. But how about both losing?

Maybe Lauren is not interested in either guy, but instead has feelings for a fourth character called Mark.

Is Mark interested in Lauren? Is he with someone else? Is Lauren brave enough to ask him out? Is there another character who's interested in James or Tom?

Each group member must THINK about a scenario.
The group discusses the ideas and chooses one idea.
Develop the story.

Don't forget to fill in your Group Work Self Assessment and Peer Assessment on **page 33** of your **PORTFOLIO**.

Characterisation

Think about the different types of characters developed by the writer in the following extract from *The Same Stuff as Stars* by Katherine Paterson.

 # The Same Stuff as Stars

by Katherine Paterson

Katherine Paterson was born in China and lived both there and in the USA on and off for a number of years. She graduated from college with a degree in English, then worked in Japan as a Christian missionary and teacher. One of her most successful novels is *Bridge to Terabithia*, which was also made into a film. She has won two Newbery Medals and two National Book Awards in the USA.

In this extract, Angel and her brother Bernie have been left in their grandma's house because their dad is in jail and their mum couldn't cope with minding them. Angel is upset because, shortly after leaving both children with their grandma, their mother Verna returned to the house and secretly took Bernie away. Angel is very protective of Bernie and fears that Verna will not look after him properly.

…although she liked the thought of Grandma's lap, it was about as comfortable as cuddling with kindling. She went into the bathroom and got some toilet paper to blow her nose, not daring to look at herself in the streaky mirror. She knew she was a mess. "Grandma," she called from the doorway. "How about I make us some tea?"

"Well, that sounds downright civilised."

After the tea, even though it was still afternoon, Angel made supper for the two of them. They didn't talk much. They tried not to look at the place where Bernie should have been sitting. Grandma even ate her broccoli without complaining. Angel started to say something about it, but she could feel the tears start as she formed the sentence in her mind, and kept quiet. She washed the dishes and left them to dry beside the sink.

"I think I'll do my homework upstairs and then go on to bed," she said.

Grandma nodded from the rocker. Trying to be a comfort seemed to have worn her out.

Angel lay on her stomach under the bare bulb and opened *Know the Stars*. It was a page she'd read so often she could almost recite it.

> *Polaris (stress on LAR) is the only star that never changes its place in the sky, at least not so that you can notice it. It always stays put while the other stars and constellations are moving…*

That was what she needed—a Polaris, a North Star, that never moved. Something steady so that she could always find her way. But what about Bernie? She'd been his Polaris, hadn't she? When everything else had changed, at least he'd had her. Now he had Verna, who switched around faster than a whirling planet. She wished she knew how to pray. She wanted to pray for Bernie, for Verna, even for Wayne.

Wayne. He was her daddy. He never would have run off with Bernie and left her behind like Verna had. It wasn't his fault the police had thrown him in jail. He didn't even do it, whatever it was they said he did. He'd never even smacked her when she was little. He'd bought her Grizzle and given her her name, Angel. Did a man who named his baby girl Angel sound like somebody who would go off and commit a crime?

Even as she crept down the stairs, even as she took the phone off the hook, even when with her finger shaking she yanked around the dial the numbers she had memorised without ever meaning to, even until the moment the voice at the other end answered—something in her stomach warned her not to go ahead, her whispery voice as trembly as her body.

"This is Angel Morgan. I need to get a message to my daddy, Wayne Morgan. Just say… just say Verna's come and took Bernie off. Just tell him that."

She hung up the phone and went to the kitchen door to look out. She could smell frost in the air and hear the wind wailing in the changing leaves. It was a night of no stars.

*****

Like a sleepwalker, she stumbled through the next day at school. She hadn't wanted to go at all. She'd wanted to stay by the phone, in case. But Grandma made her go. "It's like sitting in the garden watching cabbage come to a head. The phone'll never ring long as you're waiting beside it. Ask me. I know about such things."

She spent most of lunchtime in the bathroom and was still there in the stall when a group of girls swept in. "What did she say when you asked her about the robbery, Megan?"

Angel froze as Megan's voice answered the question. "Oh, she pretended she didn't know what I was talking about, but my grandma told my daddy and he told my mom that she's Wayne Morgan's girl. Grandma even had the clippings. She saves everything, and Daddy was in grade school with Wayne Morgan, so she thought he'd be interested."

Angel strained to hear the details. They might think she was pretending, but she really *didn't* know. It made her feel the fool to have Megan Armstrong know more about her daddy than she did.

"Did he shoot somebody?"

"He said he didn't, but the clerk had a bullet in him, didn't he? One of those guys in the ski masks shot him, and the other guys said Wayne Morgan did it. So it was two against one. They shouldn't ever let somebody like that out of jail."

But he didn't do it. Angel broke out in a cold sweat. *Wayne wouldn't hurt anybody.* But how did she know? She hardly knew her own daddy. It had happened when she was five, and all she could remember before that was the yelling. There must have been good times, too. Yes, when he bought her Grizzle. She remembered how happy she was when he gave her Grizzle. Verna had snorted something like "Blue bear? I swear," but Angel had loved it from the first. It was the only present he had ever given her, although for a while Verna would give her something and say "It's from your daddy and me." She had stopped saying it years ago. There hadn't been many presents, just the toys they got from the Salvation Army Santa Claus. That hardly counted.

The girls were still whispering, but whether about Wayne or something or somebody else, she didn't know. She wished they'd leave so she could come out of the stall. She read the dirty words and looked at the pictures scratched into the back of the door. You'd think the school would paint them over. Then again, some were dug deep in the door, so they'd probably show through the paint. She wished she had something with a sharp point, so she could scratch something nasty about Megan Armstrong on the door. Something that would last for years.

"Megan, shh! There's somebody in there."

"What of it?" Megan's voice answered. "Hey, you in there. You're not supposed to eavesdrop."

Angel stayed still, but she was seething inside. She'd been here when they came in, hadn't she?

"You scared to come out?" It was the voice of one of Megan's gang, Heather Somebody-or-other.

There was a giggle. "Hea-*thur!*"

Then suddenly Heather's head appeared under the stall door. The eyes went wide and quickly disappeared. "It's her in there!'" she whispered fiercely.

"Everything I said was true. It was in the newspapers."

Angel could almost see Megan tossing her bouncy curls.

"Let's get out of here," someone said. She could hear them scuffling out into the hall, whispering and giggling as they went. Angel was almost glad. For a few minutes she was able to think how much she hated those girls instead of the fact that Bernie was gone. *Gone.*

*****

She slumped onto her bus seat with something like relief. The worst day of her life was coming to an end. Soon she'd be home. It was strange to think of Grandma's house as home, but it was. Home with a hole bigger than a moon crater, now that there was no Bernie in it.

"It didn't ring," Grandma said. She wasn't in her rocker. She was standing by the hot plate. "I'm fixing me some tea," she said. "You want some, too?"

Angel nodded. "Then I think I'll walk up to the library."

Grandma stiffened. "It's getting dark early," she said. "Tomorrow's Saddidy. Wait till tomorrow. Then you'll have time to shop, too. We must be out of one of them precious food groups by now."

Angel giggled despite herself. "You're catching on, Grandma. I'll have you trained yet."

They drank their tea in the darkening kitchen, their bodies in knots, fighting to keep from turning to stare at the phone. She'd always tried to defend Verna, always tried to see her mother's side of things, but it was hard to do this time.

*****

She woke up in the night. She couldn't quite remember the dream that had awakened her. Someone—Bernie, she thought—had been crying, but the only fragment of the dream that had stayed with her was the sight of the pickup pulling away with Bernie's arm sticking out the window on the passenger side. "Pull in your arm, Bernie," she'd yelled. "How many times do I have to tell you? Get your arm out of the window!" She sat up, her throat as hoarse as though she'd been yelling out loud instead of in a dream.

She could still hear the crying. After countless nights of negotiating that black staircase, she was like a skilful blind person in the dark, making her way down to the kitchen and around the furniture until she reached the bedroom door. She leaned her head against the wood. Behind it she could hear the shuddering sobs of a broken old heart.

GLOSSARY

Constellations: A group of stars forming a pattern.

Salvation Army: A charity organisation.

Eavesdropping: Secretly listening to a conversation.

A. Reading

Rate this text for readability. Write the word/phrase of your choice into your copy.

VERY EASY ☐   **EASY** ☐   **OKAY** ☐   **HARD** ☐   **VERY HARD** ☐

B. Literacy Questions

1. Who is Angel living with?
2. Who has been taken away from Angel?
3. What trouble do you think Angel's dad Wayne is involved in?
4. Do you think Angel has friends in school? Explain your answer.
5. Why do you think her grandmother is crying?
6. Angel is the main character. Is she a well-written and interesting main character? Explain your answer.
7. List the bad characters. What is their role in the story?
8. Would you like to read more of this story? Discuss this with the person beside you.

C. Writing

Imagine you have been asked by the author Katherine Paterson to help develop Angel as a character. Fill in the following sentences about Angel.

Angel is _____ years old.

What Angel really wants in the story is _____.

Angel as a person is brave and kind because _____.

Angel is a dreamer because _____.

Angel is a loner but would like to _____.

The next challenge Angel faces is _____.

D. Drawing

Draw the story, mapping out the plot in images. Use the storyboard format on **page 413**.

Scene 1 – Supper in Grandma's kitchen.
Scene 2 – The phone call.
Scene 3 – School.
Scene 4 – Home with Grandma.

E. Reading – Self Assessment

Fill out the Self Assessment on **page 34** of your **PORTFOLIO**.

Focus on Narrator

Read the following extract and see if you can identify what type of narrator is telling the story and some of the common features of this type of narration.

The Adventures of Huckleberry Finn

by Mark Twain

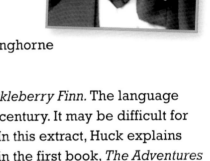

Mark Twain was born in Missouri in the United States and lived in a small town along the Mississippi river called Hannibal. He had a varied career, beginning as a printer's apprentice with the *Missouri Courier* newspaper, and then training to become a steamboat pilot in 1857 after a trip down the Mississippi. After 18 months of training, he qualified and loved sailing up and down the river. It inspired him to write *The Adventures of Tom Sawyer* and a sequel, *The Adventures of Huckleberry Finn*. Mark Twain was a pen name. 'Mark twain' was a frequent call on a steamboat. It meant that the water was two fathoms (12 feet) deep – a safe depth. His real name was Samuel Langhorne Clemens.

This is the opening chapter from *The Adventures of Huckleberry Finn.* The language and dialect are from Mississippi during the nineteenth century. It may be difficult for a modern reader to understand some of the language. In this extract, Huck explains briefly what has happened to himself and Tom Sawyer in the first book, *The Adventures of Tom Sawyer.* He is now living with the Widow Douglas and he explains how he feels living there. At midnight Tom creeps along to secretly meet Huck.

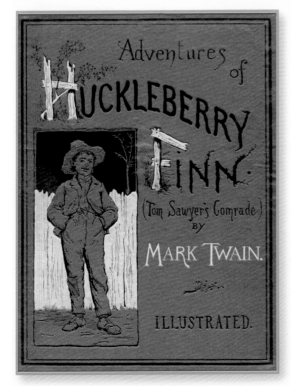

You don't know about me, without you have read a book by the name of *The Adventures of Tom Sawyer,* but that ain't no matter. That book was made by Mr Mark Twain, and he told the truth, mainly. There was things which he stretched, but mainly he told the truth. That is nothing. I never seen anybody but lied, one time or another, without it was Aunt Polly, or the widow, or maybe Mary. Aunt Polly – Tom's Aunt Polly, she is – and Mary, and the Widow Douglas, is all told about in that book – which is mostly a true book; with some stretchers, as I said before.

Now the way that the book winds up, is this: Tom and me found the money that the robbers hid in the cave, and it made us rich. We got six thousand dollars apiece – all gold. It was an awful sight of money when it was piled up. Well, Judge Thatcher, he took it and put it out at interest, and it fetched us a dollar a day apiece, all the year round – more than a body could tell what to do with. The Widow Douglas, she took me for her son, and allowed she would sivilise me; but it was rough living in the house all the time, considering how dismal regular and decent the widow was in all her ways; and so when I couldn't stand it no longer, I lit out. I got into my old rags and my sugar-hogshead again, and was free and satisfied. But Tom Sawyer he hunted me up and said he was going to start a band of robbers, and I might join if I would go back to the widow and be respectable. So I went back.

The widow she cried over me, and called me a poor lost lamb, and she called me a lot of other names, too, but she never meant no harm by it. She put me in them new clothes again, and I couldn't do nothing but sweat and sweat, and feel all cramped up. Well, then, the old thing commenced again. The widow rung a bell for supper, and you had to come to time. When you got to the table you couldn't go right to eating, but you had to wait for the widow to tuck down her head and grumble a little over the victuals, though there warn't really anything the matter with them. That is, nothing only everything was cooked by itself. In a barrel of odds and ends it is different; things get mixed up, and the juice kind of swaps around, and the things go better.

After supper she got out her book and learned me about Moses and the Bulrushers; and I was in a sweat to find out all about him; but by-and-by she let it out that Moses had been dead a considerable long time; so then I didn't care no more about him; because I don't take no stock in dead people.

Pretty soon I wanted to smoke, and asked the widow to let me. But she wouldn't. She said it was a mean practice and wasn't clean, and I must try to not do it any more. That is just

Focus on Plot

Plot is the action and the order of events in a story. When a writer thinks of a story and creates events, the events have consequences. Like a 'domino effect', one event causes something else to happen and so on.

In the following extract, Mr Toad is part good, part bad – a likeable rogue. He has done wrong but we still like him and want him to prosper. Notice the events in the story that propel the story forward and that maintain your interest. Think about the action. First one thing happens, and then something else, which leads to something else happening. Figure out how the writer structured the incidents or events.

 The Wind in the Willows by Kenneth Grahame

Kenneth Grahame was born in Edinburgh in Scotland, but at the age of five moved with his siblings to Berkshire in England to live with their grandmother. Her house was on spacious grounds near a river and a wood, which is believed to have inspired the setting for *The Wind in the Willows.* Grahame excelled in school and went on to work in a bank, but he also wrote stories. These stories were published in the 1890s. In 1908, his most famous book, *The Wind in the Willows*, was published and became an instant bestseller.

This is one story about Mr Toad, who has been held captive in a castle for stealing the magistrate's car. In this extract, the gaoler's daughter takes pity on Mr Toad and helps him to escape.

One morning the girl was very thoughtful, and answered at random, and did not seem to Toad to be paying proper attention to his witty sayings and sparkling comments.

"Toad," she said presently, "just listen, please. I have an aunt who is a washerwoman."

"There, there," said Toad graciously and affably, "never mind; think no more about it. I have several aunts who ought to be washerwomen."

"Do be quiet a minute, Toad," said the girl. "You talk too much, that's your chief fault, and I'm trying to think, and you hurt my head. As I said, I have an aunt who is a washerwoman; she does washing for all the prisoners in this castle – we try to keep any paying business of that sort in the family, you understand. She takes out the washing on Monday morning, and brings it in on Friday evening. This is a Thursday. Now, this is what occurs to me: you're very rich – at least you're always telling me so – and she's very poor. A few pounds wouldn't make any difference to you, and it would mean a lot to her. Now, I think if she were properly approached – squared, I believe, is the word you animals use – you could come to some arrangement by which she would let you have her dress and bonnet and so on, and you could escape from the castle as the official washerwoman. You're very alike in many respects – particularly about the figure."

"We're *not*," said the Toad in a huff. "I have a very elegant figure – for what I am.'

"So has my aunt," replied the girl, "for what she is. But have it your own way. You horrid, proud ungrateful animal, when I'm sorry for you, and trying to help you!"

"Yes, yes, that's all right; thank you very much indeed," said the Toad hurriedly. "But look here! You wouldn't surely have Mr Toad, of Toad Hall, going about the country disguised as a washerwoman!"

"Then you can stop here as a Toad," replied the girl with much spirit. "I suppose you want to go off in a coach-and-four!"

Honest Toad was always ready to admit himself in the wrong. "You are a good, kind, clever girl," he said, "and I am indeed a proud and stupid toad. Introduce me to your worthy aunt, if you will be so kind, and I have no doubt that the excellent lady and I will be able to arrange terms satisfactory to both parties."

Next evening the girl ushered her aunt into Toad's cell, bearing his week's washing pinned up in a towel. The old lady had been prepared beforehand for the interview, and the sight of certain gold sovereigns that Toad had thoughtfully placed on the table in full view practically completed the matter and left little further to discuss. In return for his cash, Toad received a cotton print gown, an apron, a shawl, and a rusty black bonnet; the only stipulation the old lady made being that she should be gagged and bound and dumped down in a corner. By this not very convincing artifice, she explained, aided by picturesque fiction which she could supply herself, she hoped to retain her situation, in spite of the suspicious appearance of things.

Toad was delighted with the suggestion. It would enable him to leave the prison in some style, and with his reputation for being a desperate and dangerous fellow untarnished; and he readily helped the gaoler's daughter to make her aunt appear as much as possible the victim of circumstances over which she had no control.

"Now it's your turn, Toad," said the girl. "Take off that coat and waistcoat of yours; you're fat enough as it is."

Shaking with laughter, she proceeded to 'hook-and-eye' him into the cotton print gown, arranged the shawl with a professional fold, and tied the strings of the rusty bonnet under his chin.

"You're the very image of her," she giggled, "only I'm sure you

half so respectable in all your life before. Now, good-bye, Toad, and good luck.
own the way you came up; and if anyone says anything to you, as they probably
men, you can chaff back a bit, of course, but remember you're a widow
alone in the world, with a character to lose."

heart, but as firm a footstep as he could command, Toad set forth cautiously
to be a most hare-brained and hazardous undertaking; but he was soon
ed to find how easy everything was made for him, and a little humbled
both his popularity, and the sex that seemed to inspire it, were really
herwoman's squat figure in its familiar cotton print seemed a passport
door and grim gateway; even when he hesitated, uncertain as to the right
take, he found himself helped out of his difficulty by the warder at the next gate,
us to be off to his tea, summoning him to come along sharp and not keep him waiting
there all night. The chaff and the humorous sallies to which he was subjected, and to which,
of course, he had to provide prompt and effective reply, formed, indeed, his chief danger;
for Toad was an animal with a strong sense of his own dignity, and the chaff was mostly (he
thought) poor and clumsy, and the humour of the sallies entirely lacking. However, he kept
his temper, though with great difficulty, suited his retorts to his company and his supposed
character, and did his best not to overstep the limits of good taste.

It seemed hours before he crossed the last courtyard, rejected the pressing invitation from
the last guardroom, and dodged the outspread arms of the last warder, pleading with
simulated passion for just one farewell embrace. But at last he heard the wicket-gate in the
great outer door click behind him, felt the fresh air of the outer world upon his anxious brow,
and knew that he was free.

Dizzy with the easy success of his daring exploit, he walked quickly towards the lights of the
town, not knowing in the least what he should do next, only quite certain of one thing, that
he must remove himself as quickly as possible from a neighbourhood where the lady he was
forced to represent was so well-known and so popular a character.

As he walked along, considering, his attention was caught by some red and green lights a little
way off, to one side of the town, and the sound of puffing and snorting of engines and the
banging of shunted trucks fell on his ear. "Aha", he thought, "this is a piece of luck! A railway-
station is the thing I want most in the whole world at this moment; and what's more, I needn't
go through the town to get to it, and shan't have to support this humiliating character by
repartees which, though thoroughly effective, do not assist one's sense of self-respect."

He made his way to the station accordingly, consulted a time-table; and found that a train,
bound more or less in the direction of his home, was due to start in half an hour. "More
luck!" said Toad, his spirits rising rapidly, and went off to the booking-office to buy his ticket.

He gave the name of the station that he knew to be nearest to the village of which Toad
Hall was the principal feature, and mechanically put his fingers, in search of the necessary
money, where his waistcoat pocket should have been. But here the cotton gown, which had
nobly stood by him so far, and which he had basely forgotten, intervened, and frustrated
his efforts. In a sort of nightmare he struggled with the strange uncanny thing that seemed
to hold his hands, turn all muscular strivings to water, and laugh at him all the time; while
other travellers, forming up in a line behind, waited with impatience, making suggestions of
more or less value and comments of more or less stringency and point. At last – somehow –
he never rightly understood how – he burst the barriers, attained the goal, arrived at where
all waistcoat pockets are eternally situated, and found – not only no money, but no pocket to
hold it, and no waistcoat to hold the pocket!

To his horror he recollected that he had left both coat and waistcoat behind
and with them his pocketbook, money, keys, watch, matches, pencil-case – a
life worth living, all that distinguishes the many pocketed animal, the lord of cr
the inferior onepocketed or no-pocketed productions that hop or trip about peri
unequipped for the real contest.

In his misery he made one desperate effort to carry the thing off, and, with a return to
fine old manner – a blend of the Squire and the College Don – he said, "Look here! I fir
left my purse behind. Just give me the ticket, will you, and I'll send the money on tomorr
I'm well known in these parts."

The clerk stared at him and the rusty black bonnet a moment, and then laughed. "I should
think you were pretty well known in these parts," he said, "if you've tried this game on often.
Here, stand away from the window, please, madam; you're obstructing the other passengers!"

An old gentleman who had been prodding him in the back for some moments here thrust
him away, and, what was worse, addressed him as his good woman, which angered Toad
more than anything that had occurred that evening.

Baffled and full of despair, he wandered blindly down the platform where the train was
standing, and tears trickled down each side of his nose. It was hard, he thought, to be within
sight of safety and almost of home, and to be baulked by the want of a few wretched shillings
and by the pettifogging mistrustfulness of paid officials. Very soon his escape would be
discovered, the hunt would be up, he would be caught, reviled, loaded with chains, dragged
back again to prison and bread-and-water and straw; his guards and penalties would be
doubled; and O, what sarcastic remarks the girl would make! What was to be done? He was
not swift of foot; his figure was unfortunately recognisable. Could he not squeeze under the
seat of a carriage? He had seen this method adopted by schoolboys, when the journey-money
provided by thoughtful parents had been diverted to other and better ends. As he pondered,

he found himself opposite the engine, which was being oiled, wiped, and generally caressed by its affectionate driver, a burly man with an oil can in one hand and a lump of cotton-waste in the other.

"Hullo, mother!" said the engine-driver, "what's the trouble? You don't look particularly cheerful."

"O sir!" said Toad, crying afresh, "I am a poor unhappy washerwoman, and I've lost all my money, and can't pay for a ticket, and I must get home tonight somehow, and whatever am to do I don't know. O dear, O dear!"

"That's a bad business, indeed," said the engine driver reflectively. "Lost your money – and can't get home – and got some kids, too, waiting for you, I dare say?"

"Any amount of 'em," sobbed Toad. "And they'll be hungry – and playing with matches – and upsetting lamps, the little innocents! – and quarrelling, and going on generally. O dear, O dear!"

"Well, I'll tell you what I'll do," said the good engine driver. "You're a washerwoman to your trade, says you. Very well, that's that. And I'm an engine driver, as you may well see, and there's no denying it's terrible dirty work. Uses up a power of shirts, it does, till my missus is fair tired of washing of 'em. If you'll wash a few shirts for me when you get home, and send 'em along, I'll give you a ride on my engine. It's against Company regulations, but we're not so very particular in these out-of-the-way parts."

The Toad's misery turned into rapture as he eagerly scrambled up into the cab of the engine. Of course, he had never washed a shirt in his life, and couldn't if he tried and, anyhow, he wasn't going to begin; but he thought: "When I get safely home to Toad Hall, and have money back again, and pockets to put it in, I will send the engine-driver enough to pay for quite a quantity of washing, and that will be the same thing, or better."

The guard waved his welcome flag, the engine driver whistled in cheerful response, and the train moved out of the station. As the speed increased, and the Toad could see on either side of him real fields, and trees, and hedges, and cows, and horses, all flying past him, and as he thought how every minute was bringing him nearer to Toad Hall, and sympathetic friends, and money to chink in his pocket, and a soft bed to sleep in, and good things to eat, and praise and admiration at the recital of his adventures and his surpassing cleverness, he began to skip up and down and shout and sing snatches of song, to the great astonishment of the engine driver, who had come across washerwomen before, at long intervals, but never one at all like this.

They had covered many and many a mile, and Toad was already considering what he would have for supper as soon as he got home, when he noticed that the engine driver, with a puzzled expression on his face, was leaning over the side of the engine and listening hard. Then he saw him climb on to the coals and gaze out over the top of the train; then he returned and said to Toad: "It's very strange; we're the last train running in this direction tonight, yet I could be sworn that I heard another following us!"

Toad ceased his frivolous antics at once. He became grave and depressed, and a dull pain in the lower part of his spine, communicating itself to his leg, made him want to sit down and try desperately not to think of all the possibilities.

By this time the moon was shining brightly, and the engine driver, steadying himself on the coal, could command a view of the line behind them for a long distance.

Presently he called out, "I can see it clearly now! It is an engine, on our rails, coming along at a great pace! It looks as if we were being pursued!"

The miserable Toad, crouching in the coal-dust, tried hard to think of something to do, with dismal want of success.

"They are gaining on us fast!" cried the engine driver. "And the engine is crowded with the queerest lot of people! Men like ancient warders, waving halberds; policeman in their helmets, waving truncheons; and shabbily dressed men in pot-hats, obvious and unmistakable plain-clothes detectives even at this distance, waving revolvers and walking sticks; all waving, and all shouting the same thing – 'Stop, stop, stop!'"

Then Toad fell on his knees among the coals and, raising his clasped paw in supplication, cried, "Save me, only save me, dear kind Mr Engine-driver, and I will confess everything! I am not the simple washerwoman I seem to be! I have no children waiting for me, innocent or otherwise! I am a toad – the well-known and popular Mr Toad, a landed proprietor; I have just escaped, by my great daring and cleverness, from a loathsome dungeon into which my enemies had flung me; and if those fellows on that engine recapture me, it will be chains and bread-and-water and straw and misery once more for poor, unhappy, innocent Toad!"

The engine driver looked down upon him very sternly, and said, "Now tell the truth; what were you put in prison for?"

"It was nothing very much," said poor Toad, colouring deeply. "I only borrowed a motor-car while the owners were at lunch; they had no need of it at the time. I didn't mean to steal it, really; but people – especially magistrates – take such harsh views of thoughtless and high-spirited actions."

The engine driver looked very grave and said, "I fear that you have indeed been a wicked toad, and by rights I ought to give you up to offended justice. But you are evidently in sore trouble and distress, so I will not desert you. I don't hold with motor, for one thing; and I don't hold with being ordered about by policeman when I'm on my own engine, for another. And the sight of an animal in tears always makes me feel queer and soft-hearted. So cheer up, Toad! I'll do my best, and we may beat them yet!"

They piled on more coals, shovelling furiously; the furnace roared, the sparks flew, the engine leapt and swung, but still their pursuers slowly gained. The engine-driver, with a sigh, wiped his brow with a handful of cotton-waste, and said, "I'm afraid it's no good, Toad. You see, they are running light, and they have the better engine. There's only one thing left for us to do, and it's your only chance, so attend very carefully to what I tell you. A short way ahead of us is a long tunnel, and on the other side of that the line passes through a thick wood. Now, I will put on all the speed I can while we are running through the tunnel, but the other fellows will slow down a bit, naturally, for fear of an accident. When we are through, I will shut off steam and put on the brakes as hard as I can, and the moment it's safe to do so you must jump and hide in the wood, before they get through the tunnel and see you. Then I will go at full speed ahead again, and they can chase me if they like, for as long as they like, and as far as they like. Now mind and be ready to jump when I tell you!"

They piled on more coals, and the train shot into the tunnel, and the engine rushed and roared and rattled, till at last they shot out at the other end into fresh air and the peaceful moonlight, and saw the wood lying dark and helpful upon either side of the line. The driver shut off the steam and put on the brakes, the Toad got down on the step, and as the train slowed down to almost a walking pace he heard the driver call out, "Now, jump!"

Focus on Plot Structure

A plot or story has to be good if we are to continue reading and be interested in what will happen next. A plot has to have:

- Action
- Problems
- Roadblocks and obstacles for protagonists and antagonists to face.

Every story needs an element of surprise or the unexpected. You also have to figure out the structure of the story and the order of events. Will you tell the story from the beginning, in chronological order? Or will you give away the ending in the first chapter, before explaining how this ending happened using flashback?

Stories generally have four elements:

- Introduction
- Development
- Climax
- Resolution.

Introduction

- The beginning is important, it must be interesting and must draw in or engage the reader. It doesn't have to tell the story from the start. It can begin close to a key moment in the story, before going back to explain how the story reached that point. It can give away the resolution at the start, then trace all the action backwards.

Development and Climax

- The action has been building, and it will reach a high point, a climax, a point where the story turns and it heads towards the end. You should be engaged, even engrossed in the story at this point.

Resolution

- How are the problems resolved? What happens to the characters? Is it the ending you expected or is it unexpected? Is there a surprise or a twist in the end? To what extent are you satisfied with the ending? Is it clear cut or is it ambiguous with some loose ends left hanging? Would you have preferred a different ending?

Once Upon a Time

Deciding the Order of Events

- Think about how the four elements will be put together when developing a plot. A straightforward option is to tell the story in chronological order. Start at the beginning, develop the action, build it to a climax and then a resolution.

- However, many novels and stories give the ending away at the start or perhaps the writer drops you into the middle of the climax or crisis and then traces back through all the events that led to that point – i.e. brings you back to the beginning.

- Writers think carefully about how they will structure their story, just like an architect carefully designs the structure of a building. When planning your plot, think about whether you will tell your story from the beginning in chronological order or begin at a different point in the action.

Flashback

A writer might begin a story in the present. For example, they might describe the murder of a main character and then use flashback to fill in the details that led to the murder. You may be told the ending of the story in the opening chapter, before the writer uses flashbacks to trace all the previous events leading up to the murder. For example, we are about to read an extract from *The Grass is Singing* by Doris Lessing. Think about how the author begins the story. Do you think this is an interesting introduction?

Flashback

The Grass is Singing *by Doris Lessing*

Murder Mystery
By Special Correspondent

Mary Turner, wife of Richard Turner, a farmer at Ngesi, was found murdered on the front verandah of their homestead yesterday morning. The houseboy, who has been arrested, has confessed to the crime. No motive has been discovered.

It is thought he was in search of valuables.

The newspaper did not say much. People all over the country must have glanced at the paragraph with its sensational heading and felt a little spurt of anger mingled with what was almost satisfaction, as if some belief had been confirmed, as if something had happened which could only have been expected. When natives steal, murder or rape, that is the feeling white people have.

And then they turned the page to something else.

But the people in 'the district' who knew the Turners, either by sight, or from gossiping about them for so many years, did not turn the page so quickly. Many must have snipped out the paragraph, put it among old letters, or between the pages of a book, keeping it perhaps as an omen or a warning, glancing at the yellowing piece of paper with closed, secretive faces. For they did not discuss the murder; that was the most extraordinary thing about it. It was as if they had a sixth sense which told them everything there was to be known, although the three people in a position to explain the facts said nothing. The murder was simply not discussed. 'A bad business,' someone would remark; and the faces of the people round about would put on that reserved and guarded look. 'A very bad business,' came the reply – and that was the end of it. There was, it seemed, a tacit agreement that the Turner case should not be given undue publicity by gossip. Yet it was a farming district, where those isolated white families met only very occasionally, hungry for contact with their own kind, to talk and discuss and pull to pieces, all speaking at once, making the most of an hour or so's companionship before returning to their farms where they saw only their own faces and the faces of their black servants for weeks on end. Normally that murder would have been discussed for months; people would have been positively grateful for something to talk about.

The Nice and the Good *by Iris Murdoch*

Similarly, Iris Murdoch's novel *The Nice and the Good* opens with a murder and the rest of the story traces the reason for it.

A head of department, working quietly in his room in Whitehall on a summer afternoon, is not accustomed to being disturbed by the nearby and indubitable sound of a revolver shot.

At one moment a lazy fat man, a perfect sphere his loving wife called him, his name Octavian Gray, was slowly writing a witty sentence in a neat tiny hand upon creamy official paper while he inhaled from his breath the pleasant sleepy smell of an excellent lunch-time burgundy. Then came the shot.

Octavian sat up, stood up. The shot had been somewhere not far away from him in the building. There was no mistaking that sound. Octavian knew the sound well though it was many years since, as a soldier, he had last heard it. His body knew it as he stood there rigid with memory and with the sense, now so unfamiliar to him, of confronting the demands of the awful, of the utterly new.

Octavian went to the door. The hot stuffy corridor, amid the rushing murmur of London, was quite still. He wished to call out "What is it? What has happened?" but found he could not. He turned back into the room with an instinctive movement in the direction of his telephone, his natural lifeline and connection with the world. Just then he heard running steps.

"Sir, Sir, something terrible has occurred!"

The office messenger, McGrath, a pale-blue-eyed ginger-haired man with a white face and a pink mouth, stood shuddering in the doorway.

"Get out." Richard Biranne, one of Octavian's Under Secretaries, pushed past McGrath, propelled McGrath out of the door, closed the door.

"What on earth is it?" said Octavian.

Biranne leaned back against the door. He breathed deepiy for a moment and then said in his usual high-pitched and rather precise voice, "Look, Octavian, I know this is *scarcely* credible, but Radeechy has just shot himself."

"Radeechy? Good God. Is he dead?"

"Yes."

Octavian sat down. He straightened out the piece of cream-coloured paper on the red blotter. He read the unfinished sentence. Then he got up again. "I'd better come and—see." He moved to the door which Biranne held open for him. "I suppose we'd better call Scotland Yard."

"I've already taken the liberty of doing so," said Biranne.

Radeechy's room was on the floor below. A little crowd of people stood at its closed door, arms pendant, mouths open.

Development and Climax

Mockingjay *by Suzanne Collins*

In the middle of a story or narrative, the action progresses towards a high point or climax. Tension and suspense usually build up, leaving the reader anxious to know what will happen next. Read the following extract from *Mockingjay,* book three of *The Hunger Games* series.

Wounded, but alive. I call his name, start towards him until a nurse pushes me back and shuts me out.

"Finnick!" Something between a shriek and a cry of joy. A lovely if somewhat bedraggled young woman—dark tangled hair, sea green eyes—runs towards us in nothing but a sheet. "Finnick!" And suddenly, it's as if there's no one in the world but these two, crashing through space to reach each other. They collide, enfold, lose their balance and slam against a wall, where they stay. Clinging into one being. Indivisible.

A pang of jealousy hits me. Not for either Finnick or Annie but for their certainty. No one seeing them could doubt their love.

Boggs, looking a little worse for wear but uninjured, finds Haymitch and me. "We got them all out. Except Enobaria. But since she's from Two, we doubt she's being held anyway. Peeta's at the end of the hall. The effects of the gas are just wearing off. You should be there when he wakes."

Peeta.

Alive and well—maybe not well but alive and here. Away from Snow. Safe. Here. With me. In a minute I can touch him. See his smile. Hear his laugh. Haymitch's grinning at me. "Come on, then," he says. I'm light-headed with giddiness. What will I say? Oh, who cares what I say? Peeta will be ecstatic no matter what I do. He'll probably be kissing me anyway. I wonder if it will feel like those last kisses on the beach in the arena, the ones I haven't dared let myself consider until this moment.

Peeta's awake already, sitting on the side of the bed, looking bewildered as a trio of doctors reassure him, flash lights in his eyes, check his pulse. I'm disappointed that mine was not the first face he saw when he woke, but he sees it now. His features register disbelief and something more intense that I can't quite place. Desire? Desperation? Surely both, for he sweeps the doctors aside, leaps to his feet and moves towards me. I run to meet him, my arms extended to embrace him. His hands are reaching for me, too, to caress my face, I think.

My lips are just forming his name when his fingers lock around my throat.

Group Work

Task A – On **page 37** of your **PORTFOLIO**, fill in the template on Plot Structure: beginning, middle, end (i.e. introduction, development, climax and resolution).

Task B – In groups, work out the plot structure in the novels that you are reading for the JCSA and fill out the template on **page 38** of your **PORTFOLIO**.

Flash Fiction

Flash fiction can help you to think of plots, plot structure and characters.

Flash fiction is quick, short flashes of fiction that can be a full short story or a snippet of a story. You don't have to have the entire story or plot to write flash fiction. You might simply write a piece of it, maybe some dialogue or a descriptive opening scene or an ending. Here are some ideas to get you started:

- A farmer and his wife, who run a small farm and sell organic produce at the market every Saturday, are volunteers with a local charity and often do readings at mass, but are also secretly involved in crime…

- A good-looking, charming crook escapes from prison on Christmas Eve and hitches a lift to the seaside. He squats in an unused holiday home, passes himself off as an artist and wins the heart of the bank manager's daughter, Linda, who is already engaged to sensible Steven…

- 'Load the gun now, Sophie,' she snarled, furiously stubbing out her cigarette on the beige leather dash of her new Mercedes…

- The drop was sheer, at least a hundred feet. Stars twinkled in the night sky. A gentle breeze caressed their shoulders…

- I remember that one particular present, which I had wished and wished for, begged my parents to buy me when I was…

- Eternal Youth Elixir, only €19.99 a bottle – a 250 ml bottle at that. A steal! She had sold at least 900 bottles on day one of the ploughing championships. How gullible people were! First it was angels she'd made a million with, manufactured in Taiwan for a pittance; then fairies, made in China for even less; and now a miracle anti-wrinkle lotion! Dream Company Inc. really was a dream come true. As long as she flung a few per cent at the taxman, she'd stay out of jail. If only she could sort out Sylvester, who was still blackmailing her…

Group Work

Complete the following on **page 39** of your **PORTFOLIO**.

1. Suggest a suitable title for each of the stories above.

2. Choose one of the scenarios above and, as a group, brainstorm and develop it. Or invent your own scenario and write a story from it as a group. Once you have a plot, think about how you will structure it. Will it be chronological or will it use flashbacks?

Focus on Descriptive Writing

Writers draw you into the story by using great words – carefully chosen adverbs, verbs, adjectives, similes, metaphors and personification.

For example:

Only the rock-strewn seashore to the south, where the great grey ocean thundered and rolled; and the barren desert wastes to the north, stretching all the way to the distant mountains. No food out there; no comfort, no safety.

The Wind Singer by **William Nicholson**

Night's well and truly fallen. The swamp seems even thicker here, as black as anything. We rush on back a ways to get my rucksack and then around and a little bit further away in the dark to get some distance between us and Aaron's body (please let it be a body). We clamber round trees and over roots, getting deeper into the swamp. When we get to a small clearing where there's a bit of flat land and a break in the trees, I stop us.

The Knife of Never Letting Go by **Patrick Ness**

Its grey front stood out well from the background of a rookery, whose cawing tenants were now on the wing: they flew over the lawn and grounds to alight in a great meadow, from which these were separated by a sunk fence, and where an array of mighty old thorn trees, strong, knotty, and broad as oaks, at once explained the etymology of the mansion's designation.

Jane Eyre by **Charlotte Brontë**

Pans bubbled and steamed all morning on the stove, and she humped bucket after bucket of hot water up and down the stairs. The house was filled with the sound of her scrubbing brush working over the floors and banging against the walls, and also with the smell of soapy steam. By the end of the day her hands and the lower parts of her arms were red, and wrinkled like the nuts you see in the shops round Hallowe'en.

Shadows on Our Skin by **Jennifer Johnston**

Verbs and Adverbs

Let's focus on verbs and adverbs and practise using them. This will help you to improve your writing.

Verbs

Verbs are action words, used when something is being done or is happening. For example:

scream	dance	clap	sing	jump
talked	cheered	ate	knotted	saved
ripping	drawing	sharing	cooking	slicing

Remember that 'to be' is a **verb**: I am, you are, he is, she was, we were, they will be.

WHAT KIND OF WORD SHOULD YOU INVITE TO A FANCY TEA PARTY?

A PROPER NOUN!

Adverbs

Adverbs modify or change **verbs, adjectives or other adverbs**. They usually end in 'ly'. For example:

yawned *stiffly*	stretched *lazily*	laughed *idiotically*	danced *dreamily*
roared *angrily*	ate *ravenously*	spoke *hoarsely*	ran *lithely*
chatted *flippantly*	stood *assertively*	posed *elegantly*	smiled *smugly*

There are many types of adverb:

Adverbs of manner (how): She danced *serenely*; they ran *quickly*; he laughed *heartily*.

Adverbs of time (when): Tim went *yesterday*; she arrived *today*; he will stop *now*.

Adverbs of place (where): They raced *down*; it fell *here*; I sped *away*.

Adverbs of degree (how much): They *entirely* approve; he *almost* died; it *nearly* worked.

Interrogative adverbs (questions): *Why* is he crying? *What* is happening? *How* was it?

Adverbs can also change or modify **adjectives**, e.g. the *very* tiny kitten. *Very* is the **adverb** which **modifies** the **adjective** *tiny*. The *fairly* hot soup – *fairly* **modifies** *hot*.

 **Writing**

A. Write the following sentences into your copy, inserting adverbs into the blanks.

1. The thieves ran _____ towards the exit.

2. Killian roared _____ when he stepped on the nail.

3. She walked _____ towards the departing train.

4. Clouds scudded _____ across the calm, blue sky.

5. 'Not now, silly!' she yelled _____.

6. The elephant plodded _____ to the water tank.

7. The nightingale sang _____ in the enchanted wood.

8. Jubilant fans cheered _____, rejoicing in their victory.

9. They swam _____, desperate to reach the safety of the shore.

10. Eva and Tony laughed _____ as they approached the funfair.

B. Put the following adverbs into sentences. Write them in your copy.

frantically	nervously	happily	carelessly
casually	frequently	noisily	gracefully
mockingly	patiently	awkwardly	suspiciously
cautiously	defiantly	energetically	boisterously

C. In your copy, write the opposite of these adverbs.

slowly	quietly	confidently	widely
eagerly	harshly	untidily	sadly
honestly	arrogantly	benevolently	wisely

Adjectives and Nouns

A **noun** is the name of a person, a place or a thing.

cat   room   mouse   pear   Canada   Morocco   Marilyn

Adjectives describe **nouns** and **pronouns**.

crazy teacher   *first* flight   *my* puppy   *two* dinosaurs   *rotten* apple

Adjectives of quality: *Excited* child, *red* car, *noisy* dog, *happy* home, *quiet* street.

Adjectives of quantity: *Most* men, *ten* bikes, *third* illness, *many* birds, *second* scene.

Possessive adjectives: *My* iPad, *your* tea, *his/her* pen, *our* game, *your* keys, *their* lives.

Demonstrative adjectives: *This* book, *that* chair, *these* mice, *those* pianos.

Interrogative adjectives: *Which* tablet? *Whose* child? *What* picture?

We often use adjectives to describe the characters we write and read about. Characters have traits or features, aspects of their personalities that a reader can identify by looking at the character's actions, words and thoughts.

Examples of character traits include:

adventurous	shy	humble	meek	modest
greedy	cautious	daring	loud	bossy
brave	independent	imaginative	creative	funny
honest	wicked	wise	innocent	immature
spontaneous	jealous	lazy	generous	optimistic

Describing Characters

When you are writing, you use adjectives to describe characters. Choose one character from the novels you are studying and list some adjectives that describe him/her. Fill in the table on **page 39** of your **PORTFOLIO**. Some examples have been given below. Use a thesaurus to find more interesting adjectives.

nice	kind	hardworking	reliable	mysterious
pleasant and amiable	benevolent	diligent	conscientious	enigmatic

Focus on Atmosphere

Atmosphere refers to the mood and the feeling created by the writer. The atmosphere may be tense, calm, frantic, serious, full of suspense, happy or sad. Read the following extract and think about the words that create the atmosphere.

Code Name Verity *by Elizabeth Wein*

Published to great acclaim in 2012, this award-winning novel set during World War II tells the story of British spy Queenie, code name 'Verity', and pilot Maddie, code name 'Kittyhawk'. When their plane crashes, they are captured by the Nazis in German-occupied France. The following extract is set in England during an air-raid attack by the Luftwaffe on a British airfield.

The **air-raid siren** went. Every head in the room looked up in dismay and exhaustion at the canteen's pasteboard ceiling, as if they could see through it. Then everybody rocketed from their borrowed church hall wooden folding chairs to meet the next battle.

Maddie stood facing her new friend by the table they had just abandoned, people around her whirling into action. She felt as though she were at the eye of a tropical storm. The still point of the turning world.

'Come on!' Queenie cried, just like the Red Queen in *Through the Looking Glass*, and grabbed Maddie by the arm to pull her outside.

'You go on duty at one, what have you got –' she glanced at her watch '– an hour? Quick nap in the shelter before they need you in the radio room – pity you haven't brought your brolly along. Come on, I'll go with you.'

The pilots were already racing for the **Spitfires**, and Maddie tried to fix her mind on the practical problem of how best to take off from the half-mended runway – taxiing would be the hardest, as you wouldn't be able to see the holes in the surface past the high nose of the little fighter planes. She tried not to think about what it would be like running across the airfield to the radio room an hour from now, under fire.

But she did it. Because you do. It is incredible what you do, knowing you have to. A bit less than an hour later – to allow themselves some extra time for dodging bombs – the two girls were outside again, in the moonscape that was now RAF Maidsend.

Queenie steered Maddie at a trot, both of them bent nearly double, hugging the sides of buildings and zigzagging across the open spaces. They'd heard how during the retreat from France the low-flying planes of the **Luftwaffe** would **strafe** people on the ground with machine-gun fire, just for the hell of it, and right now there were two or three German fighters buzzing low over the runway like wasps with the sun on their wings, drilling holes in windows and parked aircraft.

'Over here! Here!' someone yelled desperately. 'Hey, you two, come and help here!'

For a few seconds Maddie, doggedly coping with her own private hell of rational or irrational fear, did not even notice Queenie's change of direction as she headed towards the cry for help. Then sense came back to Maddie for a minute and she realised that Queenie was dragging her to the nearest anti-aircraft **gun emplacement**.

Or what was left of it. Most of the protective concrete barrier and the sandbags surrounding it had been blown to bits, taking with it two of the Army **gunners** who had been valiantly trying to keep the runway fit for the Spitfire squadron who would have to land there after the battle. One of the dead gunners was easily younger than Maddie. A third man who was still standing looked like a butcher, without the apron, soaked from neck to thighs in blood. He turned wearily and said, 'Thanks for the relief. I'm beat.' Then he sat down on the ruined platform and closed his eyes. Maddie cowered next to him, her arms over her head, listening to the hideous rattle of the gunner sucking air into blood-filled lungs. Queenie slapped her.

'Get up, girl!' she ordered. 'I won't have this. I'm your superior officer giving orders now. Get up, Brodatt. If you're scared *do something*. See if you can make this gun work. Get moving!'

'The **shell** needs loading first,' the gunner whispered, lifting a finger to point. 'The Prime Minister don't like girls firing guns.'

'Bother the Prime Minister!' exclaimed the superior officer. 'Load the damned gun, Brodatt.'

Maddie, nothing if not mechanically minded and trained to react positively to orders from people in authority, clawed her way up the gun.

'That slip of a lass'll never shift that shell,' croaked the gunner. 'Weighs 30 pounds, that does.'

Maddie wasn't listening. She was reckoning. After a minute's rational thought and with strength that she later couldn't explain, she loaded the shell.

Queenie worked frantically over the fallen gunner trying to plug the holes in his chest and stomach. Maddie did not watch. After some time Queenie took her by the shoulders and showed her how to aim.

'You've got to anticipate – it's like shooting birds, you have to fire a little ahead of where they'll be next –'

'Shoot a lot of birds, do you?' Maddie gasped, anger and fear making her peevish about the other girl's seemingly limitless talents.

'I was born in the middle of a **grouse** moor on the opening day of the shooting season! I could fire a gun before I could read! But this poxy thing is just a wee bit bigger than a Diana air rifle, and I don't know how it works, so we have to do it together. Like yesterday, all right?' She gave a sudden gasp and asked anxiously, 'That's not one of our planes, is it?'

'Can't you tell?'

'Not really.' Maddie relented.

'It's a **Messerschmitt 109**.'

'Well, clobber it! Point this way – now wait till he comes back, he doesn't know this station's still operational – just wait.' Maddie waited. Queenie was right: doing something, focusing, took away the fear.

'Now go!'

The blast momentarily blinded them both. They did not see what happened. Maddie swore, afterwards, that the plane did not go down in a ball of flame until it had made at least two more passes over the runway. But no one else ever claimed to have shot down that Me-109 (oh, how many aircraft I know after all!), and God knows the fighter pilots were a competitive lot of bean counters. So that kill – I expect the Luftwaffe also call it a kill when someone shoots down a plane, like deer – was credited to two off-duty **WAAF** officers working together at an unmanned gun station.

'I don't think our gun did that,' Maddie told her friend, **whey-faced**, as the black, oily smoke rose from the turnip field where the plane had come down. 'It must have been one of our lot, firing from the air. And if it was this gun, it wasn't you.'

It was bad enough she suspected the reason Queenie was at her side now was because she'd had to give up on the lad whose gun they'd taken over. Bad enough. But there had also been a pilot in that ball of flame, a living young man with not much more training than Maddie herself.

'Stay here,' Queenie choked. 'Can you load another shell? I'll find someone who knows what they're doing to take over – you'll be needed in the Tower now –'

Queenie paused a moment. 'Which way to the north-east air-raid shelter from here?' she asked anxiously. 'I get so muddled in the smoke.'

Maddie pointed. 'Straight line across the grass. Easy peasy if you're brave enough – like finding Neverland, "Second to the right, and then straight on till morning."'

'What about you? Brave enough?'

'I'll be all right. Now I've got something to do –'

They both ducked instinctively as something exploded at the other end of the runway. Queenie squeezed Maddie round the waist and gave her a quick peck on the cheek. '"Kiss me, Hardy!" Weren't those Nelson's last words at the **Battle of Trafalgar**? Don't cry. We're still alive and we make a *sensational* team.'

Then she hitched up her hair to its two-inch above the collar regulation point, swabbed her own tears and the grease and the concrete dust and the gunner's blood from her cheeks with the back of her hand, and she was off running again, like the Red Queen.

A. Reading

Rate this text for readability. Write the word/phrase of your choice into your copy.

VERY EASY ☐   **EASY** ☐   **OKAY** ☐   **HARD** ☐   **VERY HARD** ☐

B. Literacy Questions

1. Describe the location/setting in the above extract.
2. What kind of person do you think Maddie is? Quote from the extract to support your answer.
3. Identify two sentences that convey the atmosphere in the extract.

C. Dictionary

Use a dictionary to find the meaning of the words in **bold** in the above extract.

D. Research

Research one of the topics listed below and give a presentation on it to your class.

Topic 1: Aircraft used in World War II.

Topic 2: The role of women in the air forces during World War II.

Topic 3: Spies – their successes or failures during World War II.

Focus on Setting

Setting means the place or location of a story and the time period in which it is set. A story must happen in a place and at a particular time. For example, *Jane Eyre* by Charlotte Brontë is set in the 1840s in England. Most of the action occurs in a big house in the countryside. In contrast to this, *The Book of Lost Things* by John Connolly is set in two worlds: the real world and the fantasy world 12-year-old David escapes to after his mother's death.

Read the following extract and concentrate on the details that describe/convey the setting.

One Day in the Life of Ivan Denisovich

by Aleksandr Solzhenitsyn

Aleksandr Solzhenitsyn was born in Kislovodsk, Russia, in 1918. He graduated with a degree in mathematics from Rostov University, where he also studied literature. He served in the Russian army, was twice decorated and reached the rank of captain. In early 1945, he was arrested and charged with criticising the Soviet leader Stalin. Solzhenitsyn spent eight years in labour camps. In his novella *One Day in the Life of Ivan Denisovich*, Solzhenitsyn describes life in a camp in Karaganda in northern Kazakhstan. Released in 1953 on Stalin's death, Solzhenitsyn remained in exile for three years but then returned to Russia. During the 1960s he published short stories. In 1974 the novel *The Gulag Archipelago* was published and serialised in 1989. Solzhenitsyn won the Nobel Prize in Literature in 1970.

In the following extract, Shukov and his friends are in the labour camp. It is winter and is bitterly cold. They have just finished work and it is dinnertime. They go into the canteen and Shukov tricks the cook and manages to receive an extra bowl of food.

Pavlo and Shukhov, with Gopchik bringing up the rear, walked into the canteen. The men stood there so close to one another that you couldn't see either tables or benches. Some ate sitting down but most stood. The lads of the 82nd who'd been pecking at those holes half a day without a chance of getting warm, had been the first to get in after the hooter: now even after they'd finished eating they didn't leave. Where else could they warm up? The oaths fell off them like water off a duck's back: it was so much more comfortable here than in the cold. Pavlo and Shukhov elbowed their way in. They'd arrived at a good moment: one team was being served, another was awaiting its turn, and there was only one deputy team-leader near the hatch. So they were well ahead of the rest.

'Bowls, bowls,' the cook shouted through the hatch and people hurriedly handed them over. Shukhov was collecting another lot and turning them in, not to get extra porridge but to get what was coming to him quicker.

Behind the partitions some 'helpers' were already washing bowls – for extra porridge.

The cook began to serve the deputy team-leaders who stood ahead of Pavlo in the queue.

'Gopchik,' Pavlo shouted, over the heads of the men behind him.

'Here I am,' came Gopchik's thin bleat from the door.

'Call the team.'

Off he went.

The main thing today was that the porridge was good – oatmeal porridge, the best sort. It wasn't often they had it. More often they got magara twice a day – a bran mash. But oatmeal is filling, it's good.

How often had Shukhov in his youth fed oats to horses! Never had it occurred to him that there'd come a time when his whole soul would crave for a handful of them.

'Bowls, bowls,' shouted the cook.

Now the 104th was in the queue. That team-leader's deputy, up ahead, got his double helping and bounced away from the hatch.

This extra helping, too, was at the zeks' expense – but no one objected. The cook gave double helpings to all the team-leaders, and they either ate the extra helping themselves or gave it to their deputies. Tiurin gave his to Pavlo.

Shukhov's job now was to wedge himself in behind a table, oust two dawdlers, politely ask another prisoner to move, and clear a little space in front of him – for twelve bowls (to stand close together), with a second row of six, and two more on top. Next he had to take the bowls from Pavlo, repeating the number as he did so and keeping his eyes skinned – in case some outsider should nab a bowl from the table. And he had to see he wasn't jolted by someone's elbow so as to upset a bowl – right beside him people were leaving the table, stepping over the benches or squeezing in to eat. Yes, you had to keep your eyes skinned: was that fellow eating out of his own bowl? Or had he wormed his way up to one of the 104th's?

'Two, four, six,' the cook counted at the hatch. He handed out the bowls two at a time – it was easier for him that way, otherwise he might count wrong.

'Two, four, six,' Pavlo repeated quietly to himself, there at the hatch, in Ukrainian, and at once gave the bowls, in pairs, to Shukhov, who put them on the table. Shukhov didn't repeat the numbers aloud – but he counted more sharply than anyone.

'Eight, ten.'

Why wasn't Gopchik bringing in the team?

'Twelve, fourteen,' the counting continued.

The kitchen ran out of bowls. Shukhov had a clear view through the hatch, past Pavlo's head and shoulders. The cook put down two bowls on it and, keeping his hands on them, paused as though thinking. Must be bawling out the dishwashers. But just then another lot of dirty bowls was pushed on to the hatch. The cook let go of the two clean ones he'd filled and pushed back the pile of dirty ones.

Shukhov left the fourteen bowls he'd already stacked on the table, straddled a bench, took the two filled ones from the hatch, and said quietly to Pavlo rather than the cook:

'Fourteen.'

'Stop! Where are you taking those bowls?' shouted the cook.

'He's from our team,' Pavlo confirmed.

'"Our team", but he's mixed up the count.'

'Fourteen,' Pavlo said with a shrug. Himself he wouldn't have filched the extra bowls, for as deputy team-leader he had to maintain his dignity: but now he was simply repeating what Shukhov had said – he could always blame him for the mistake.

'I've already counted fourteen,' the cook expostulated.

'So you did, but you didn't pass them out. You kept your hands on them,' Shukhov shouted. 'Come and count for yourself if you don't believe us. Look, they're all here on the table.'

As he spoke he'd noticed the two Estonians pushing through to him, and he shoved the two bowls into their hands as they passed. And he'd managed to get back to the table to see that all the bowls were in place – the next tables hadn't pinched any, though they'd had ample opportunity to do so.

The cook's red face loomed large in the hatch.

'Where are those bowls?' he asked sternly.

'Here they are, at your service,' yelled Shukhov. 'Move along, scum, you're spoiling his view,' he said to someone, giving him a shove. 'Here they are, the pair of them.' He picked up two bowls from the second row. 'Here we have three rows of four, all nice and tidy. Count them.'

'Hasn't your team come?' the cook asked, looking suspiciously round the small segment of the canteen he could see through the hatch – it had been kept narrow to prevent anyone looking into the kitchen and seeing how much was left in the cauldron.

'No, none of 'em are here yet,' said Pavlo, shaking his head.

'Then why the hell are you taking bowls when the team's not here?'

'Here they come,' yelled Shukhov.

And everyone heard the peremptory shouts of the captain at the door: 'Why are you hanging on here?' he yelled, in his best quarter-deck voice. 'If you've eaten, clear out and let others in.'

The cook muttered something into the hatch. Then he drew himself up, and his hands could again be seen giving out the bowls:

'Sixteen, eighteen.'

Then he ladled the last portion, a double helping:

'Twenty-three. That's all. Next team.'

GLOSSARY

Hooter: A horn or bell that sounded at certain times.

Zeks: Forced labour camp inmates/prisoners.

Filched: Stolen.

A. Reading

Rate this text for readability. Write the word/phrase of your choice into your copy.

VERY EASY ☐   **EASY** ☐   **OKAY** ☐   **HARD** ☐   **VERY HARD** ☐

B. Literacy Questions

1. Describe the setting and surroundings in the above extract. Quote to support your points.
2. Explain how Shukhov tricks the cook.
3. Identify a moment of tension in the extract. What words create the tension? Explain how this is achieved.

C. Group Work

Identify the features of the story. Complete the following table on **page 40** of your **PORTFOLIO**.

Name of story/book		
Main plot		
Setting		
Main character		
Other characters		
Action – First		
Action – Next		
Action – Then		
Excitement/tension		
Dialogue		
Language		
Personification		
Similes/metaphors		
Descriptive verbs/adverbs		
Descriptive adjectives		

D. Research

Aleksandr Solzhenitsyn led a very interesting life. Do some further research on any of the following topics:

- His other novels and short stories.
- His life after he was released from the labour camp.
- Russia after Stalin's death in 1953.
- Russia today.

Short Stories

Short stories are much shorter than novels. Often it can be harder to write a short story than to write a novel. Short stories offer only a brief glimpse of a character even though the plot might span a long time such as months or years. Due to their length, short stories often focus on a smaller cast of characters. Read the following stories and think about how you feel as you are reading each one.

While the Auto Waits *by O. Henry*

O. Henry was the pseudonym, or pen name, of William Sydney Porter (1862–1910). Porter worked as a pharmacist, journalist and bank clerk but was imprisoned for three years for embezzling funds. He began writing stories in prison and became highly respected as a short story writer. He was known for his witty and humorous style and for writing stories with an unexpected twist.

Promptly at the beginning of twilight, came again to that quiet corner of that quiet, small park the girl in gray. She sat upon a bench and read a book, for there was yet to come a half hour in which print could be read.

To repeat: Her dress was gray, and plain but perfect in style and fit. A large-meshed veil imprisoned her hat and a face that shone through it with a calm and unconscious beauty. She had come there at the same hour on the previous day, and on the day before that; and there was one who knew it.

The young man who knew it was waiting near by. His patience was rewarded, for, in turning a page, her book slipped from her fingers and bounded from the bench a full yard away.

The young man seized it with great audacity, returning it to its owner with a look of gallantry and hope. In a pleasant voice, he risked a simple remark upon the weather – that introductory subject responsible for so much of the world's unhappiness – and stood by for a moment, awaiting his fate.

The girl looked him over leisurely; at his ordinary neat dress and his features that showed no particular expression.

'You may sit down, if you like,' she said, in a full, slow contralto. 'Really, I would like to have you do so. The light is too bad for reading. I would prefer to talk.'

He slid upon the seat by her side with politeness.

'Do you know,' he said, speaking the formula with which park chairmen open their meetings, 'that you are quite the most beautiful girl I have seen in a long time? I had my eye on you yesterday. Didn't know somebody was knocked down by those pretty lamps of yours, did you, honeysuckle?'

'Whoever you are,' said the girl in icy tones, 'you must remember that I am a lady. I will excuse the remark you have just made because the mistake was, doubtless, not an unnatural one — in your circle. I asked you to sit down; if the invitation must make me your honeysuckle, consider it withdrawn.'

'I earnestly beg your pardon,' pleaded the young man. 'It was my fault, you know, — I mean, there are girls in parks, you know — that is, of course, you don't know, but —'

'Abandon the subject, if you please. Of course I know. Now, tell me about these people passing and crowding, each way, along these paths. Where are they going? Why do they hurry so? Are they happy?'

The young man could not guess the role he would be expected to play. 'It is interesting to watch them,' he replied. 'It's the wonderful drama of life. Some are going to supper and some to — er — other places. One wonders what their histories are.'

'I do not,' said the girl; 'I am not so curious. I come here to sit because here, only, can I be near the great, common, beating heart of humanity. My part in life is played where its beats are never felt. Can you guess why I spoke to you, Mr—?'

'Parkenstacker,' said the young man. Then he looked eager and hopeful.

'No,' said the girl, holding up a slender finger, and smiling slightly. 'You would recognise it immediately. It is impossible to keep one's name out of print. Or even one's portrait. This veil and this hat of my maid's hide my identity. You should have seen the chauffeur stare at it when he thought I did not see. Frankly, there are five or six names that belong in the holy of holies, and mine, by accident of birth, is one of them. I spoke to you, Mr Stackenpot—'

'Parkenstacker,' corrected the young man, modestly.

' — Mr Parkenstacker, because I wanted to talk, for once, with a natural man — one unspoiled by wealth and supposed social superiority. Oh! you do not know how weary I am of it — money, money, money! And of the men who surround me, dancing like dolls all cut by the same pattern. I am sick of pleasure, of jewels, of travel, of society, of luxuries of all kinds.'

'I always had an idea,' uttered the young man, hesitatingly, 'that money must be a pretty good thing.'

'Enough money for living comfortably is to be desired. But when you have so many millions that — !' She concluded the sentence with a gesture of despair. 'It is the monotony of it,' she continued, 'that bores. Drives, dinners, theatres, balls, suppers, with the gilding of too much wealth over it all. Sometimes the very tinkle of the ice in my champagne glass nearly drives me mad.'

Mr Parkenstacker looked frankly interested.

'I have always liked,' he said, 'to read and hear about the ways of wealthy and fashionable folks. I suppose I am a bit of a snob. But I like to have my information accurate. Now, I had formed the opinion that champagne is cooled in the bottle and not by placing ice in the glass.'

The girl gave a musical laugh of real amusement.

'You should know,' she explained, in a patient tone, 'that we of the non-useful class depend for our amusement upon change. Just now it is the fashion to put ice in champagne. The idea was originated by a visiting Prince of Tartary while dining at the Waldorf. It will soon give way to some other new idea. Just as at a dinner party this week on Madison Avenue a green glove was laid by the plate of each guest to be put on and used while eating olives.'

'I see,' admitted the young man, humbly. 'These special amusements of the inner circle do not become known to the common public.'

'Sometimes,' continued the girl, acknowledging his confession of error by a slight bow, 'I have thought that if I ever should love a man it would be one of lowly station. One who is a worker and not a drone. But, doubtless, the demands of caste and wealth will be stronger than my wishes. What is it that makes me tell you these things, Mr Packenstarker?'

'Parkenstacker,' breathed the young man. 'Indeed, you cannot know how much I appreciate your confidences.'

The girl regarded him with the calm, impersonal look that befitted the difference in their stations.

'What is your line of business, Mr Parkenstacker?' she asked.

'A very humble one. But I hope to rise in the world. Were you really in earnest when you said that you could love a man of lowly position?'

'Indeed I was. But I said "might". There is a Grand Duke and a Marquis pursuing me. Yes; no position could be too humble were the man what I would wish him to be.'

'I work,' declared Mr Parkenstacker, 'in a restaurant.'

The girl shrank slightly.

'Not as a waiter?' she said, almost pleading. 'Labour is noble, but, — personal service, you know — valets and —'

'I am not a waiter. I am cashier in' — on the street they faced beyond the opposite side of the park was the brilliant electric sign 'RESTAURANT' — 'I am cashier in that restaurant you see there.'

The girl glanced at a tiny watch set in a bracelet upon her left wrist, and rose, hurriedly. She pushed her book into a glittering bag, for which, however, the book was too large.

'Why are you not at work?' she asked.

'I am on the night turn,' said the young man; 'it is yet an hour before my period begins. May I not hope to see you again?'

'I do not know. Perhaps — but the fancy may not seize me again. I must go quickly now. There is a dinner, and a box at the play — and oh! the same old round. Perhaps you noticed an automobile at the upper corner of the park as you came. One with a white body.'

'And red wheels?' asked the young man, frowning thoughtfully.

'Yes, I always come in that. Pierre waits for me there. He supposes me to be shopping in the department store across the square. Imagine a life wherein we must deceive even our chauffeurs. Goodnight.'

'But it is dark now,' said Mr Parkenstacker, 'and the park is full of rude men. May I not walk — ?'

'If you have the slightest regard for my wishes,' said the girl, firmly, 'you will remain at this bench for ten minutes after I have left. I do not mean to accuse you, but you are probably aware that autos generally bear the monogram of their owner. Again, good-night.'

Swift and stately she moved away through the dusk. The young man watched her graceful form as she reached the pavement at the park's edge, and turned up along it toward the corner where stood the automobile. Then he treacherously and unhesitatingly began to slide along the park trees and bushes in a course parallel to her route, keeping her well in sight.

When she reached the corner she turned her head to glance at the motor car, and then passed it, continuing on across the street. Sheltered behind a standing cab, the young man followed her movements closely with his eyes. Passing down the sidewalk of the street opposite the park, she entered the restaurant with the blazing sign. The place was one of those glaring establishments, all white paint and glass, where one may dine cheaply. The girl entered the restaurant and went to some place at the back, whence she quickly returned without her hat and veil.

The cashier's desk was well to the front. A red-haired girl on the stool climbed down, glancing pointedly at the clock as she did so. The girl in gray mounted in her place.

The young man pushed his hands into his pockets and walked slowly back along the sidewalk. At the corner his foot struck a small, paper-covered volume lying there. By its picturesque cover he recognised it as the book the girl had been reading. He picked it up carelessly, and saw that its title was *New Arabian Nights*, the author being of the name of Stevenson. He dropped it again upon the grass, and stood, hesitating, for a minute. Then he stepped into the automobile, reclined upon the cushions, and said two words to the chauffeur:

'Club, Henri.'

GLOSSARY

Monogram: Name or initials.
Audacity: Boldness.
Gallantry: Politeness shown by a man to a woman.
Contralto: Lowest female singing voice.
Caste: Social class.

A. Reading

Rate this text for readability. Write the word/phrase of your choice into your copy.

VERY EASY ☐   **EASY** ☐   **OKAY** ☐   **HARD** ☐   **VERY HARD** ☐

B. Literacy Questions

1. Identify the narrative voice in the story, using quotations to prove your point.
2. Describe the girl, using details from the extract.
3. Describe Mr Parkenstacker, using quotes from the extract.
4. What did you think of the ending of the story? Did you expect it to end as it did?

C. Group Work

Think about unusual and unexpected endings in novels that you have read, or in films that you have watched. As a group, make a list of these and discuss them.

D. Oral Language

'The young man could not guess the role he would be expected to play.'
In pairs, discuss:

- The two roles the young man played in the short story.
- The two roles the girl played in the story.
- The extent to which everyone plays many different roles in life.

Louise *by W. Somerset Maugham*

William Somerset Maugham was an English novelist, playwright and short story writer. Maugham qualified as a doctor but after the success of his first novel (*Liza of Lambeth*, 1897) he gave up medicine to write full-time. During World War I, he worked in the ambulance corps and later in the British Secret Service. He travelled to Switzerland, Russia, India and South-east Asia and his experiences abroad provided inspiration for his novels and short stories.

I could never understand why Louise bothered with me. She disliked me and I knew that behind my back, in that gentle way of hers, she seldom lost the opportunity of saying a **disagreeable** thing about me. She had too much delicacy ever to make a direct statement, but with a hint and a sigh and a little flutter of her beautiful hands she was able to make her meaning plain. She was a mistress of cold praise. It was true that we had known one another almost intimately, for five-and-twenty years, but it was impossible for me to believe that she could be affected by the claims of old association. She thought me a **coarse**, brutal, **cynical**, and **vulgar** fellow. I was puzzled at her not taking the obvious course and dropping me. She did nothing of the kind; indeed, she would not leave me alone; she was constantly asking me to lunch and dine with her and once or twice a year invited me to spend a week-end at her house in the country. At last I thought that I had discovered her motive. She had an uneasy suspicion that I did not believe in her; and if that was why she did not like me, it was also why she sought my acquaintance: it **galled** her that I alone should look upon her as a comic figure and she could not rest till I acknowledged myself mistaken and defeated. Perhaps she had an inkling that I saw the face behind the mask and because I alone held out was determined that sooner or later I too should take the mask for the face. I was never quite certain that she was a complete **humbug**. I wondered whether she fooled herself as thoroughly as she fooled the world or whether there was some spark of humour at the bottom of her heart. If there was it might be that she was attracted to me, as a pair of crooks might be attracted to one another, by the knowledge that we shared a secret that was hidden from everybody else.

I knew Louise before she married. She was then a frail, delicate girl with large and melancholy eyes. Her father and mother worshipped her with an anxious adoration, for some illness, scarlet fever I think, had left her with a weak heart and she had to take the greatest care of herself. When Tom Maitland proposed to her they were dismayed, for they were convinced that she was much too delicate for the strenuous state of marriage. But they were not too well off and Tom Maitland was rich. He promised to do everything in the world for Louise and finally they entrusted her to him as a sacred charge. Tom Maitland was a big, husky fellow, very good-looking and a fine athlete. He doted on Louise. With her weak heart he could not hope to keep her with him long and he made up his mind to do everything he could to make her few years on earth happy. He gave up the games he excelled in, not because she wished him to, she was glad that he should play golf and hunt, but because by a coincidence she had a heart attack whenever he proposed to leave her for a day. If they had a difference of opinion she gave in to him at once, for she was the most **submissive** wife a man could have, but her heart failed her and she would be laid up, sweet and uncomplaining, for a week. He would not be such a brute as to cross her. Then they would have quite a little **tussle** about which should yield and it was only with difficulty that at last he persuaded her to have her own way. On one occasion seeing her walk eight miles on an expedition that she particularly wanted to make, I suggested to Tom Maitland that she was stronger than one would have thought. He shook his head and sighed.

'No, no, she's dreadfully delicate. She's been to all the best heart specialists in the world and they all say that her life hangs on a thread. But she has an unconquerable spirit.'

He told her that I had remarked on her endurance.

'I shall pay for it tomorrow,' she said to me in her **plaintive** way. 'I shall be at death's door.'

'I sometimes think that you're quite strong enough to do the things you want to,' I murmured.

I had noticed that if a party was amusing she could dance till five in the morning, but if it was dull she felt very poorly and Tom had to take her home early. I am afraid she did not like my reply, for though she gave me a pathetic little smile I saw no amusement in her large blue eyes.

'You can't very well expect me to fall down dead just to please you,' she answered.

Louise outlived her husband. He caught his death of cold one day when they were sailing and Louise needed all the rugs there were to keep her warm. He left her a comfortable fortune and a daughter. Louise was inconsolable. It was wonderful that she managed to survive the shock. Her friends expected her speedily to follow poor Tom Maitland to the grave. Indeed they already felt dreadfully sorry for Iris, her daughter, who would be left an orphan. They **redoubled** their attentions towards Louise. They would not let her stir a finger; they insisted on doing everything in the world to save her trouble. They had to, because if she was called upon to do anything tiresome or inconvenient her heart went back on her and there she was at death's door. She was entirely lost without a man to take care of her, she said, and she did not know how, with her delicate health, she was going to bring up her dear Iris. Her friends asked why she did not marry again. Oh, with her heart it was out of the question, though of course she knew that dear Tom would have wished her to, and perhaps it would be the best thing for Iris if she did; but who would want to be bothered with a wretched **invalid** like herself? Oddly enough more than one young man showed himself quite ready to undertake the charge and a year after Tom's death she allowed George Hobhouse to lead her to the altar. He was a fine, upstanding fellow and he was not at all badly off. I never saw anyone so grateful as he for the privilege of being allowed to take care of this frail little thing.

'I shan't live to trouble you long,' she said.

He was a soldier and an ambitious one, but he resigned his **commission**. Louise's health forced her to spend the winter at Monte Carlo and the summer at Deauville. He hesitated a little at throwing up his career, and Louise at first would not hear of it; but at last she yielded as she always yielded, and he prepared to make his wife's last few years as happy as might be.

'It can't be very long now,' she said. 'I'll try not to be troublesome.'

For the next two or three years Louise managed, **notwithstanding** her weak heart, to go beautifully dressed to all the most lively parties, to gamble very heavily, to dance and even to flirt with tall slim young men. But George Hobhouse had not the **stamina** of Louise's first husband and he had to brace himself now and then with a stiff drink for his day's work as Louise's second husband. It is possible that the habit would have grown on him, which Louise would not have liked at all, but very fortunately (for her) the war broke out. He rejoined his regiment and three months later was killed. It was a great shock to Louise. She felt, however, that in such a crisis she must not give way to a private grief; and if she had a heart attack nobody heard of it. In order to distract her mind she turned her villa at Monte Carlo into a hospital for **convalescent** officers. Her friends told her that she would never survive the strain.

'Of course it will kill me,' she said, 'I know that. But what does it matter? I must do my bit.'

It didn't kill her. She had the time of her life. There was no convalescent home in France that was more popular. I met her by chance in Paris. She was lunching at the Ritz with a tall and very handsome young Frenchman. She explained that she was there on business connected with the hospital. She told me that the officers were too charming to her. They knew how delicate she was and they wouldn't let her do a single thing. They took care of her, well – as though they were all her husbands. She sighed.

'Poor George, who would ever have thought that I, with my heart, should survive him?'

'And poor Tom!' I said.

I don't know why she didn't like my saying that. She gave me her plaintive smile and her beautiful eyes filled with tears.

'You always speak as though you grudged me the few years that I can expect to live.'

'By the way, your heart's much better, isn't it?'

'It'll never be better. I saw a specialist this morning and he said I must be prepared for the worst.'

'Oh, well, you've been prepared for that for nearly twenty years now, haven't you?'

When the war came to an end Louise settled in London. She was now a woman of over forty, thin and frail still, with large eyes and pale cheeks, but she did not look a day more than twenty-five. Iris, who had been at school and was now grown up, came to live with her.

'She'll take care of me,' said Louise. 'Of course, it'll be hard on her to live with such a great invalid as I am, but it can only be for such a little while, I'm sure she won't mind.'

Iris was a nice girl. She had been brought up with the knowledge that her mother's health was precarious. As a child she had never been allowed to make a noise. She had always realised that her mother must on no account be upset. And though Louise told her now that she would not hear of her sacrificing herself for a tiresome old woman the girl simply would not listen. It wasn't a question of sacrificing herself, it was a happiness to do what she could for her poor dear mother. With a sigh her mother let her do a great deal.

'It pleases the child to think she's making herself useful,' she said.

'Don't you think she ought to go out and about more?' I asked.

'That's what I'm always telling her. I can't get her to enjoy herself. Heaven knows, I never want anyone to put themselves out on my account.'

And Iris, when I remonstrated with her, said: 'Poor dear mother, she wants me to go and stay with friends and go to parties, but the moment I start off anywhere she has one of her heart attacks, so I much prefer to stay at home.'

But presently she fell in love. A young friend of mine, a very good lad, asked her to marry him and she consented. I liked the child and was glad that she was to be given at last the chance to lead a life of her own. She had never seemed to suspect that such a thing was possible. But one day the young man came to me in great distress and told me that his marriage was indefinitely postponed. Iris felt that she could not desert her mother. Of course it was really no business of mine, but I made the opportunity to go and see Louise. She was always glad to receive her friends at tea-time and now that she was older she cultivated the society of painters and writers.

'Well, I hear that Iris isn't going to be married,' I said after a little.

'I don't know about that. She's not going to be married quite as soon as I could have wished. I've begged her on my bended knees not to consider me, but she absolutely refuses to leave me.'

'Don't you think it's rather hard on her?'

'Dreadfully. Of course it can only be for a few months, but I hate the thought of anyone sacrificing themselves for me.'

'My dear Louise, you've buried two husbands, I can't see the least reason why you shouldn't bury at least two more.'

'Do you think that's funny?' she asked me in a tone that she made as offensive as she could.

'I suppose it's never struck you as strange that you're always strong enough to do anything you want to and that your weak heart only prevents you from doing things that bore you?'

'Oh, I know, I know what you've always thought of me. You've never believed that I had anything the matter with me, have you?'

I looked at her full and square.

'Never. I think you've carried out for twenty-five years a stupendous bluff. I think you're the most selfish and monstrous woman I have ever known. You ruined the lives of those two wretched men you married and now you're going to ruin the life of your daughter.'

I should not have been surprised if Louise had had a heart attack then. I fully expected her to fly into a passion. She merely gave me a gentle smile.

'My poor friend, one of these days you'll be so dreadfully sorry you said this to me.'

'Have you quite determined that Iris shall not marry this boy?'

'I've begged her to marry him. I know it'll kill me, but I don't mind. Nobody cares for me. I'm just a burden to everybody.'

'Did you tell her it would kill you?'

'She made me.'

'As if anyone ever made you do anything that you were not yourself quite determined to do.'

'She can marry her young man tomorrow if she likes. If it kills me, it kills me.'

'Well, let's risk it, shall we?'

'Haven't you got any compassion for me?'

'One can't pity anyone who amuses one as much as you amuse me,' I answered.

A faint spot of colour appeared on Louise's pale cheeks and though she smiled still her eyes were hard and angry.

'Iris shall marry in a month's time,' she said, 'and if anything happens to me I hope you and she will be able to forgive yourselves.'

Louise was as good as her word. A date was fixed, a **trousseau** of great magnificence was ordered, and invitations were issued. Iris and the very good lad were radiant. On the wedding-day, at ten o'clock in the morning, Louise, that devilish woman, had one of her heart attacks – and died. She died gently forgiving Iris for having killed her.

A. Reading

Rate this text for readability. Write the word/phrase of your choice into your copy.

VERY EASY ☐   **EASY** ☐   **OKAY** ☐   **HARD** ☐   **VERY HARD** ☐

B. Literacy Questions

1. How did Louise die?
2. The narrator of the story thinks that Louise is a fraud. Find two pieces of evidence from the extract to support his view.
3. Describe the character of Louise. Find good and bad points about her.
4. What is your opinion of Louise? Is she a manipulator or is she genuinely weak and frail? Use quotes from the extract to support your answer.
5. The story spans 25 years, covering Louise's early twenties, two marriages and her death. What techniques does the author use in this short story to cover so much time?

C. Dictionary

Use a dictionary to find the meaning of the words in **bold** in the above extract. Note that some words have more than one meaning. Try to find the meaning that fits best with the story and its context.

D. Group Work

In your group, create another ending for the story. For example, imagine that Louise does not die. Perhaps she wreaks revenge on the narrator. Or perhaps Iris tires of being the good, dutiful daughter and takes a different route…

Step 1: Discuss a range of possible endings.

Step 2: Choose and agree on one ending.

Step 3: Each person writes a paragraph of this ending.

Step 4: Swap the work. As a group, write ONE paragraph based on what you have all written.

Step 5: Write a few drafts until you are all happy with the ending.

Step 6: One person reads it aloud to the class.

Read and Enjoy

To Every Thing There is a Season

by Alistair MacLeod

Alistair MacLeod's Scottish ancestors emigrated to Canada in the 1790s and settled in Cape Breton, Nova Scotia. MacLeod was born in Saskatchewan in 1936. When he was ten, the family moved to Cape Breton. He was good at English in school and trained to be a teacher, before attaining a Master's degree and a PhD. To finance his university years, MacLeod worked in the mines in British Colombia and on a logging camp in Vancouver. He taught English at Indiana University and at the University of Windsor and his work in the universities took up much of his time. He published one novel and 20 short stories during his lifetime and won numerous awards. MacLeod died in April 2014.

The following story, written in 1977, is from a collection entitled *Island*. In his foreword to the collection, Irish writer John McGahern noted that MacLeod writes about 'people and a way of life on Cape Breton, that has continued relatively unchanged for several generations since the first settlers went there from Scotland… They work as fishermen, miners, smallholders, loggers, light-house keepers, migrant workers. They live in a dramatically beautiful setting provided mostly by nature and hostile to much human endeavour.'

I am speaking here of a time when I was eleven and lived with my family on our small farm on the west coast of Cape Breton. My family had been there for a long, long time and so it seemed had I. And much of that time seems like the proverbial yesterday. Yet when I speak on this Christmas 1977, I am not sure how much I speak with the voice of that time or how much in the voice of what I have since become. And I am not sure how many liberties I may be taking with the boy I think I was. For Christmas is a time of both past and present and often the two are imperfectly blended. As we step into its nowness we often look behind.

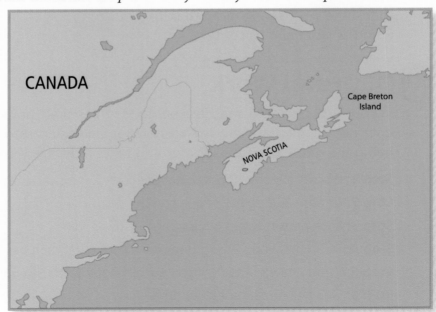

We have been waiting now, it seems, forever. Actually, it has been most intense since Hallowe'en when the first snow fell upon us as we moved like muffled mummers upon darkened country roads. The large flakes were soft and new then and almost generous, and the earth to which they fell was still warm and as yet unfrozen. They fell in silence into the puddles and into the sea where they disappeared at the moment of contact. They disappeared, too, upon touching the heated redness of our necks and hands or the faces of those who did not wear masks. We carried our pillowcases from house to house, knocking on doors to become silhouettes in the light thrown out from kitchens (white pillowcases held out by whitened forms). The snow fell between us and the doors and was transformed in shimmering golden beams. When we turned to leave, it fell upon our footprints, and as the night wore on obliterated them and all the records of our movements. In the morning everything was soft and still and November had come upon us.

My brother Kenneth, who is two and a half, is unsure of his last Christmas. It is Hallowe'en that looms largest in his memory as an exceptional time of being up late in magic darkness and falling snow. "Who are you going to dress up as at Christmas?" he asks. "I think I'll be a snowman." All of us laugh at that and tell him Santa Claus will find him if he is good and that he need not dress up at all. We go about our appointed tasks waiting for it to happen.

I am troubled myself about the nature of Santa Claus and I am trying to hang on to him in any way that I can. It is true that at my age I no longer really believe in him, yet I have hoped in all his possibilities as fiercely as I can; much in the same way, I think, that the drowning man waves desperately to the lights of the passing ship on the high sea's darkness. For without him, as without the man's ship, it seems our fragile lives would be so much more desperate.

My mother has been fairly tolerant of my attempted perpetuation. Perhaps because she has encountered it before. Once I overheard her speaking about my sister Anne to one of her neighbours. "I thought Anne would *believe* forever," she said. "I practically had to tell her." I have somehow always wished I had not heard her say that as I seek sanctuary and reinforcement even in an ignorance I know I dare not trust.

Kenneth, however, believes with an unadulterated fervour, and so do Bruce and Barry, who are six-year-old twins. Beyond me there is Anne who is thirteen and Mary who is fifteen, both of whom seem to be leaving childhood at an alarming rate. My mother has told us that she was already married when she was seventeen, which is only two years older than Mary is now. That, too, seems strange to contemplate and perhaps childhood is shorter for some than it is for others. I think of this sometimes in the evenings when we have finished our chores and the supper dishes have been cleared away and we are supposed to be doing our homework. I glance sideways at my mother, who is always knitting or mending, and at my father, who mostly sits by the stove coughing quietly with his handkerchief at his mouth. He has "not been well" for over two years and has difficulty breathing whenever he moves at more than the slowest pace. He is most sympathetic of all concerning my extended hopes, and says we should hang on to the good things in our lives as long as we are able. As I look at him out of the corner of my eye, it does not seem that he has many of them left. He is old, we think, at forty-two.

Yet Christmas, in spite of all the doubts of our different ages, is a fine and splendid time, and now as we pass the midpoint of December our expectations are heightened by the increasing coldness that has settled down upon us. The ocean is flat and calm and along the coast, in the scooped-out coves, has turned to an icy slush. The brook that flows past our house is almost totally frozen and there is only a small channel of rushing water that flows openly at its very centre. When we let the cattle out to drink, we chop holes with the axe at the brook's edge so that they can drink without venturing onto the ice.

The sheep move in and out of their lean-to shelter, restlessly stamping their feet or huddling together in tightly packed groups. A conspiracy of wool against the cold. The hens perch high on their roosts with their feathers fluffed out about them, hardly feeling it worthwhile to descend to the floor for their few scant kernels of grain. The pig, who has little time before his butchering, squeals his displeasure to the cold and with his snout tosses his wooden trough high in the icy air. The splendid young horse paws the planking of his stall and gnaws the wooden cribwork of his manger.

We have put a protective barricade of spruce boughs about our kitchen door and banked our house with additional boughs and billows of eel grass. Still, the pail of water we leave standing in the porch is solid in the morning and has to be broken with the hammer. The clothes my mother hangs on the line are frozen almost instantly and sway and creak from their suspending clothespins like sections of dismantled robots: the stiff-legged rasping trousers and the shirts and sweaters with unyielding arms outstretched. In the morning we race from our frigid upstairs bedrooms to finish dressing around the kitchen stove.

We would extend our coldness half a continent away to the Great Lakes of Ontario so that it might hasten the Christmas coming of my older brother, Neil. He is nineteen and employed on the "lake boats," the long flat carriers of grain and iron ore whose season ends any day after December 10, depending on the ice conditions. We wish it to be cold, cold on the Great Lakes of Ontario, so that he may come home to us as soon as possible. Already his cartons have arrived. They come from different places: Cobourg, Toronto, St. Catharines, Welland, Windsor, Sarnia, Sault Ste. Marie. Places that we, with the exception of my father, have never been. We locate them excitedly on the map, tracing their outlines with eager fingers. The cartons bear the lettering of Canada Steamship Lines, and are bound with rope knotted intricately in the fashion of sailors. My mother says they contain his "clothes" and we are not allowed to open them.

For us it is impossible to know the time or manner of his coming. If the lakes freeze early, he may come by train because it is cheaper. If the lakes stay open until December 20, he will have to fly because his time will be more precious than his money. He will hitchhike the last sixty or hundred miles from either station or airport. On our part, we can do nothing but listen with straining ears to radio reports of distant ice formations. His coming seems to depend on so many factors which are out there far beyond us and over which we lack control.

The days go by in fevered slowness until finally on the morning of December 23 the strange car rolls into our yard. My mother touches her hand to her lips and whispers "Thank God." My father gets up unsteadily from his chair to look through the window. Their longed-for son and our golden older brother is here at last. He is here with his reddish hair and beard and we can hear his hearty laugh. He will be happy and strong and confident for us all.

There are three other young men with him who look much the same as he. They too, are from the boats and are trying to get home to Newfoundland. They must still drive a hundred miles to reach the ferry at North Sydney. The car seems very old. They purchased it in Thorold for two hundred dollars because they were too late to make any reservations, and they have driven steadily since they began. In northern New Brunswick their windshield wipers failed, but instead of stopping they tied lengths of cord to the wipers' arms and passed them through the front window vents. Since that time, in whatever precipitation, one of them has pulled the cords back and forth to make the wipers function. This information falls tiredly but excitedly from their lips and we greedily gather it in. My father pours them drinks of rum and my mother takes out her mincemeat and the fruitcakes she has been carefully hoarding. We lean on the furniture or look from the safety of sheltered doorways. We would like to hug our brother but are too shy with strangers present. In the kitchen's warmth, the young men begin to nod and doze, their heads dropping suddenly to their chests. They nudge each other with their feet in an attempt to keep awake. They will not stay and rest because they have come so far and tomorrow is Christmas Eve and stretches of mountains and water still lie between them and those they love. After they leave we pounce upon our brother physically and verbally. He laughs and shouts and lifts us over his head and swings us in his muscular arms. Yet in spite of his happiness he seems surprised at the appearance of his father, whom he has not seen since March. My father merely smiles at him, while my mother bites her lip.

Now that he is here there is a great flurry of activity. We have left everything we could until the time he might be with us. Eagerly I show him the fir tree on the hill which I have been watching for months and marvel at how easily he fells it and carries it down the hill. We fall over one another in the excitement of decoration.

He promises that on Christmas Eve he will take us to church in the sleigh behind the splendid horse that until his coming we are all afraid to handle. And on the afternoon of Christmas Eve he shoes the horse, lifting each hoof and rasping it fine and hammering the cherry-red horseshoes into shape upon the anvil. Later he drops them hissingly into the steaming tub of water. My father sits beside him on an overturned pail and tells him what to do. Sometimes we argue with our father, but our brother does everything he says.

That night, bundled in hay and voluminous coats, and with heated stones at our feet, we start upon our journey. Our parents and Kenneth remain at home, but all the rest of us go. Before we leave we feed the cattle and sheep and even the pig all that they can possibly eat, so that they will be contented on Christmas Eve. Our parents wave to us from the doorway. We go four miles across the mountain road. It is a primitive logging trail and there will be no cars or other vehicles upon it. At first the horse is wild with excitement and lack of exercise and my brother has to stand at the front of the sleigh and lean backwards on the reins. Later he settles down to a trot and still later to a walk as the mountain rises before him. We sing all the Christmas songs we know and watch for the rabbits and foxes scudding across the open patches of snow and listen to the drumming of partridge wings. We are never cold.

When we descend to the country church we tie the horse in a grove of trees where he will be sheltered and not frightened by the many cars. We put a blanket over him and give him oats. At the church door the neighbours shake hands with my brother. "Hello, Neil," they say. "How is your father?"

"Oh," he says, just "Oh."

The church is very beautiful at night with its festooned branches and glowing candles and the booming, joyous sounds that come from the choir loft. We go through the service as if we are mesmerised.

On the way home, although the stones have cooled, we remain happy and warm. We listen to the creak of the leather harness and the hiss of runners on the snow and begin to think of the potentiality of presents. When we are about a mile from home the horse senses his destination and breaks into a trot and then into a confident lope. My brother lets him go and we move across the winter landscape like figures freed from a Christmas card. The snow from the horse's hooves falls about our heads like the whiteness of the stars.

After we have stabled the horse we talk with our parents and eat the meal our mother has prepared. And then I am sleepy and it is time for the younger children to be in bed. But tonight my father says to me, "We would like you to stay up with us a while," and so I stay quietly with the older members of my family. When all is silent upstairs Neil brings in the cartons that contain his "clothes" and begins to open them. He unties the intricate knots quickly, their whorls falling away before his agile fingers. The boxes are filled with gifts neatly wrapped and bearing tags. The ones for my younger brothers say "from Santa Claus" but mine are not among them any more, as I know with certainty they will never be again. Yet I am not so much surprised as touched by a pang of loss at being here on the adult side of the world. It is as if I have suddenly moved into another room and heard a door click lastingly behind me. I am jabbed by my own small wound.

But then I look at those before me. I look at my parents drawn together before the Christmas tree. My mother has her hand upon my father's shoulder and he is holding his ever-present handkerchief. I look at my sisters, who have crossed this threshold ahead of me and now each day journey farther from the lives they knew as girls. I look at my magic older brother who has come to us this Christmas from half a continent away, bringing everything he has and is. All of them are captured in the tableau of their care.

"Every man moves on," says my father quietly, and I think he speaks of Santa Claus, "but there is no need to grieve. He leaves good things behind."

GLOSSARY

Tolerant: To allow or to put up with.

Perpetuation: Making something continue or last indefinitely.

Unadulterated: Unchanged, remaining pure.

Frigid: Very cold.

Voluminous: Very loose or full, lots of fabric.

Tableau: A group of motionless figures representing a scene.

ASSESSMENT

Complete this assessment on **page 41** of your **PORTFOLIO**.

Written Assessment

A. Descriptive Writing – Adjectives

List the adjectives used to describe the nouns in the following extract from *Stay Where You Are and Then Leave* by **John Boyne**.

The shoeshine box was made of dark brown mahogany. It was twice as long as it was wide, with a gold-coloured clasp to unlock the lid from the base which, when opened, revealed three compartments within.

The first contained two horsehair brushes, one black, one brown, with corrugated grips on the handles; the second revealed a set of four grey shining cloths and a pair of sponge daubers; the third held two tins of polish which had been almost full when Alfie found the box. Carved into the side was the word *Holzknecht* and an emblem that displayed an eagle soaring above a mountain, wild-eyed and dangerous. Secured to the underside of the lid was a footrest that could be taken out and attached to the top of the sealed box through a pair of thin grooves etched into the side. This was where a customer laid his foot when he was having his shoes shined.

When Alfie first brought the box back to his own bedroom, he had stared at it for a long time, running his fingers across the elegant woodwork and taking careful sniffs of the polish, which sent an irritating tickle up his nose. He had seen boxes like this before, of course, although none as beautifully designed and well cared for as Mr Janáček's. A few days after signing up, his father had taken him to King's Cross – he'd said they were going there to look at the trains, but that wasn't the real reason – and Alfie had seen Leonard Hopkins from number two shining shoes in a corner by the ticket counter and charging a penny a shine. It seemed to take him a long time to finish each shoe, though, for every time a pretty girl walked by, Leonard's eyes followed her as if he had become hypnotised, and only when his customer tapped him on the head did he turn back again.

Adjectives

Peer Assessment – *Swap what you have written with the person beside you and compare your lists.*

ASSESSMENT

B. Descriptive Writing – Verbs and Adjectives

Identify verbs and adjectives that you think are effective in the following text.

Bleak House *by Charles Dickens*

Fog everywhere. Fog up the river, where it flows among green aits and meadows; fog down the river, where it rolls defiled among the tiers of shipping, and the waterside pollutions of a great (and dirty) city. Fog on the Essex marshes, fog on the Kentish heights. Fog creeping into the cabooses of collier-brigs, fog lying out on the yards, and hovering in the rigging of great ships; fog drooping on the gunwales of barges and small boats. Fog in the eyes and throats of ancient Greenwich pensioners, wheezing by the firesides of their wards; fog in the stem and bowl of the afternoon pipe of the wrathful skipper, down in his close cabin; fog cruelly pinching the toes and fingers of his shivering little 'prentice boy on deck. Chance people on the bridges peeping over the parapets onto a nether sky of fog, with fog all around them, as if they were up in a balloon, and hanging in the misty clouds.

Verbs	Adjectives

Peer Assessment – *Swap what you have written with the person beside you and compare your lists.*

C. Reading Comprehension

Focus on Setting and Characterisation

Chalkline *by Jane Mitchell*

"Jameela. Go and find your brothers. Food's ready and your father wants them here."

Her mother's voice had an edge of impatience to it. She was squatting next to the cooking stove beneath the shade of the walnut tree, grinding spices and patting out chapattis. The meal was prepared, her husband was home from his day's work in the bicycle shop, yet her older sons were nowhere to be seen. Seven-year-old Jameela immediately tossed away the small heap of stones and twigs with which she had been amusing her little sister, Afrah, and jumped up, taking the toddler by the hand.

ASSESSMENT

"Come on, Afrah. Let's go and find Rafiq so Papa's not waiting."

"Take Imraan also," her mother said, indicating the infant gurgling on the mat beside her.

Jameela scooped up the baby, propping him on her hip, and the little trio headed out of their small courtyard and down the dirt track to the square in front of the mosque.

"We'll look in the square first," she told Afrah. "That's where they always go after school."

Sure enough, there was Rafiq, racing around with his friends, dodging behind the plum trees and swinging from the lower branches. Spits of dust lacked up from his bare heels as he ran. On the wall at one side of the square stood little Mahmood, jumping up and down and waving his arms above his head. "Run, Rafiq, run! They'll catch you. Quick! Quick!" He didn't even see Jameela approach.

"Mahmood, you're to come home now. Dinner's ready."

He turned to her, a scowl darkening his small face. "What about Rafiq? Does he have to come too?"

Mahmood only did what his big brother did, copying him at everything.

Jameela tugged his arm. "You both have to come. Mamma said to get you."

He pulled away from her and clambered down from the wall so she couldn't reach him. "Then call him. I'll wait."

He stood crossly with his arms folded, turned slightly away from her. Jameela knew Rafiq wouldn't want to come home. He might be angry.

"You call him," she suggested to Mahmood archly. "I can't run after him with Afrah and Imraan. And girls don't run after their big brothers. But you can. Show me how quickly you can catch him."

Mahmood was delighted to have an excuse to race after Rafiq and needed no further encouragement. He forgot about being annoyed and sprinted across the square to where the older boys were now playing.

"Rafiq! Rafiq!" he shouted.

Rafiq stopped his play and stood talking to Mahmood for a moment. He looked over and, after a pause, took leave of his friends and crossed the square. He was hot from running, his face flushed. As Jameela expected, he was not pleased at having to stop. And he certainly did not like being summoned home by his sister.

"Why do we have to go home?" he demanded once Jameela was within earshot.

"Papa's waiting," she told him. 'You have to come."

"Mahmood said Mamma sent you."

Jameela grinned. "But it is Papa who wants you."

He knew there was no answer to that. Their father's word was final. Rafiq went in search

ASSESSMENT

of his cloth slippers, heaped with the other boys' under one of the plum trees, and slipped them on. They turned up the street and made for home.

"I can run faster than all the boys in my class," Rafiq told Jameela, dancing along beside her. "That's because I'm the tallest."

Jameela kept walking.

"And I'm the best writer also." And when she didn't respond: "Did you hear me?"

'Yes but I already know," she said, glancing at him. "You don't need to tell me."

"How do you know?" he asked, suddenly curious.

"Because when you teach me from your books, I see the teacher's marks and there are always stars beside your work."

Now it was Rafiq's turn to grin. "You're smart," he said, "for a girl."

Jameela longed to go to school, but in her village, girls didn't attend lessons. Instead they stayed at home and helped their mothers with cooking and cleaning and household tasks. Only the boys went to school, where they learned prayers and writing and reading. Rafiq was clever in school, but once it was over for the day, he threw his books aside to run and play football with his friends in the square.

That evening, when the meal was over and all the village boys were in their homes for the night, the family sat in the courtyard. Rafiq pulled out his books to teach Jameela, as he did most evenings.

"You're wasting your time, Rafiq," their father said as he came out of the house, picking his teeth with the tip of his long knife. "What use has a girl for reading and writing?"

"Teacher says to learn something new every day, Papa," Rafiq dared to answer. "Jameela's learning to read. She's clever. She knows her numbers already."

Jameela smiled up at her father, but he spat against the wall the red juice from the betel nut he was chewing.

"And she'll forget them quickly enough when she is married and she is busy preparing food, taking care of her husband and giving him children. Those are the skills she needs to learn."

"I can write my name, Papa," Jameela piped up.

ASSESSMENT

He looked down at her. "Just make sure you've done your chores first, and Rafiq, your homework."

Rafiq dropped his eyes immediately, in deference to their father's final word, but he wished he would say good things about Jameela's reading and writing. It was true that she didn't need to learn schoolwork, but she enjoyed it and Rafiq liked teaching her, sitting close on the step and reading out the words so she could repeat them. Rafiq thought that sometime, if he felt very brave, he might try to explain this to his papa, even though he knew it would anger him.

As their father left the courtyard to meet with the other men before evening prayers, he glanced to where the golden sun was dipping towards the distant hills. "Rafiq, meet me at the mosque before the sun settles in the Haji Pir pass."

Once her husband had gone, the children's mother spoke up. "It's useful to be able to read and write, Jameela," she said. "Then the traders won't try to cheat you with their prices at market."

Until now she had remained silent, squatting on a mat spread in the corner, where she was busy stitching pieces of brightly coloured cloth into new clothes for her children. She squinted into the last beams of the evening sun to thread the needle she held tightly in one hand.

Jameela smiled at her. "I'll keep learning, Mamma." She looked at Rafiq. "As long as you keep teaching me."

"I like teaching," Rafiq said, his solemn thoughts brightening. "I'd like to be a teacher some day. I'll have girls in my class too, not just boys."

"Can I be in your class, Rafiq?" Mahmood asked, jumping up from where he was drawing in the dust with a small stick. He leaned on his brother's knee.

"You'll be too old to be my pupil," Rafiq told him. "But in less than one year from now, little brother, you'll start school and we can go together."

"And me," cried Afrah, toddling over to join in the chatter.

"Afrah, Afrah!" Rafiq picked her up, laughing, and swung her in the air so she squealed with excitement. "Yes! I'll have you in my class. But not Jameela."

"Why can she be in your class and I can't?" Jameela demanded playfully. Her hands were on her hips, her head cocked to one side, and her mother smiled to see her own mannerisms echoed in her daughter's movements.

Rafiq arched an eyebrow. "Because you'll be married and living far away with your husband."

ASSESSMENT

"I will not!" Jameela spluttered. "I'm not leaving here" – she swept her hand around the courtyard – "to go and get married. I'm staying."

"Ah you'll change, Jameela. Wait and see," he teased her.

"No I won't. I will never go away from you, Rafiq," she told him, her face suddenly earnest.

Questions (40 marks)

1. How many children are in the family? Name each one and guess their age. (5 marks)
2. Identify two pieces of good descriptive writing in the text. (5 marks)
3. Describe the setting of the story. What country is it set in? What kind of place is the action happening in? Use quotes to support your answer. (10 marks)
4. Describe the characters of Rafiq and Jameela. Use quotes to support your answer. (10 marks)
5. What is your impression of the children's father? Use quotes to support your answer. (10 marks)

Focus on Plot and Atmosphere

Private Peaceful *by Michael Morpurgo*

It takes an eternity to cross no-man's-land. I begin to wonder if we'll ever find their trenches at all. Then we see their wire up ahead. We wriggle through a gap, and still undetected we drop down into their trench. It looks deserted, but we know it can't be. We can still hear the voices and the music. I notice the trench is much deeper than ours, wider too and altogether more solidly constructed. I grip my rifle tighter and follow Charlie along the trench, bent double like everyone else. We're trying not to, but we're making too much noise. I can't understand why no one has heard us. Where are their sentries, for God's sake? Up ahead I can see Wilkie waving us on with his revolver. There is a flickering of light now coming from a dugout ahead, where the voices are, where the music is. From the sound of it there could be half a dozen men in there at least. We only need one prisoner. How are we going to manage half a dozen of them?

At that moment the light floods into the trench as the dugout curtain opens. A soldier comes out shrugging on his coat, the curtain closing behind him. He is alone, just what we are after. He doesn't seem to see us right away. Then he does. For a split second the Hun does nothing and neither do we. We just stand and look at one another. He could so easily have done what he should have done, just put up his hands and come with us. Instead he lets out a shriek and turns, blundering through the curtain back into the dugout. I don't know who threw the grenade in after him, but there is a blast that throws me back against the trench wall. I sit there stunned. There is screaming and firing from inside the dugout, then silence. The music has stopped.

By the time I get in there Little Les is lying on his side shot through the head, his eyes staring at me. He looks so surprised. Several Germans are sprawled across their dugout, all still, all dead – except one. He stands there naked, blood spattered and shaking. I too am shaking. He has his hands in the air and is whimpering. Wilkie throws a coat over him and Pete bundles

ASSESSMENT

him out of the dugout. Frantic now to get back we scrabble our way up out of the trench, the Hun still whimpering. He is beside himself with terror. Pete is shouting at him to stop, but he's only making it worse. We follow the captain through the German wire and run.

For a while I think we have got away with it, but then a flare goes up and we are caught suddenly in broad daylight. I hurl myself to the ground and bury my face in the snow. Their flares last so much longer than ours, shine so much brighter. I know we're for it. I press myself into the ground, eyes closed. I'm praying and thinking of Molly. If I'm going to die I want her to be my last thought. But she's not. Instead I'm saying sorry to Father for what I did, that I didn't mean to do it. A machine gun opens up behind us and then rifles fire. There is nowhere to hide, so we pretend to be dead. We wait till the light dies and the night is suddenly black again. Wilkie gets us to our feet and we go on, running, stumbling, until more lights go up, and the machine gunners start up again. We dive into a crater and roll down crashing through the ice into the watery bottom. Then the shelling starts. It seems as if we have woken up the entire German army. I cower in the stinking water with the German and Charlie, the three of us clinging together, heads buried in one another as the shells fall all about us. Our own guns are answering now but it is little comfort to us. Charlie and I drag the Hun prisoner out of the water. Either he is talking to himself or he's saying a prayer, it's difficult to tell.

Then we see Wilkie lying higher up the slope, too close to the lip of the crater. When Charlie calls out to him he doesn't reply. Charlie goes to him and turns him over. "It's my legs," I hear the captain whisper. "I can't seem to move my legs." He's too exposed up there, so Charlie drags him back down as gently as he can. We try to make him comfortable. The Hun keeps praying out loud. I'm quite sure he's praying now. "*Du lieber Gott*," I hear. They call God by the same name. Pete and Nipper are crawling over towards us from the far side of the crater. We are together at least. The ground shudders, and with every impact we are bombarded by showers of mud and stone and snow. But the sound I hate and fear most is not the sound of the explosion – by then it's done and over with, and you're either dead or not. No, it's the whistle and whine and shriek of the shells as they come over. It's the not knowing where they will land, whether this one is for you.

Then, as suddenly as the barrage begins, it stops. There is silence. Darkness hides us again. Smoke drifts over us and down into our hole, filling our nostrils with the stench of cordite. We stifle our coughing. The Hun has stopped his praying, and is lying curled up in his overcoat, his hands over his ears. He's rocking like a child, like Big Joe.

Questions (40 marks)

1. Why are Charlie and the narrator crossing 'no-man's-land'? (5 marks)

2. How does the German prisoner (the Hun) react when he is being captured by the British? Use quotes to support your answer. (5 marks)

3. 'There is nowhere to hide so we pretend to be dead.' Explain what happens to the soldiers as they try to bring the prisoner back across no-man's-land. (10 marks)

4. What sound does the narrator hate the most? Why? Use quotes to support your answer. (10 marks)

5. How does the author create tension and an atmosphere of horror in this extract? Identify the words that effectively create the atmosphere for the reader. (10 marks)

CHAPTER 3

Songs and Poetry

My Learning Expectations

In this chapter I will:

- **Figure out** how lyrics are written and try to write them

- **Figure out** how **lyrics, rhythm** and **music** are connected

- **Think about** and **figure out** how poems appeal to the **five senses**

- Notice the different **formats** of poems

- Study work by individual poets and various poems according to **themes**

- Understand the mix of **colloquial/conversational** and **aesthetic/descriptive language** used by poets

- Write my own poems and **experiment** with **rhyme, rhythm, syllables, structure, free verse**, etc.

- **Read** for enjoyment

Songs and Poetry

Songs

What is a song?
Is it the lyrics, music, passion and emotion? Some songs make you want to jump up and dance; others make you sad.

How is a song written? How are the music and lyrics written? Which comes first? How do the words and the music connect?

There are many ways to compose songs.

You can begin by simply strumming a chord or a phrase on a guitar, humming and adding words to it or you can write the words first and put them to music.

Your Response to Music

Music appeals to our sense of hearing. It affects our mood. It can be soothing or energising. It can make us want to jump around wildly, or it can tug at our emotions and make us cry. Music is powerful.

How do you respond to music? How does it make it you feel? How does music move you? How can words and sound have an impact on you?

A. Oral Language

In pairs or groups:

- Discuss the answers to the above questions.

- Reflect on your favourite songs or lyrics. Talk about why you like particular songs. Think about summer hits, favourite dance songs, Christmas songs, or whatever your favourite type of song is.

- Discuss why you like these and talk about the impact that songs and music have on you.

B. Group Work

1. Figure out how music affects people's moods. Listen (in class or at home) to some sad and some happy songs. Think about the features of these songs that have an impact on the listener. Then, write down suggestions.

2. Why not try to write a short, simple song. How is it done? Has anyone in your class tried to write a song? Is anyone in a band?

Songwriting Tips

Create a melody first, perhaps on the guitar, and then try to write a few lyrics.

OR

If you have even one line or lyric that sticks in your head, compose a melody around that line.

Start small and build from either that early melody or that one first line.

Tone

How do the lyrics you've written make you feel? Try to match that feeling with a particular chord or chord sequence. For example, some minor chords, such as E minor and A minor, can sound mellow and sad and could be fitting for a sombre tone.

Other brighter, fuller chords, such as E major and G major, can sound more optimistic and vibrant and may suit a more upbeat tone.

Chorus

Work on creating a chorus that suits the overall tone of your song. Your main message should be in the chorus. Try to have one strong lyric that you can build the chorus around.

 ## Research

Do some research on songwriting and present your findings to the class. This is good practice for the Oral Language Assessment. For example, research on the origins of the word 'lyric' reveals the following information:

The word 'lyric' stems from the Greek words *lurikos* and *lura*, meaning lyre. 'Lyre' is a noun. A lyre is a stringed musical instrument. Lyric is the adjective that comes from lyre. The Latin word is *lyricus* and the French is *lyrique*.

Early lyric poems were dramatic stories and may have been accompanied by music or may have been sung. 'Lyric' is associated both with poetry (a lyric poem) and with songwriting, i.e. writing lyrics.

Read the lyrics of Ed Sheeran's song 'Thinking Out Loud' and listen to the song. Which features of the song do you think made it so popular?

Thinking Out Loud *by Ed Sheeran*

When your legs don't work like they used to before
And I can't sweep you off of your feet
Will your mouth still remember the taste of my love?
Will your eyes still smile from your cheeks?

And, darling, I will be loving you 'til we're 70
And, baby, my heart could still fall as hard at 23
And I'm thinking 'bout how people fall in love in mysterious ways
Maybe just the touch of a hand
Well, me—I fall in love with you every single day
And I just wanna tell you I am

So honey now
Take me into your loving arms
Kiss me under the light of a thousand stars
Place your head on my beating heart
I'm thinking out loud
That maybe we found love right where we are

When my hair's all but gone and my memory fades
And the crowds don't remember my name
When my hands don't play the strings the same way
I know you will still love me the same

'Cause honey your soul could never grow old, it's evergreen
And, baby, your smile's forever in my mind and memory
I'm thinking 'bout how people fall in love in mysterious ways
Maybe it's all part of a plan
Well, I'll just keep on making the same mistakes
Hoping that you'll understand

But, baby, now
Take me into your loving arms
Kiss me under the light of a thousand stars
Place your head on my beating heart
Thinking out loud
That maybe we found love right where we are

Words are powerful and can have a huge impact on us. Think about how happy you are when someone compliments or praises you, or how hurt you are when you are criticised. Think about times when you have cried listening to a particular song or reading a novel, because the main character has died or suffered unjustly. You were involved in the story and the power of words evoked a response from you. Think about a song that evokes a sad response from you. How does it do this?

How do mere words have power? Writers craft their songs, stories, poems and dramas very carefully. They write drafts until they're happy with the words, the sentences and the impact that the final text will have on a reader or listener. They focus on appealing to your senses to help you imagine and visualise the world they have created. You need to develop some of these skills with words to improve your own writing.

Next time you're listening to a song or reading a poem, short story or novel, pause at a beautiful image, a gorgeous description, a cleverly chosen adjective, a striking verb. Think about this. Store what strikes you, like a squirrel hoarding nuts for winter. Record your stash of words and images in your **PORTFOLIO**. With regular reading, soon you'll find that your memory will automatically save this precious stash and your unconscious mind will release these words when you are writing.

My Quote Wall

Think about your favourite lyrics, poem, quotes, or any type of text that appeals to you. Write this text into **page 47** of your **PORTFOLIO**.

The Five Senses

In Chapter 1, you read about how writers use the five senses to help to recreate scenes, build atmosphere and bring the story to life for the reader. Let's examine how the five senses work in poetry.

Taste

I have eaten
the plums
that were in
the icebox

and which
you were probably
saving
for breakfast

Forgive me
they were delicious
*so sweet
and so cold*

'This is Just to Say' by **William Carlos Williams**

Touch

Consider the grass growing
As it grew last year and the year before,
Cool about the ankles like summer rivers,
When we walked on a May evening through the meadows
To watch the mare that was going to foal.

'Consider the Grass Growing' by **Patrick Kavanagh**

Sound

… the *squelch* and *slap* of soggy peat…

From **'Digging'** by **Seamus Heaney**

Sight

I was six when I first saw kittens drown…

Like wet gloves they bobbed and shone till he sluiced
Them out on the dunghill, glossy and dead…

… for days I sadly hung
Round the yard watching the *three sogged remains*
Turn mealy and crisp as old summer dung.

From **'The Early Purges'** by **Seamus Heaney**

Smell

My mother's old leather handbag,
Crowded with letters she carried
All through the war. The smell
of my mother's handbag: *mints*
and lipstick and Coty powder…

Odour of *leather and powder…*

From **'Handbag'** by **Ruth Fainlight**

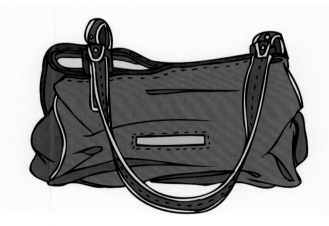

Writers appeal to our five senses to help us to visualise, to imagine, to almost feel, almost taste, touch, smell and see whatever it is that they are describing. Once we identify with the senses, we relate to and connect with the description, the scene, the character and the mood.

The writing of some poets may be described as 'sensuous' because it appeals to our senses. For example, the British Romantic poets such as William Wordsworth and John Keats, the Latino poet Richard Blanco, the Caribbean poet Derek Walcott and the American poet Elizabeth Bishop all appeal to the readers' senses in their writing.

How Language Works in Poetry

Poets choose their words very carefully, selecting only the most suitable. Like connoisseurs (experts in matters of skill), they are very careful craftspeople.

If a poet wrote plain, straightforward lines, it wouldn't be very interesting. It would be the ordinary, humdrum words that you hear, see and understand every day.

So, poets create mystery, a puzzle, a thing of beauty. They use aesthetic language, which is very descriptive. They craft their poem using similes, metaphors, personification and so on.

Poets work hard to create alliteration, rhyme, assonance, sibilance, onomatopoeia and similar effects.

You might remember some of these terms from *Great Expectations 1*, but if you need to revise them, go to **page 151** of this chapter.

Poets also use colloquial, conversational language. Some poets mix both types of language in their poems. The conversational, everyday language is easy to follow but the aesthetic language is usually harder to figure out. For example, think about what is conversational and what is aesthetic in the following poem:

The sea is never the same twice. Today
the waves open their lions' mouths hungry
for the shore, and I feel the earth helpless.

'Some Days the Sea' by **Richard Blanco**

My Response to Poetry

Read the following poem and see if you can identify some of the features of poetry you have studied.

 Frozen Food *by Doireann Ní Ghríofa*

'The Iceman was carrying a sloe, presumably to eat' — *Mandy Haggith*

In the frozen foods aisle, I think of him
when I shiver among shelves of green-flecked
garlic breads and chunks of frozen fish.
I touch the cold door until my thumbs numb.

Strangers unpacked his body in a lab
and thawed his hand, watched long-frozen fingers
unfurl one by one, until his fist finally opened,
let go, and from his grasp rolled
a single sloe,
ice-black with a purple-blue waxy bloom.

Inside the sloe,
a blackthorn stone.
Inside the stone,
a seed.

Standing in the supermarket aisle,
I watch my breath freeze

 ## A. Reading

Rate this text for readability. Write the word/phrase of your choice into your copy.

VERY EASY ☐   **EASY** ☐   **OKAY** ☐   **HARD** ☐   **VERY HARD** ☐

 ## B. Literacy Questions

 In pairs, answer the following questions.

1. Think about what you imagined and how you felt as you read this poem. Discuss your response with the person beside you, read the poem again and share your thoughts about it with your partner.

2. List the words or images that had an impact on you.

3. Comment on the title of the poem.

4. Figure out whether the language in the poem is colloquial or aesthetic, or a combination of the two.

C. Writing

Make two headings in your copy: Aesthetic Language and Colloquial Language.
Read the poem 'Frozen Food' again. Match up the lines of the poem under the
headings in the columns.

Aesthetic Descriptive, figurative language	Colloquial Conversational, casual, everyday language

You can use the following checklist to help your understanding when you read a poem for the
first time. Over the next few pages we will look at some common types and features
of poetry.

MY RESPONSE CHECKLIST ☑

- ☑ How do you respond to what you read?
- ☑ What impact do the words in a poem have on you?
- ☑ What senses do you think the poem appeals to?
- ☑ What word or image strikes you, has an effect on you or makes you think about something or someone? What word or image makes you feel a certain way, reminds you of something, triggers a memory, helps you to imagine or see something new?
- ☑ What kinds of things reach out to you in the poem? Is it the beauty of a word or an image?
- ☑ Can you identify any common features of poetry in what you have just read, such as assonance or rhyme?
- ☑ What kind of language does the poet use?

Styles of Poetry

Over the following pages we will look at some of the common styles of poetry that you will encounter.

Blank verse means there is no rhyme and the lines may be almost conversational, so there are no stanzas (verses). However, long blank verse poems often have verse paragraphs. For example, 'Mending Wall' by Robert Frost and 'The Schooner Flight' by Derek Walcott.

Ballads (from the Latin *ballare*, meaning to dance) were originally songs that told a story. Many ballads were sung or read aloud in public. Ballad poems are therefore long, narrative poems, often written in quatrains (four line stanzas) with a refrain (lines repeated like a chorus). An example would be 'The Ballad of Reading Gaol' by Oscar Wilde.

Blank Verse

Down *by Brendan Kennelly*

why does a poem
always
go
down
the page
like
a shooting
star
or a spade
cutting
into earth
making way
for seeds
to nestle
in darkness
and slowly
begin
to become
(for example)
a small
white
flower
perfect
in the
light?

Ballad

The Boys of Barr na Sráide *by Sigerson Clifford*

The Irish poet Sigerson Clifford wrote, 'The Boys of Barr na Sráide' about his childhood, going out with his friends for the 'wran' on Stephen's Day during the War of Independence, 1919–21, and the Civil War, 1921–22.

Oh the town it climbs the mountain and looks upon the sea,
And sleeping time or waking 'tis there I long to be,
To walk again that kindly street, the place I grew a man
And the Boys of Barr na Sráide went hunting for the wran.

With cudgels stout we roamed about to hunt the droileen
We looked for birds in every furze from Letter to Dooneen:
We sang for joy beneath the sky, life held no print or plan
And we Boys in Barr na Sráide, hunting for the wran.

And when the hills were bleeding and the rifles were aflame,
To the rebel homes of Kerry the Saxon stranger came,
But the men who dared the Auxies and beat the Black and Tans
Were the Boys of Barr na Sráide hunting for the wran.

And here's a toast to them tonight, the lads who laughed with me,
By the groves of Carhan river or the slopes of Beenatee,
John Dawley and Batt Andy, and the Sheehans Con and Dan,
And the Boys of Barr na Sráide who hunted for the wran.

And now they toil on foreign soil, where they have gone their way
Deep in the heart of London town or over on Broadway.
And I am left to sing their deeds, and praise them while I can
Those Boys of Barr na Sráide who hunted for the wran.

And when the wheel of life runs down and peace comes over me,
O lay me down in that old town between the hills and sea,
I'll take my sleep in those green fields the place my life began,
Where the Boys of Barr na Sráide went hunting for the wran.

GLOSSARY

Barr na Sráide: A street in Caherciveen, Co. Kerry.

Droileen: The Irish for wren, usually spelt *dreoilín*.

Letter, Dooneen: Places in South Kerry on the Iveragh Peninsula.

Saxon: English.

Auxies: Auxiliaries, English soldiers from the RIC, set up to counter rebellion.

Epic poems are long narratives or stories, collected from the oral tradition of storytelling. They often deal with the heroic exploits of a person. For example, Seamus Heaney's translation of the Old English epic *Beowulf*.

Elegies are songs and poems of lamentation, grieving the death or loss of someone or lamenting some other great loss. For example, 'Funeral Blues' by W. H. Auden.

Odes are poems addressed to a specific person or thing. For example, 'Ode to a Nightingale' and 'Ode on a Grecian Urn' by John Keats.

Sestinas have 39 lines, written in six sestets (six lines) and a tercet (three lines). 'Sestina' means 'song of sixes'. The rhyme words of the first sestet recur in different order as the rhyme words in every subsequent sestet. For example, Elizabeth Bishop's poem 'Sestina'.

Villanelles are usually 19-line poems with a refrain or repetition to emphasise a mood or feeling. In Italian, *vilano* is the word for peasant. For example, 'Do Not Go Gentle Into That Good Night' by Dylan Thomas.

Sonnets have 14 lines, arranged either in Shakespeare's style as three quatrains (a quatrain is made up of four lines) and a rhyming couplet, or following Petrarch's style of eight lines (an octave) and six lines (a sestet).

Sonnet

Sonnet XVIII *by William Shakespeare*

Shall I compare thee to a summer's day?
Thou art more lovely and more temperate:
Rough winds do shake the darling buds of May,
And summer's lease hath all too short a date:
Sometime too hot the eye of heaven shines,
And often is his gold complexion dimm'd;
And every fair from fair sometime declines,
By chance, or nature's changing course untrimm'd:
But thy eternal summer shall not fade,
Nor loose possession of that fair thou ow'st;
Nor shall death brag thou wand'rest in his shade,
When in eternal lines to time thou grow'st:
     So long as men can breathe or eyes can see,
     So long lives this and this gives life to thee.

GLOSSARY

Temperate: Mild, moderate.

Complexion: The general character of a thing.

Sonnets are 14-line poems. Shakespeare's sonnets are made up of three quatrains and a rhyming couplet. A quatrain is four lines. In each quatrain the poet explains a point. The points are developed quatrain by quatrain and the last two lines sum up the poet's belief. For example, in the first quatrain of 'Sonnet XVIII', Shakespeare says that the girl is more beautiful than a summer's day. In the second quatrain, he says that nature has flaws. Sometimes the sun is too hot or nature changes abruptly. In the third quatrain, he says the girl and her beauty will outlive the changes in nature. She will not be in the shadow of death. In the final couplet, he explains that this sonnet will keep the girl 'alive' because people will read it for years to come.

Revision: Features of Poetry

Before we move on, let's revise some of the features of poetry that you may remember learning about last year in *Great Expectations 1*.

Similes: A comparison using 'like' or 'as'. For example, 'long icicles like crystal daggers hung down from the eaves of the houses', from 'The Happy Prince' by Oscar Wilde.

Metaphors: A comparison that doesn't use 'like' or 'as'. For example, 'her smile is a summer's day' and 'hunger is a wolf howling at the moon'.

Personification: Giving something human qualities. For example, 'the trees sighed and whispered.'

Alliteration: When the first consonant is repeated in a series of words. For example, 'the tall trees towered tremendously over the tiny child'.

Assonance: Vowel sounds repeated in a series of words. The broad vowels are 'a', 'o' and 'u' and these give a slow, soft effect. The slender vowels are 'i' and 'e', which give a harsher sound effect.

Sibilance: The repetition of the letter 's'. A few or many 's'es in a series of words creates a certain sound effect.

Onomatopoeia: You can almost hear the sound in onomatopoeic words such as whizz, bang, clang, crash and clash.

Rhythm: Your heart has a rhythm as it beats. In poetry, rhythm is the beat the poem has. Rhyme creates rhythm, as does following a particular pattern with syllables and word length.

Repetition: Repeating words or lines. Repetition is used to emphasise a point, mood or feeling.

Refrain: This is like a chorus or repetition. Lines in a refrain are repeated to emphasise a mood or feeling. For example, 'There should be nothing here I don't remember' from 'Looking for the Gulf Motel' by Richard Blanco.

Rhyme: Words that sound the same are presented in a pattern, perhaps at the end of every line. For example, know/though/snow/go.

Couplet: Two lines, one after the other, that are usually rhyming and the same length. Couplets at the end of a poem are often used to moralise and to summarise. For example, the final couplet in 'Sonnet XVIII' by Shakespeare.

Rhyming couplets: Two lines together which have end-rhyme are called rhyming couplets. For example:

I went to turn the grass once after one
Who mowed it in the dew before the sun.

From **'The Tuft of Flowers'** by **Robert Frost**

Iambic pentameter: In a line of poetry, words are parcelled or separated into what is called a foot. This is the repetition of a basic unit. For example, the following line from 'Sonnet XII' by Shakespeare:

'When I do count the clock that tells the time'

Separated into feet, it becomes:

When **I** / do **count** / the **clock** / that **tells** / the **time**

The stress is on the words in bold.

An iamb is one of the basic feet or part of a line. There are five iambs in this line. The Greek for five is *pente*, so the line is an example of iambic pentameter.

If a line has four iambs, it is an iambic tetrameter.

The word 'iamb' is a noun; 'iambic' is an adjective.

Syllables: These are units of sound. Every word is made up of syllables. For example, the word 'music' has two syllables: 'mu' and 'sic'. Poets use syllables to create sound patterns. These patterns create rhythm.

Windrush Child *by John Agard*

Behind you
Windrush child
palm trees wave goodbye

above you
Windrush child
seabirds asking why

around you
Windrush child
blue water rolling by

beside you
Windrush child
your Windrush mum and dad

think of storytime yard
and mango mornings

and new beginnings
doors closing and opening

will things turn out right?
At least the ship will arrive
in midsummer light

and you Windrush child
think of grandmother
telling you don't forget to write

and with one last hug
walk good walk good
and the sea's wheel carries on spinning

and from that place England
you tell her in a letter
of your Windrush adventure

stepping in a big ship
not knowing how long the journey
or that you're stepping into history

bringing your Caribbean eye
to another horizon
grandmother's words your shining beacon

learning how to fly
the kite of your dreams
in an English sky

Windrush child
walking good walking good
in a mind-opening
meeting of snow and sun

A. Reading

Rate this text for readability. Write the word/phrase of your choice into your copy.

VERY EASY ☐   **EASY** ☐   **OKAY** ☐   **HARD** ☐   **VERY HARD** ☐

B. Group Work

Examine the poem 'Windrush Child' by John Agard.

1. Comment on or explain the style/format/layout of the poem.
2. Identify and list the features used in the poem. Use the features on **pages 151 and 152**.

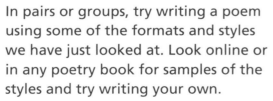

C. Writing – My Own Poem

In pairs or groups, try writing a poem using some of the formats and styles we have just looked at. Look online or in any poetry book for samples of the styles and try writing your own.

You could try Creative Modelling by copying the format and style of an existing poem, but using your own words. For example, look at the poem Scott Westerfeld tweeted based on 'This is Just to Say' by William Carlos Williams. You can read the original poem on **page 142**.

Write your poem on **page 48** of your **PORTFOLIO**.

Scott Westerfeld
@ScottWesterfeld   Following

I tweeted
the joke
that you said
last night

and which
you were probably
saving
for yourself

Forgive me
it was funny
and got
lots of RTs

RETWEETS   FAVORITES
452   767

2:51 AM - 4 Mar 2015

Winter Days *by Gareth Owen*

Biting air
Winds blow
City streets
Under snow

Noses red
Lips sore
Runny eyes
Hands raw

Chimneys smoke
Cars crawl
Piled snow
On garden wall

Slush in gutters
Ice in lines
Frosty patterns
On window panes

Morning call
Lift up head
Nipped by winter
Stay in bed

 ## A. Reading

Rate this text for readability. Write the word/phrase of your choice into your copy.

VERY EASY ☐   **EASY** ☐   **OKAY** ☐   **HARD** ☐   **VERY HARD** ☐

 ## B. Literacy Questions

1. List the rhyming words in the poem.

2. Explain how the cold wind affects the people. Quote from the poem to support your answer.

3. Explain the effect of the cold weather on the traffic and on the streets. Quote from the poem to support your answer.

The Siege *by Helen Dunmore*

Helen Dunmore is an English poet, novelist and children's writer. Her novels are on syllabi in schools and she has won awards for her fiction and poetry. She lives in Bristol.

The following excerpt from one of Dunmore's novels is very descriptive and is an example of how text can be written in paragraphs or in the format of a poem. Notice that a story is being told. Why not take a descriptive piece of fiction from any book you are reading and rewrite it as a poem?

When the first snow falls, Anna always goes to the Summer Garden. Then, the noise of the city is muffled, and the park is eerily luminous. Small, naked-looking sparrows hop from twig to twig, dislodging a powder of snow. The trees are lit up like candelabra by the whiteness they hold in their arms. Underfoot, she hears for the first time the squeak of snow packing into the treads of her boots. She bends down, scoops up a handful of the new snow, throws it up into the air and watches it scatter into powdery fragments as it falls for the second time. And although she's cold and she ought to get home, she always stays much longer than she means to, because she knows that this feeling won't come again for another year.

Now, here is how the same text might be laid out as a poem:

When the first snow falls,
Anna always goes to the Summer
Garden. Then, the noise of the
city is muffled, and the park is
eerily luminous. Small, naked-
looking sparrows hop from twig
to twig, dislodging a powder of
snow. The trees are lit up like
candelabra by the whiteness they
hold in their arms. Underfoot,
she hears for the first time the
squeak of snow packing into the
treads of her boots. She bends
down, scoops up a handful of
the new snow, throws it up into
the air and watches it scatter into
powdery fragments as it falls for
the second time. And
although she's cold and
she ought to get home, she always
stays much longer than she
means to, because she knows
that this feeling won't come again
for another year.

A. Reading

Rate this text for readability. Write the word/phrase of your choice into your copy.

VERY EASY ☐   **EASY** ☐   **OKAY** ☐   **HARD** ☐   **VERY HARD** ☐

B. Literacy Questions

1. Where does Anna go when the first snow falls?
2. Find a line that personifies trees.
3. What does Anna hear in the garden?
4. Why do you think the snow is described as 'powder' and 'powdery'?
5. Why do you think Anna stays 'much longer than she means to' in the garden?
6. Comment on the name of the garden.

The next three poems examine relationships between parents and children. Themes include father–son relationships, childhood and growing up.

 # Walking Away *by Cecil Day-Lewis*

For Seán

It is eighteen years ago, almost to the day –
A sunny day with the leaves just turning,
The touch-lines new-ruled – since I watched you play
Your first game of football, then, like a satellite
Wrenched from its orbit, go drifting away.

Behind a scatter of boys. I can see
You walking away from me towards the school
With the pathos of a half-fledged thing set free
Into a wilderness, the gait of one
Who finds no path where the path should be.

That hesitant figure, eddying away
Like a winged seed loosened from its parent stem,
Has something I never quite grasp to convey
About nature's give-and-take – the small, the scorching
Ordeals which fire one's irresolute clay.

I have had worse partings, but none that so
Gnaws at my mind still. Perhaps it is roughly
Saying what God alone could perfectly show –
How selfhood begins with a walking away,
And love is proved in the letting go.

GLOSSARY

Pathos: Pity or sadness.

Gait: A person's way of walking.

Eddying: Something moving in a circular way (water, smoke, air).

Convey: In the context of the poem, it may mean to show or understand, put across.

Irresolute: Hesitant or uncertain.

A. Reading

Rate this text for readability. Write the word/phrase of your choice into your copy.

VERY EASY ☐   **EASY** ☐   **OKAY** ☐   **HARD** ☐   **VERY HARD** ☐

 B. Group Work

In groups, figure out the answers to the following questions and write them into your copy.

1. Imagine you are creating a short film based on the story or action in the poem. Figure out the scenes in the poem. Try to number them in sequence. Decide the sequence of screen shots to film. Choose suitable music to accompany the short film.

2. How do you think the young child felt in stanza three?

3. How does the narrator feel about his son 'drifting away'?

4. What age do you think the narrator's son is in the 'present time' in the poem?

 C. Writing

Imagine you are the son in the poem. Write a paragraph or a poem giving your viewpoint on growing up and gaining independence from your dad.

  D. Writing

Daily life presents challenges, big and small. Some days are good and we're happy. Other days are bad – we make mistakes and have regrets, we encounter people we don't like, we suffer situations we'd rather not be in. Ultimately, we learn from all of our experiences, good and bad.

Think about 'the small, the scorching ordeals which fire one's irresolute clay'. On **page 49** of your **PORTFOLIO**, write one paragraph or more about 'What shapes and moulds your clay'. What mistakes have you made and learned from? What good things inspire or motivate you? For example, think about friends/sport/hobbies.

Adrian Mitchell

Adrian Mitchell was an English poet, novelist and playwright. He studied English at Oxford, where he was taught by Christopher Tolkien, son of J. R. R. Tolkien. Mitchell began his career as a journalist before becoming a full-time writer. In 1998, he adapted *The Lion, the Witch and the Wardrobe* for the stage. Mitchell had a very interesting and varied career – you might consider doing further research on his life.

Five Years Old *by Adrian Mitchell*

Five-year-olds dream of becoming giants –
Golden-bearded, striding around the map,
Gulping streams, munching sandwiches
Of crushed ice and white-hot anthracite
Between two slices of slate.
They sit on the edge of Salisbury Plain
Bawling huge songs across the counties
For ten days at a time,
Eating trees, cuddling carthorses,
Before stomping home to Windsor Castle.
They name clouds. They fall in love with buses,
They lick the stars, they are amazed by hoses,
They dance all the time because they don't think about dancing...

They long to be allowed into the big good schools
Which will teach them to be giants with wings.

GLOSSARY
Anthracite: Coal.
Salisbury Plain: A chalk plateau in central southern England known for its archaeology, notably Stonehenge.
Windsor Castle: A castle in Berkshire, used by the British royal family as a holiday home and for state visits.

A. Reading

Rate this text for readability. Write the word/phrase of your choice into your copy.

VERY EASY ☐   **EASY** ☐   **OKAY** ☐   **HARD** ☐   **VERY HARD** ☐

B. Literacy Questions

1. According to the poem, what do five-year-olds dream of?
2. What do five-year-olds long for? Explain why.
3. Five-year-olds seem to be very busy. Make a list of the verbs used in the poem to describe their actions. For example, 'striding', 'gulping'.
4. Identify one image that you liked in the poem and explain why you liked it.

C. Writing

Do you remember how energetic and fun-loving you were when you were five? Write a paragraph or a page about the games you really enjoyed playing at that age.

Beatrix is Three *by Adrian Mitchell*

At the top of the stairs
I ask for her hand. O.K.
She gives it to me.
How her fist fits my palm,
A bunch of consolation.
We take our time
Down the steep carpetway
As I wish silently
That the stairs were endless.

 ## A. Reading

Rate this text for readability. Write the word/phrase of your choice into your copy.

VERY EASY ☐   **EASY** ☐   **OKAY** ☐   **HARD** ☐   **VERY HARD** ☐

 ## B. Literacy Questions

1. Explain what is happening in the poem.
2. How do you think the poet feels towards Beatrix? Explain your answer using quotes.

 ## C. Pairwork

Think about connections that you can make between the poems 'Walking Away', 'Five Years Old' and 'Beatrix is Three'.

In pairs, compare the themes and feelings in the poems.

George Harding

George Harding is from Cork. He is an environmentalist, booklover and hurling fanatic and is married with three children. He has performed at many literary festivals around Munster and his poetry has been featured in various Irish, British and American publications. His first collection, *My Stolen City*, was published by Revival Press in 2011, and his second book, *Last Bus to Pewterhole Cross*, was published in 2015.

 # First Snow *by George Harding*

"Look Daddy – look at the snow
it's snowing – look, snow!"
Black dark and there it was
and she nosed on the window.

"Come on Daddy – can we go
and make snowballs outside?
Oh! It's snowing – look at the snow!
I can't believe it!" she cried.

But the snow was late in coming
for play and innocent delight
and she dreamt of snow and snowing
all that long winter's night.

 ## A. Reading

Rate this text for readability. Write the word/phrase of your choice into your copy.

VERY EASY ☐   EASY ☐   OKAY ☐   HARD ☐   VERY HARD ☐

 ## B. Oral Language

 In pairs, discuss your childhood memories of snow. Where were you? How old were you? Did you play in the snow?

 ## C. Writing

On **page 50** of your **PORTFOLIO**, write a paragraph or a poem about your childhood memories or experiences of snow.

The Music of Hurling *by George Harding*

(for John Liddy)

I heard the furious buzz of hurling
hurtling on my window pane
a wasp wearing his Kilkenny jersey
tapping the glass like a sliotar on a boss.

He tapped and buzzed for sixty seconds
until my patience snapped
and then trapped him in a glass, before
releasing him, with a flick of the wrist,

into the brilliant sunshine
and surviving the brutal toss
he revived immediately
with something in his fist

a sliotar probably, but I could not see
his venom for one last strike
making his final point
as usual, and me wishing he would miss.

Hurling is indeed a game for the Gods. Hurling, which can claim to be the parent of every game played with a stick and ball, stands still unapproached as the greatest game ever devised for the diversion of men. Like the race that begot it, it is old, yet young, virile and fascinating, and though its origin dates away back in prehistoric eras, could Oisín come back again today from Tír na nÓg, he would find in an all-too-changed world, by Lee and Suir and Nore and Shannon, at least one familiar sight to gladden his heart.

GAA journalist, Seamus O'Ceallaigh

A. Reading

Rate this poem for readability. Write the word/phrase of your choice into your copy.

VERY EASY ☐ **EASY** ☐ **OKAY** ☐ **HARD** ☐ **VERY HARD** ☐

B. Group Work

The poet is comparing his encounter with the wasp to the game of hurling. In groups, discuss why you think the poet makes this comparison.

C. Writing

Explain the 'story' in the poem using a maximum of five sentences.

Fleur Adcock

Fleur Adcock was born in Auckland, New Zealand, but has spent much of her life in England. She graduated from college with a degree in Classics. She has worked as a lecturer and librarian, as well as a poet and freelance writer.

For a Five-Year-Old *by Fleur Adcock*

A snail is climbing up the window-sill
into your room, after a night of rain.
You call me in to see, and I explain
that it would be unkind to leave it there:
it might crawl to the floor; we must take care
that no one squashes it. You understand,
and carry it outside, with careful hand,
to eat a daffodil.

I see, then, that a kind of faith prevails:
your gentleness is moulded still by words
from me, who drowned your kittens, who betrayed
your closest relatives, and who purveyed
the harshest kind of truth to many another.
But that is how things are: I am your mother,
And we are kind to snails.

GLOSSARY

Prevails: Current, existing or widespread.

Purveyed: A purveyor is a person who promotes or sells an idea or goods.

A. Reading

Rate this text for readability. Write the word/phrase of your choice into your copy.

VERY EASY ☐   **EASY ☐**   **OKAY ☐**   **HARD ☐**   **VERY HARD ☐**

B. Group Work

In your group, figure out the following:

1. Who is the 'You' and who is the 'I' in the poem? What is their relationship?
2. What kind act is done in stanza one?
3. How does stanza two contrast with stanza one?
4. What does the poet mean by 'But that is how things are'?
5. List some good and some bad deeds that you have done.

Things *by Fleur Adcock*

There are worse things than having behaved foolishly in public.
There are worse things than these miniature betrayals,
committed or endured or suspected; there are worse things
than not being able to sleep for thinking about them.
It is 5 a.m. All the worse things come stalking in
and stand icily about the bed looking worse and worse and worse.

 ## A. Reading

Rate this text for readability. Write the word/phrase of your choice into your copy.

VERY EASY ☐   **EASY** ☐   **OKAY** ☐   **HARD** ☐   **VERY HARD** ☐

 ## B. Group Work

In your group, figure out the following:

1. The title of the poem: why is it called 'Things'?
2. The location/setting of the poem and the time of day/night.
3. The person in the poem: is the speaker a child, a teenager or an adult?
4. Is the activity and energy in the poem from the person or nature or both?
5. Identify the images or words that strike you. Explain why and how they have an impact on you.

 ## C. Writing

Write a paragraph about your own experiences of waking up in the middle of the night due to nightmares, worries, fears or anxieties.

W. B. Yeats

W. B. Yeats is considered by many to be one of Ireland's greatest poets. He won the Nobel Prize in Literature in 1923. He was passionate about Irish mythology and the folklore, culture and landscape of Ireland. In particular, he loved Sligo, which is often referred to fondly as 'Yeats country'.

The themes expressed in the following poems are love and old age. In the first two poems Yeats is thinking about the autumn, or the later stage, in his life. There is a sense of nostalgia and fondness for the woman he loves. We see that love changes as people grow older together. In the next two poems, love is in its early, youthful stages and there's a sense of excitement and great joy.

The Falling of the Leaves *by W. B. Yeats*

Autumn is over the long leaves that love us,
And over the mice in the barley sheaves;
Yellow the leaves of the rowan above us,
And yellow the wet wild-strawberry leaves.

The hour of the waning of love has beset us,
And weary and worn are our sad souls now;
Let us part, 'ere the season of passion forget us,
With a kiss and a tear on thy drooping brow.

GLOSSARY
Rowan: A small deciduous tree with red berries.
Waning: Becoming weaker or smaller.
Beset: Faced with or surrounded by.

A. Reading

Rate this text for readability. Write the word/phrase of your choice into your copy.

VERY EASY ☐   **EASY** ☐   **OKAY** ☐   **HARD** ☐   **VERY HARD** ☐

B. Literacy Questions

1. List the words in the poem that you associate with the season of autumn.
2. List the words in the poem that rhyme.
3. What kind of mood or atmosphere does the poem have? Use quotations to support your answer.

C. Writing

In pairs, write your own poem on the theme of autumn. See the examples on **page 51** of your **PORTFOLIO**.

Alfred, Lord Tennyson

Tennyson was born in Somersby, Lincolnshire, England in 1809. He began writing poetry in his teenage years, as did two of his brothers. Together, the three brothers published a book of poetry when Alfred was 17. In 1827, Tennyson went to Cambridge University and had his first solo collection of poetry published. In 1850 he was appointed Poet Laureate of Great Britain and Ireland. He is known for his short lyric poems, such as 'Break, Break, Break' and 'Charge of the Light Brigade', and for his poems based on mythology, such as 'Ulysses'. Tennyson also wrote epic poems and blank verse. He died on 6 October 1892.

Lines from Tennyson's poem are often quoted, such as:

''Tis better to have loved and lost/Than never to have loved at all.'
'Theirs is not to reason why/Theirs but to do and die.'
'My strength is as the strength of ten,/Because my heart is pure.'

 # The Song of the Brook *by Alfred, Lord Tennyson*

I come from haunts of coot and hern,
    I make a sudden sally,
And sparkle out among the fern,
    To bicker down a valley.

By thirty hills I hurry down,
    Or slip between the ridges,
By twenty thorps, a little town,
    And half a hundred bridges.

Till last by Philip's farm I flow
    To join the brimming river,
For men may come and men may go,
    But I go on for ever.

I chatter over stony ways,
    In little sharps and trebles,
I bubble into eddying bays,
    I babble on the pebbles.

With many a curve my banks I fret
    By many a field and fallow,
And many a fairy foreland set
    With willow-weed and mallow.

I chatter, chatter, as I flow
    To join the brimming river,
For men may come and men may go,
    But I go on for ever.

I wind about, and in and out,
    With here a blossom sailing,
And here and there a lusty trout,
    And here and there a grayling,

And here and there a foamy flake
    Upon me, as I travel
With many a silvery water-break
    Above the golden gravel,

And draw them all along, and flow
    To join the brimming river,
For men may come and men may go,
    But I go on for ever.

GLOSSARY

Brook: An old word for river or stream.

Coot and hern: A coot is a bird with black plumage; a hern is also a bird, maybe a heron.

Sudden sally: Rush suddenly, leap out.

Thorps: Villages or hamlets.

Grayling: An edible freshwater fish that is silvery grey with violet stripes.

 ## A. Reading

Rate this text for readability. Write the word/phrase of your choice into your copy.

VERY EASY ☐   EASY ☐   OKAY ☐   HARD ☐   VERY HARD ☐

 ## B. Literacy Questions

1. Who or what is the speaker in the poem, the 'I'?
2. Find and explain one example of personification in the poem.
3. Find and explain one example of noise made by the brook on its journey.
4. List three examples of alliteration in the poem.
5. List four examples of rhyme in the poem.
6. What things does the brook see as it flows?

 ## C. Numeracy Questions

1. How many hills, thorps and bridges does the little brook flow through?
2. How many stanzas are there in the poem?
3. How many times is the line 'but I go on for ever' repeated?

The Lotos-Eaters *by Alfred, Lord Tennyson*

'The Lotos-Eaters' tells the story of hard-working sailors whose ship lands unexpectedly on a strange, enchanted island awash with beautiful music and fruit. When the sailors eat the lotos fruit, which is plentiful on the island, they become drowsy and sleepy, reluctant to sail home to their loved ones. The following extract, from the sailors' 'choric song', captures a particular mood or feeling.

There is sweet music here that softer falls
Than petals from blown roses on the grass,
Or night dews on still waters between walls
Of shadowy granite, in a gleaming pass;
Music that gentlier on the spirit lies,
Than tired eyelids upon tired eyes;
Music that brings sweet sleep down from the blissful skies.
Here are cool mosses deep,
And thro' the moss the ivies creep,
And in the stream the long-leaved flowers weep,
And from the craggy ledge the poppy hangs in sleep.

A. Reading

Rate this text for readability. Write the word/phrase of your choice into your copy.

VERY EASY ☐   **EASY** ☐   **OKAY** ☐   **HARD** ☐   **VERY HARD** ☐

B. Literacy Questions

1. List the words that rhyme in the poem.
2. Which of the five senses does this extract appeal to? Quote from the poem to support your answer.
3. Identify and list examples of alliteration and assonance in the poem.

C. Visual Literacy

Draw the scene as described above: the roses with their petals blown onto the grass, the shadowy, wet granite walls by the water's edge in darkness…

Eavan Boland

Eavan Boland was born in Dublin in 1944 but spent her early childhood in London, where her father worked as a diplomat. Boland's mother was an artist. Her family returned to Dublin when she was 14. She attended secondary school in Killiney, after which she completed a degree in English Literature and Language at Trinity College. From the 1960s to the 1980s, Boland worked as a freelance journalist and broadcaster. She has won numerous awards for her work and is currently a professor at Stanford University, California. Themes in her poetry include history, politics, nature, love, children and motherhood.

In the following three poems, Boland looks at simple, ordinary aspects of life – the moment at dusk when a child runs to its mother, a holiday in Clare and feeding a baby at night. She captures the moments and the feelings that a mother experiences: relief, fear, anxiety and happiness.

This Moment *by Eavan Boland*

A neighbourhood.
At dusk.

Things are getting ready
to happen
out of sight.

Stars and moths.
And rinds slanting around fruit.

But not yet.

One tree is black.
One window is yellow as butter.

A woman leans down to catch a child
who has run into her arms
this moment.

Stars rise.
Moths flutter.
Apples sweeten in the dark.

A. Reading

Rate this text for readability. Write the word/phrase of your choice into your copy.

VERY EASY ☐   EASY ☐   OKAY ☐   HARD ☐   VERY HARD ☐

 # B. Group Work

In your group, imagine your task is to draw suitable pictures/illustrations to explain each stanza in the poem.

Think about the following:

1. Setting (place/location).
2. The time of day or night or both.
3. The objects or things mentioned in the poem.
4. What colours you will you use to create mood/atmosphere.
5. The action that occurs in the poem.

Give each member of the group at least one scene to work on. Decide the order of the finished pages/scenes. As a group, assess the strengths and weaknesses of each page. Do the pictures effectively tell the story? Agree an overall grade for the work.

 ## Group Work Assessment

Don't forget to fill in a Group Work Self Assessment and Peer Assessment on **page 54** of your **PORTFOLIO**.

 ## C. Writing – Creative Modelling

Write your own poem on your own topic, but copy the format of the poem 'This Moment'. See the example on **page 55** of your **PORTFOLIO**.

 # D. Pairwork

Think about how poets make ordinary things extraordinary.

In pairs, compile a list of the simple, everyday things that Boland captures in these three poems.

On Holiday *by Eavan Boland*

Ballyvaughan.
Peat and salt.
How the wind bawls
across these mountains
scalds the orchids
of the Burren.

They used to leave milk
out once on these windowsills
to ward away
the child-stealing spirits.

The sheets are damp.
We sleep between the blankets.
The light cotton of the curtains
lets the light in.

You wake first thing
and in your five-year-size
striped nightie you are
everywhere trying everything:
the springs on the bed,
the hinges on the window.

You know your a's and b's
But there's a limit now
to what you'll believe.

When dark comes I leave
a superstitious feast
of wheat biscuits, apples,
orange juice out for you
and wake to find it eaten.

GLOSSARY

Superstitious: Believing in things or events that are not based on reason.

A. Reading

Rate this text for readability. Write the word/phrase of your choice into your copy.

VERY EASY ☐   **EASY** ☐   **OKAY** ☐   **HARD** ☐   **VERY HARD** ☐

B. Literacy Questions

1. Where are the mother and child?

2. From stanza one, do you think the Burren is a cold or a warm place? Explain your answer.

3. What time of year do you think it is? Are there any clues to suggest the season? What words or clues would you put into the poem to make the season more obvious?

4. Describe the activities of the five-year-old child.

5. What superstition does the mother mention in the poem?

6. Do you think that the mother believes this superstition? Think about the last stanza.

C. Writing – Imagine

Imagine the child-stealing spirits arrive at night expecting food or milk but find none because the five-year-old ate the feast. What happens next? Write another stanza of the poem or write a paragraph continuing the story.

D. Writing – Personal Response

Write a poem or a paragraph on **page 56** of your **PORTFOLIO** about a place that is special to you, somewhere you find beautiful, tranquil or heart-warming.

Hymn *by Eavan Boland*

Four a.m.
December.
A lamb would perish
out there.

The cutlery glitter
of that sky
has nothing in it
I want to follow.

Here is the star
of my nativity:
in the nursery lamp
in that suburb window,

behind which
is boiled glass, a bottle,

and a baby all
hissing like a kettle.

The light goes out.
The blackbird
takes up his part.
I wake by habit.
I know it all by heart:

these candles
and the altar
and the psaltery of dawn.

And in the dark
as we slept
the world
was made flesh.

GLOSSARY

Psaltery: A stringed musical instrument.
Perish: To die, face ruin or destruction.

A. Reading

Rate this text for readability. Write the word/phrase of your choice into your copy.

VERY EASY ☐   **EASY** ☐   **OKAY** ☐   **HARD** ☐   **VERY HARD** ☐

B. Literacy Questions

1. What links and connections can you make between the words 'December,' 'star', 'nativity' and 'baby'?

2. Explain what is happening in stanza four.

3. Boland is comparing the ritual of the baby's night-time feed with religious rituals. Can you explain the religious rituals? Use quotes to support your answer.

4. Why do you think the poem is called 'Hymn'? What kind of a song is a hymn?

5. What do you think the themes in the poem might be?

Patrick Kavanagh

Born in rural Inniskeen in Monaghan, Kavanagh was the fourth of ten children. His mother was a teacher and his father a shoemaker. Kavanagh loved reading and greatly admired nature and the land. He became a successful poet and novelist, saying in the introduction to his *Collected Poems* (1964) that 'a man innocently dabbles in words and in rhymes and finds that it is his life'.

 # Memory of My Father *by Patrick Kavanagh*

Every old man I see
Reminds me of my father
When he had fallen in love with death
One time when sheaves were gathered.

That man I saw in Gardiner Street
Stumble on the kerb was one,
He stared at me half-eyed,
I might have been his son.

And I remember the musician
Faltering over his fiddle
In Bayswater, London,
He too set me the riddle.

Every old man I see
In October-coloured weather
Seems to say to me:
'I was once your father.'

GLOSSARY

Sheaves: Bundles of grain stalks tied together after harvest.

Faltering: Losing strength or momentum, hesitating.

 ## A. Reading

Rate this text for readability. Write the word/phrase of your choice into your copy.

VERY EASY ☐   **EASY** ☐   **OKAY** ☐   **HARD** ☐   **VERY HARD** ☐

 ## B. Literacy Questions

1. Identify the season the poet might be talking about in this poem.

2. Explain why the old men remind Kavanagh of his father. Use quotes to support your answer.

3. Identify an image that particularly appeals to you. Explain why you like it.

 ## C. Writing – Creative Modelling

Write your own poem, 'Memory of My _____'. Model it on the form and structure used in 'Memory of My Father'.

A Christmas Childhood *by Patrick Kavanagh*

I
One side of the potato-pits was white with frost—
How wonderful that was, how wonderful!
And when we put our ears to the paling-post
The music that came out was magical.

The light between the ricks of hay and straw
Was a hole in Heaven's gable. An apple tree
With its December-glinting fruit we saw—
O you, Eve, were the world that tempted me

To eat the knowledge that grew in clay
And death the germ within it! Now and then
I can remember something of the gay
Garden that was childhood's. Again

The tracks of cattle to a drinking-place,
A green stone lying sideways in a ditch
Or any common sight the transfigured face
Of a beauty that the world did not touch.

II
My father played the melodion
Outside at our gate;
There were stars in the morning east
And they danced to his music.

Across the wild bogs his melodion called
To Lennons and Callans.
As I pulled on my trousers in a hurry
I knew some strange thing had happened.

Outside the cow-house my mother
Made the music of milking;
The light of her stable-lamp was a star
And the frost of Bethlehem made it twinkle.

A water-hen screeched in the bog,
Mass-going feet
Crunched the wafer-ice on the pot-holes,
Somebody wistfully twisted the bellows wheel.

My child poet picked out the letters
On the grey stone,
In silver the wonder of a Christmas townland,
The winking glitter of a frosty dawn.

Cassiopeia was over
Cassidy's hanging hill,
I looked and three whin bushes rode across
The horizon — the Three Wise Kings.

An old man passing said:
'Can't he make it talk—
The melodion'. I hid in the doorway
And tightened the belt of my box-pleated coat.

I nicked six nicks on the door-post
With my penknife's big blade—
There was a little one for cutting tobacco.
And I was six Christmases of age.

My father played the melodion,
My mother milked the cows,
And I had a prayer like a white rose pinned
 On the Virgin Mary's blouse.

GLOSSARY

Transfigured: Transformed into something more beautiful.

Cassiopeia: A constellation of stars near the north celestial pole, 'w' shaped.

A. Reading

Rate this text for readability. Write the word/phrase of your choice into your copy.

VERY EASY ☐   **EASY** ☐   **OKAY** ☐   **HARD** ☐   **VERY HARD** ☐

B. Group Work

As a group, figure out the answers to the following questions. Then write your own answers into your copy.

1. Do you think that the poet as a six-year-old child found Christmas magical? Explain your answer.
2. Identify two ordinary or common things that the child found beauty in.
3. List the musical references in the poem.
4. Find and explain the onomatopoeia in part II of the poem.
5. Identify two images or lines from the poem that appeal to you. Explain your choices.

C. Drawing

Imagine the things that are glinting, twinkling, glittering and winking in the poem. Try to draw the frosty, snowy scene in the early dawn, in hilly rural Monaghan where the poet lived.

Seamus Heaney

Seamus Heaney was born in 1939, on a small farm called Mossbawn, in Co. Derry. Heaney was the eldest of nine children. His father was a farmer and a cattle-dealer. Heaney loved nature and many of his poems recount his childhood experiences with animals and the natural world. He won a scholarship to grammar school and then studied English Language and Literature at Queen's University Belfast. Here, he met the Belfast poets, Michael Longley and Derek Mahon. Heaney became a lecturer, poet, playwright and translator, winning numerous awards over the years for his work. In 1995, he was awarded the Nobel Prize for Literature. In 1976, Heaney and his family moved to Sandymount in Dublin, where he lived until his death in 2013.

Family relationships are a recurring theme in Heaney's poems. He gives the reader a glimpse into his relationship with his parents, his grandfather and his siblings. In an honest and subtle way, Heaney offers an insight into his personal life, his real experiences, his thoughts, his fears and how he dealt with them.

 ## In Memoriam M.K.H., 1911–1984 *by Seamus Heaney*

When all the others were away at Mass
I was all hers as we peeled potatoes.
They broke the silence, let fall one by one
Like solder weeping off the soldering iron:
Cold comforts set between us, things to share
Gleaming in a bucket of clean water.
And again let fall. Little pleasant splashes
From each other's work would bring us to our senses.

So while the parish priest at her bedside
Went hammer and tongs at the prayers for the dying
And some were responding and some crying
I remembered her head bent towards my head,
Her breath in mine, our fluent dipping knives–
Never closer the whole rest of our lives.

GLOSSARY

Solder: Joining metals together.
Hammer and tongs: Literally instruments used by blacksmiths but metaphorically the phrase means to work hard or intensely at something.

 ## A. Reading

Rate this text for readability. Write the word/phrase of your choice into your copy.

VERY EASY ☐   **EASY** ☐   **OKAY** ☐   **HARD** ☐   **VERY HARD** ☐

 ## B. Literacy Questions

1. What did Heaney like most when 'all the others were away at Mass'?
2. Which words in the first stanza imply that there was a comfortable silence between mother and son?
3. What strikes Heaney as the prayers are said at his mother's deathbed in stanza two? Support your answer with quotes from the poem.
4. Identify an image that you find appealing in the poem. Explain why you like it.

Digging *by Seamus Heaney*

Between my finger and my thumb
The squat pen rests; snug as a gun.

Under my window, a clean rasping sound
When the spade sinks into gravelly ground:
My father, digging. I look down

Till his straining rump among the flowerbeds
Bends low, comes up twenty years away
Stooping in rhythm through potato drills
Where he was digging.

The coarse boot nestled on the lug, the shaft
Against the inside knee was levered firmly.
He rooted out tall tops, buried the bright edge deep
To scatter new potatoes that we picked,
Loving their cool hardness in our hands.

By God, the old man could handle a spade.
Just like his old man.

My grandfather cut more turf in a day
Than any other man on Toner's bog.
Once I carried him milk in a bottle
Corked sloppily with paper. He straightened up
To drink it, then fell to right away
Nicking and slicing neatly, heaving sods
Over his shoulder, going down and down
For the good turf. Digging.

The cold smell of potato mould, the squelch and slap
Of soggy peat, the curt cuts of an edge
Through living roots awaken in my head.
But I've no spade to follow men like them.

Between my finger and my thumb
The squat pen rests.
I'll dig with it.

A. Reading

Rate this text for readability. Write the word/phrase of your choice into your copy.

VERY EASY ☐   **EASY** ☐   **OKAY** ☐   **HARD** ☐   **VERY HARD** ☐

B. Group Work

Give each person in your group a separate task from the following list.

1. From the poem, make a list of words you associate with farming and rural life, and with family and generations. This will help you to discover the themes of the poem.

2. Identify the words or images that appeal to your senses. What can you almost hear, see, smell, taste or touch?

3. List the similes and metaphors in the poem. Similes are comparisons using 'like' or 'as'. Metaphors compare one thing to another without using 'like' or 'as'.

4. List the examples of alliteration.

5. List the possessive pronouns and the things they describe ownership of. For example, 'my finger': 'my' is the possessive pronoun and 'finger' is the object that belongs to the narrator/poet.

When each person has worked on their task, swap the results. Everyone must read everyone else's work. Then, as a group, present the information concisely to the class using the following template on **page 58** of your **PORTFOLIO**.

Title of poem	
Themes	
Words/images that appeal to the senses	
Similes	
Metaphors	
Alliteration	
My overall comment on the poem	

Mid-Term Break *by Seamus Heaney*

I sat all morning in the college sick bay,
Counting bells knelling classes to a close.
At two o'clock our neighbours drove me home.

In the porch I met my father crying –
He had always taken funerals in his stride –
And Big Jim Evans saying it was a hard blow.

The baby cooed and laughed and rocked the pram
When I came in, and I was embarrassed
By old men standing up to shake my hand

And tell me they were 'sorry for my trouble'.
Whispers informed strangers I was the eldest,
Away at school, as my mother held my hand

In hers and coughed out angry tearless sighs.
At ten o'clock the ambulance arrived
With the corpse, stanched and bandaged by the nurses.

Next morning I went up into the room. Snowdrops
And candles soothed the bedside; I saw him
For the first time in six weeks. Paler now,

Wearing a poppy bruise on his left temple,
He lay in the four foot box as in his cot.
No gaudy scars, the bumper knocked him clear.

A four foot box, a foot for every year.

GLOSSARY

Knelling: The sound of a bell.

Stanched: Bandaged to stop blood flow from a wound.

Gaudy: Very bright and showy, lacking taste.

 ## A. Reading

Rate this text for readability. Write the word/phrase of your choice into your copy.

VERY EASY ☐   **EASY** ☐   **OKAY** ☐   **HARD** ☐   **VERY HARD** ☐

 ## B. Group Work

In a group, discuss the following questions. Write the answers into your copy.

1. What is the poem about? Use quotes from the poem to support your answer.
2. How does the narrator feel in stanza three? Why does he feel like this?
3. Identify words or images that are soft and calming in stanza six.
4. How do you feel about the poem? Explain the impact that it has on you.

The Railway Children *by Seamus Heaney*

When we climbed the slopes of the cutting
We were eye-level with the white cups
Of the telegraph poles and the sizzling wires.

Like lovely freehand they curved for miles
East and miles west beyond us, sagging
Under their burden of swallows.

We were small and thought we knew nothing
Worth knowing. We thought words travelled the wires
In the shiny pouches of raindrops,

Each one seeded full with the light
Of the sky, the gleam of the lines, and ourselves
So infinitesimally scaled

We could stream through the eye of a needle.

GLOSSARY

Telegraph poles: Like telephone or electricity poles linking wires.

Freehand: Cursive writing.

Infinitesimally: Extremely small.

 ## A. Reading

Rate this text for readability. Write the word/phrase of your choice into your copy.

VERY EASY ☐   **EASY** ☐   **OKAY** ☐   **HARD** ☐   **VERY HARD** ☐

 ## B. Literacy Questions

1. What were the children doing?
2. What age do you think the children were? Quote from the poem to support your answer.
3. Identify one image that appeals to you in the poem and explain why you like it.

 ## C. Writing

'We were small and thought we knew nothing/Worth knowing…'

Think about how you can relate to the poem or connect with the experience of the children. Can you remember feeling small and knowing very little? Write one paragraph about such a feeling.

An Advancement of Learning *by Seamus Heaney*

I took the embankment path
(As always, deferring
The bridge). The river nosed past,
Pliable, oil-skinned, wearing

A transfer of gables and sky.
Hunched over the railing,
Well away from the road now, I
Considered the dirty-keeled swans.

Something slobbered curtly, close,
Smudging the silence: a rat
Slimed out of the water and
My throat sickened so quickly that

I turned down the path in cold sweat
But God, another was nimbling
Up the far bank, tracing its wet
Arcs on the stones. Incredibly then

I established a dreaded
Bridgehead. I turned to stare
With deliberate, thrilled care
At my hitherto snubbed rodent.

He clockworked aimlessly a while,
Stopped, back bunched and glistening,
Ears plastered down on his knobbed skull,
Insidiously listening.

The tapered tail that followed him,
The raindrop eye, the old snout:
One by one I took all in.
He trained on me. I stared him out

Forgetting how I used to panic
When his grey brothers scraped and fed
Behind the hen coop in our yard,
On ceiling boards above my bed.

This terror, cold, wet-furred, small-clawed,
Retreated up a pipe for sewage.
I stared a minute after him.
Then I walked on and crossed the bridge.

195

GLOSSARY

Embankment: A barrier, usually a wall of earth/stone built to prevent a river flooding.

Deferring: Putting off.

Dirty-keeled: A keel is the ridge along the breastbone of many birds.

Nimbling: Moving nimbly, agilely.

Pliable: Easily bent, flexible.

Bridgehead: A military term meaning a strong position from which to attack the enemy.

Clockworked: Worked smoothly and regularly.

Hitherto: An old word meaning 'previously'.

Tapered: Reduced or diminished.

Insidious: Proceeding in a gradual, subtle way with harmful effects.

A. Reading

Rate this text for readability. Write the word/phrase of your choice into your copy.

VERY EASY ☐   EASY ☐   OKAY ☐   HARD ☐   VERY HARD ☐

B. Literacy Questions

1. What is Heaney describing in the first two verses? Use quotes to support your answer.

2. What is Heaney's reaction to the rats in verses three and four?

3. Explain Heaney's encounters with rats and his reactions to them as a young child.

4. Verse five is written from the point of view of an adult Heaney. How does he cope with the rats? Quote from the poem to support your answer.

5. What do you think about the final line of the poem? How does the adult Heaney feel?

6. Identify a few lines in the poem that you felt were very descriptive. What images did these lines create in your mind?

C. Oral Language

Think about your own fears, during childhood or at present. Tell the person beside you about one of these fears.

The Soldier *by Rupert Brooke*

Rupert Brooke was an English poet who became well-known for his poems about World War I. He won prizes in school for his poetry and also won a scholarship to King's College, Cambridge. He died at the age of 27 from sepsis, after getting bitten by a mosquito while on duty with the Navy.

If I should die, think only this of me:
That there's some corner of a foreign field
That is forever England. There shall be
In that rich earth a richer dust concealed;
A dust whom England bore, shaped, made aware,
Gave, once, her flowers to love, her ways to roam,
A body of England's, breathing English air,
Washed by the rivers, blest by suns of home.

And think, this heart, all evil shed away,
A pulse in the eternal mind, no less
Gives somewhere back the thoughts by England given;
Her sights and sounds; dreams happy as her day;
And laughter, learnt of friends; and gentleness,
In hearts at peace, under an English heaven.

 ## A. Reading

Rate this text for readability. Write the word/phrase of your choice into your copy.

VERY EASY ☐   **EASY** ☐   **OKAY** ☐   **HARD** ☐   **VERY HARD** ☐

 ## B. Literacy Questions

1. Identify lines in the poem that prove the soldier's love of England.
2. How will the 'foreign field' have a corner that is 'forever England'?
3. Is the mood of the poem positive or negative? Explain your answer.
4. What consolation is the soldier offering to his loved ones at home in England?

Grass *by Carl Sandburg*

Born in Illinois, Carl Sandburg worked from the age of 12 at various jobs, including milkman, bricklayer, farm labourer, hotel porter and journalist. He wrote books of poetry, fiction, history, biographies and children's stories. In 1919, Sandburg's poetry collection *Corn Huskers* won a Pulitzer Prize and in 1951 he won another Pulitzer Prize for his anthology *Complete Poems*. Sandburg won the 1940 Pulitzer Prize for History for *The War Years*, his second book on Abraham Lincoln.

Pile the bodies high at Austerlitz and Waterloo.
Shovel them under and let me work –
I am the grass; I cover all.

And pile them high at Gettysburg
And pile them high at Ypres and Verdun.
Shovel them under and let me work.
Two years, ten years, and passengers ask the conductor:
What place is this?
Where are we now?

I am the grass.
Let me work.

GLOSSARY

Austerlitz: Napoleon defeated the Russo-Austrians at the Battle of Austerlitz on 2 December 1805.

Waterloo: Napoleon was defeated on 15 June 1815 by a Prussian army and an Anglo-allied army led by the Duke of Wellington.

Gettysburg: The Battle of Gettysburg was fought in 1863 in Pennsylvania, between the Union and the Confederate forces during the American Civil War. It marked a turning point in the war with the highest number of casualties of the entire war occurring here.

Ypres: Ypres, western Belgium, was strategically important during World War I. A number of battles occurred there between the Allies and the Central Powers in October and November 1914.

Verdun: The Battle of Verdun (in northeastern France) was fought in 1916 between the French and German armies.

A. Reading

Rate this text for readability. Write the word/phrase of your choice into your copy.

VERY EASY ☐   EASY ☐   OKAY ☐   HARD ☐   VERY HARD ☐

B. Group Work

In groups, figure out the answers to the following question.

Explain the personification in the poem. Think about:

- Who is at work.
- What work is being done.
- How the work is being done.
- What the consequences or the results of this work will be over time.

C. Research

Find and read some war poems written by two French poets, Guillaume Apollinaire and Albert-Paul Granier. Do the French poets give you a different perspective on the war?

The Dead *by Billy Collins*

Billy Collins was born in New York on 22 March 1941. Growing up, his mother instilled in him a love of words and verse. Collins studied English for his BA degree and Romantic poetry for his MA and PhD. He is Professor of English at Lehmann College in the Bronx, New York.

The dead are always looking down on us, they say.
while we are putting on our shoes or making a sandwich,
they are looking down through the glass bottom boats of heaven
as they row themselves slowly through eternity.

They watch the tops of our heads moving below on earth,
and when we lie down in a field or on a couch,
drugged perhaps by the hum of a long afternoon,
they think we are looking back at them,
which makes them lift their oars and fall silent
and wait, like parents, for us to close our eyes.

A. Reading

Rate this text for readability. Write the word/phrase of your choice into your copy.

VERY EASY ☐   **EASY** ☐   **OKAY** ☐   **HARD** ☐   **VERY HARD** ☐

B. Visual Literacy

On **page 59** of your **PORTFOLIO**, draw the images you can visualise or imagine when you read the poem. Think about a picture for each line. Figure out how you will arrange a series of pictures or images to tell the story in the poem.

Read and Enjoy

 Desiderata *by Max Ehrmann*

Go placidly amid the noise and the haste, and remember what peace there may be in silence. As far as possible, without surrender, be on good terms with all persons.

Speak your truth quietly and clearly; and listen to others, even to the dull and the ignorant; they too have their story.

Avoid loud and aggressive persons; they are vexatious to the spirit. If you compare yourself with others, you may become vain or bitter, for always there will be greater and lesser persons than yourself.

Enjoy your achievements as well as your plans. Keep interested in your own career, however humble; it is a real possession in the changing fortunes of time.

Exercise caution in your business affairs, for the world is full of trickery. But let this not blind you to what virtue there is; many persons strive for high ideals, and everywhere life is full of heroism.

Be yourself. Especially, do not feign affection. Neither be cynical about love; for in the face of all aridity and disenchantment, it is as perennial as the grass.

Take kindly the counsel of the years, gracefully surrendering the things of youth.

Nurture strength of spirit to shield you in sudden misfortune. But do not distress yourself with dark imaginings. Many fears are born of fatigue and loneliness.

Beyond a wholesome discipline, be gentle with yourself. You are a child of the universe no less than the trees and the stars; you have a right to be here.

And whether or not it is clear to you, no doubt the universe is unfolding as it should. Therefore be at peace with God, whatever you conceive Him to be.

And whatever your labors and aspirations, in the noisy confusion of life, keep peace in your soul. With all its sham, drudgery and broken dreams, it is still a beautiful world. Be cheerful. Strive to be happy.

ASSESSMENT

Complete this assessment on **page 60** of your **PORTFOLIO**.

Written Assessment

A. Assessment

Lyrics in songs are _____.

Rhythm means _____.

Rhyme is _____.

(2 marks each)

B. Poetic Features

Write in an example for each feature of poetic language.

Features of language/ imagery	Examples
Alliteration	
Rhyme	
Sibilance	
Assonance	
Personification	
Simile	
Metaphor	
Repetition	
Onomatopoeia	

How many are lines in a sonnet? _____

How many lines are in a quatrain? _____

How many lines are in an octet? _____

How many lines are in a sestet? _____

How many lines are in a rhyming couplet? _____

(2 marks each)

211

ASSESSMENT

C. Read and Respond 1

The Darkening Night *by Emily Brontë*

The night is darkening round me,
The wild winds coldly blow;
But a tyrant spell has bound me
And I cannot, cannot go.

The giant trees are bending
Their bare boughs weighed with snow.
And the storm is fast descending,
And yet I cannot go.

Clouds beyond clouds above me,
Wastes beyond wastes below;
But nothing drear can move me;
I will not, cannot go.

GLOSSARY

Drear: Dreary.

Questions

1. Describe the weather in the poem. Quote to support your answer.   (10 marks)
2. How does the weather contribute to the mood in the poem?   (5 marks)
3. List two examples of alliteration.   (5 marks)

ASSESSMENT

D. Read and Respond 2

Advice to a Teenage Daughter *by Isobel Thrilling*

You have found a new war game
Called love.
Here on your dressing-table
Stand arrayed
Brave ranks of lipsticks
Brandishing
Swords of cherry pink and flame.
Behold the miniature armies
Of little jars,
Packed with the scented
Dynamite of flowers.
See the dreaded tweezers;
Tiny pots
Of manufactured moonlight,
Stick-on-stars.

Beware my sweet;
Conquest may seem easy
But you can't compete with football,
Motor-cycles, cars,
Cricket, computer-games,
Or a plate of chips.

GLOSSARY

Brandishing: Waving something threateningly or in excitement.

Questions

1. List the words in the poem associated with battles or war. (5 marks)
2. Identify the two sides in the 'new war game'. (5 marks)
3. Who do you think is giving advice to the girl? Explain your answer. (5 marks)
4. Is the poem about love or war, or both? Explain your answer. (5 marks)

ASSESSMENT

E. Read and Respond 3

October *by Harry Clifton*

The big news around here is the fall of
      leaves
In Harrington Street and Synge Street,
Lying about in pockets, adrift at your feet
As you kick them away. The other news is
      the trees, –
Their yellow, as I speak, is unbelievable,
Not that you need me to tell you.
      Everywhere
The house is falling down around our ears
And it's wonderful, in the dry, spicy air,
How quietly it happens. Close your eyes,
Don't think, just listen. Hear them fall,
      the years
We came towards each other, out of a sun
Already westering. Look at us, even yet,
Exchanging tree-lore, twenty years on
In a leafless cathedral – bride and groom,
      well-met.

Questions

1. What is the 'big news'? (5 marks)

2. How do you think the poet feels about autumn? (5 marks)

3. What connections can you make between the leaves, autumn and the couple? (5 marks)

4. Identify one image that appeals to you in the poem and explain why you like it. (5 marks)

ASSESSMENT

F. Read and Respond 4

Spring Fed *by Tony Curtis*

the stone basin
fills and fills
from the swivel tap's
trickle.

The hills have shed
so much snow
and now,
the first brown grasses
clear of it,
the heifers push
up into the fields
to take the early shoots

and it comes
again,
the whole slow
turning of the season-
the softer touch of air,
the shine on the bucket,
the unclenching of things,
the lapping of the water
in the stone basin
up to the rim,
and the very first,
this
delicious overspilling
onto our boots.

Questions

1. What season is portrayed in the poem? Quote to support your answer.   (5 marks)
2. Describe two changes that take place in stanza two.
   Support your points with quotes.   (10 marks)
3. Would you agree that the imagery in stanza three appeals to the senses?
   Explain your answer.   (10 marks)
4. Comment on the title of the poem. Is it suitable or would you suggest another title?

          (5 marks)

Introductions

a 'meet and greet': one person names a second person in order to introduce
...son. The third person then greets the person they have been newly

...uctions are made between friends, family and so on, on a casual basis:

...me to
...ow are you
...o far?

Hi girls, this is Julie.
Julie is new to the school, this is
her first day. Julie, this is Lynn
and Eimear.

Hi, it's nice to
meet you.
It's ok so far.

Formal introductions are more serious and the language used is more polite. More
information may be given about the person, perhaps stating their occupation.
For example, your teacher might introduce you to an important guest speaker,
whom you in turn might have to introduce to your class group.

Teacher   Good morning, Professor Patterson. We're so
privileged to have you visit us today. I'd like to
introduce you to Tony, the class prefect.

Professor Patterson Good morning, it's lovely to be
here. Nice to meet you, Tony.

Tony   Good morning, Professor Patterson. I will introduce
you to the class. They are so excited about your
scientific success and experiments.
Good morning everyone, thank you for your
attention. Today is a very exciting day for us as we
welcome the celebrated, award-winning professor
of chemistry Professor Patterson to our school. It is
a great privilege to have her here as part of Science
Week. She is, as many of you already know, a past
pupil of this school. Having earned a scholarship to
study science in Trinity, she…

A. Writing

Distinguish between the formal and informal introductions below. [...]
into your copy and write *F* beside the formal instructions and *I* beside [...]
instructions.

Hiya, this is my best friend Tommo. Tommo, this is Charlie.
Good afternoon, ladies and gentlemen. It gives me great pleasure to introduce to you our sp[...] guest, TV and radio presenter Ms Elena Ryan.
Hi, how are ye? Sorry I'm late, this is Lisa. Lisa, Anna and Lily, now are ye okay?
Sure ye met each other yesterday, didn't ye? George, don't you know this is Marco?
Good evening, Mr Ryan. I'd like to introduce you to my assistant, Mr Watson.
This is a wonderful occasion to introduce to you all the most eminent surgeon in his field…
Good morning, Madam Bovary. May I introduce Lord and Lady Byron…
Hi, I'm Michelle. I don't think I've met you before. And you are?

B. Listening

Listen to the introductions and classify them as formal or informal.

C. Oral Language

Role-play one of the following situations.

- Introduce yourself to the class. Give background details about yourself, your family, your hobbies and interests.

- Introduce a famous writer to the class. The writer is going to read some of his/her work and talk about the writing process.

- You are the class prefect. Introduce yourself to the parents of incoming First Years. Speak to them for five minutes about First Year.

- You are nominating your classmate for the Student of the Year award. Introduce yourself, speak briefly about the award and introduce your nominee.

- You are the chairperson of a debate. Give the introductory speech. Introduce yourself to the audience, welcome the audience and introduce the opposition and the proposition.

Speeches

Speeches can be formal or informal, or can sometimes use a mix of both types of language. The speaker addresses an audience. It is important for the speaker to 'know' the audience so they can deliver a good, suitable, effective speech. The speaker should consider what the audience might expect. This depends on the context of the speech.

The purpose of a speech:

- To inform people about an unfamiliar subject.
- To persuade the audience to change their opinion.
- To inspire the audience to take a course of action.
- To entertain the audience with humour and anecdotes.

A. Oral Language

In pairs, chat about the kinds of speeches you have heard or made. For example:

Speeches in School

- Principal welcoming first years to the school.
- Success speech of a winning team.
- Guest speaker delivering a speech.

Speeches at Family Events

- Thank you
- Weddings
- Birthday parties
- Wedding anniversary parties
- Retirements
- Farewell/goodbye
- Eulogy (funeral speech).

Speeches in the Media

- Award acceptance
- President/Taoiseach/minister's address
- Eulogy at a state funeral or the funeral of a public figure. For example, poet Paul Muldoon spoke at Seamus Heaney's funeral.

B. Oral Language

Informal Impromptu Speeches

Try making an impromptu (unprepared) speech, where you think on your feet or speak off the top of your head.

Take turns speaking to the class for one minute about one of the following topics:

- Why I like sport/music/reading.
- My opinion of my city.
- A day I'll always remember.
- My pets.
- My fear of…
- I remember learning how to…
- My first day in primary/secondary school.
- My favourite TV programmes.
- The most embarrassing moment in my life.

Sample Impromptu Speech

Topic: A pet hate

Wasps! I simply hate them! I don't mind bees, even though I've never liked honey. I always found it too sweet, too gooey and gluey, messy and sticky. Bees just bumble about harmlessly but wasps are so waspish. Their drone and hum is an irritant. They're simply pests. Just as you sit down to enjoy the barbeque, a pesky wasp whizzes by,

hovers over your juicy burger and is resistant to all attempts at being swatted away. *Whizz*, swat, *whizz*, swat, *whizz*, swat… His victory sees you swipe up your plate and retreat indoors to eat in peace.

The power of this tiny insect did not strike me until I suffered two stings in my early childhood. The sharp pain, red swelling and insistent throb left an indelible memory. Now the sight of a wasp terrifies me. The instant I hear the incessant *zzzzzzzzzzzzzzzzz*, I leap up, adrenalin pumping, grab a suitable weapon and prepare to bash the wasp to bits. Not in revenge, you understand, but to save myself or some other misfortunate person from the deadly sting. My little random act of kindness to others!

C. Writing

Write a speech (1–2 minutes long) on one of the following topics and then deliver it to the class.

Personal Experience Speech

1. A frightening/dangerous/painful experience.
2. A happy/sad experience.
3. A surprising/exciting/interesting experience.

Include some of the following details in your speech:

- Where you were.
- Who was with you.
- What you were doing.
- What exactly happened.
- How you reacted.
- How you felt.
- How it ended.

Personal Opinion Speech

Certain issues evoke a response from us. We feel strongly about particular topics. We express our opinions and feelings on these issues to our friends and family.

What do you feel strongly about? Remember, you can agree or disagree with the opinions below, as long as you are able to say why.

- Exercise is energising.
- Homework should be done in school-time and the school day extended.
- School uniforms are essential.
- Our diets today are full of junk food.
- Social media is fantastic.
- Music is the best medicine.
- I can't escape peer pressure.
- There are too many rules in my world.
- It's not too hard to save the planet.
- Setting goals is important.
- Punctuality is important.

Speeches and Opinions

Maeve Binchy (1939–2012), the much-loved Irish writer, felt strongly about latecomers. Read the following newspaper article in which she condemns the unpunctual among us. As you read it, imagine it being said out loud as a speech.

Consider the following elements:

- The tone/tones she may have used.
- The attention-grabbing first line and 'shocking' final line.
- The variety of anecdotes and examples given
- Her use of exaggeration and humour.

Some of these elements are the criteria for success in writing a good article or speech.

I regard people who say they'll meet you at eight pm and then turn up at eight-thirty as liars. I had a colleague years ago in my teaching days who used to smile and say that she was always late, as if it were something outside her control, like having freckles or a Gemini star sign.

At first I went through agonies thinking she had been mown down by a bus. After that I would arrange to meet her, not on the corner of a street or at the cinema, but in a cafe where at least I could sit down while waiting. After that I stopped meeting her. There were too many main features beginning at five-twenty missed, too many buses gone, too many houses where I had to be part of an apology for an unpunctuality that was none of my making.

She lives in another country now and I met someone who had been to see her. Just as nice as ever, apparently, just as good company. Much loved by her children but treated as a dotty old lady who can't be relied on. She would never turn up to pick them up from school, so they just adapted to doing their homework in the schoolyard. So she is still at it, thinking she can say one thing and do another, and everyone will forgive her because she is unpunctual the way other people are left-handed or colour-blind.

Of course she got away with it because people are so astounded by the unpunctual that they forgive them and allow them to roam the world as ordinary people instead of as the liars they are. It's our fault for putting up with it in every walk of life and I advise people to declare war on the unpunctual. It's no longer acceptable to consider it an attractive, laid-back, national characteristic. It is in fact a lazy, self-indulgent, discourteous way of going on. Already there are a lot of signs that people do not accept it as charming.

I remember a time when the curtain never went up on time in a Dublin theatre because, as the theory went, the Irish were all so busy being witty and wonderful and entertaining in bars they couldn't do anything as pen-pushing, meticulous and prosaic as coming in and being seated before eight o'clock. But enough protests from those who objected to people shuffling in late to performances has led to their not being admitted until the first interval, and it's very interesting to see how that has concentrated the ability to get to the place before the lights go out.

Staff of Aer Lingus don't think it's charming and witty to leave late because their wonderful free-spirited clients can't be hurried, and likewise with trains, the DART and the buses. Religious services don't take account of some quirk in the national psyche by having Mass at around eleven or Matins at approximately ten.

Races, football matches, television programmes start on time. Why should business appointments and social engagements be let off this hook? And yet this week I was talking to an American publisher on the phone who said that she was expecting an Irish author in her office but he was 40 minutes late. She laughed good-naturedly and even though she was 3,000 miles away I could see her shrug forgivingly. 'Oh well, that's the Irish for you!' she said, as if somehow it explained something. To me it explained nothing.

As a race we are not naturally discourteous. In fact, if anything, we wish to please a bit too much. That's part of our national image. So where does this unpunctuality come into the stereotype? Has it something to do with being feckless and free and not seeing ourselves ever as a slave to any time-servers or time-keepers? It's a bit fancy and I don't think that it's at all part of what we are.

Not turning up at the time you promised seems quite out of character and if we do it, it must be because it has been considered acceptable for too long. If nobody were to wait for the latecomer, then things would surely change. If the unpunctual were to be left looking forlorn and foolish when they had ratted on their promise, the people would keep better time. We shouldn't go on saying that it's perfectly all right and, nonsense, they mustn't worry, and really it was quite pleasant waiting here alone wondering was it the right day, the right place, or the right time. We should never again say to latecomers that they're in perfect time when the meal is stuck to the roof of the oven and the other guests are legless with pre-dinner drinks.

Sit in any restaurant, bar or hotel foyer and listen while people greet each other. 'I'm very sorry. The traffic was terrible.' 'I'm sorry for being late I couldn't get parking…' 'I'm sorry. Are you here long? I wasn't sure whether you said one or half past…' 'I'm sorry, but better late than never.' I wouldn't forgive any of these things. In a city, people with eyes in their heads know that the traffic is terrible: they can see it. Unless they have been living for a while on the planet Mars, they're aware that it's impossible to park. If they couldn't remember whether you said one or half past, that shows great interest in the meeting in the first place. And as for better late than never, I'm not convinced.

GLOSSARY

Discourteous: Rude, impolite.

Meticulous: Careful, precise.

Prosaic: Lacking orginality.

Forlorn: Sad and hopeless.

 A. Reading

Rate this text for readability. Write the word/phrase of your choice into your copy.

VERY EASY ☐   **EASY** ☐   **OKAY** ☐   **HARD** ☐   **VERY HARD** ☐

 B. Oral Language

 In pairs or groups, discuss the points raised by Maeve Binchy in the article. To what extent do you agree or disagree with her?

1. Identify clearly the points you agree and/or disagree with.
2. Identify any exaggeration (hyperbole) in the article.
3. Identify the tones used in the article. Are they cross, angry, calm, critical, jovial?

 C. Writing

1. Identify and list briefly the points made in the article.

2. If you feel strongly about the importance of punctuality, why not write your own speech about the issue, using Maeve Binchy's speech as an example?
   - Consider your own experiences at the hands of latecomers and write about them, paragraph by paragraph.
   - Clearly state your own viewpoint or opinion on latecomers.
   - Think of a clever opening and closing sentence.

3. Choose one of the following topics and write a 1–2 minute speech on it, and then deliver it to your class. Use the tips on speechmaking on **page 227**.
   - Pets are great fun but are hard work.
   - There's too much homework.
   - Social media is a waste of precious time.
   - Exercise is fun and essential for health.
   - Manners and politeness are declining in today's society.
   - Music is beautiful.
   - Sport is too competitive and expensive.

How to Write a Speech

A speech must have the following parts:

- An introduction
- A main body
- A conclusion.

Getting Started

- **Decide on your topic/purpose:** What is the aim or purpose of the speech?
- **Brainstorm:** Think about what you might talk about.
- **Organise the material:** Put your points in logical order.
- **Conclusion:** End on an impressive note.

Writing Your Speech

1. Opening Sentences Must Grab Attention

Use:
- A quote
- Something for shock factor
- Some facts
- An amusing anecdote
- A motif or symbol to which you wish to return at the end so that you have come full circle.

Next, give a brief preview of what you're going to talk about in the speech.

2. Main Body of the Speech

- Each idea must help and relate to the main point.
- Have one idea per paragraph.
- Avoid overlap and redundant ideas and cut these out when you reread your speech.

3. Conclusion

- Reiterate the main point/purpose.
- Give a brief summary if necessary.
- End on a positive note.
- End on humour if appropriate.
- Make it memorable.

Hillary Rodham Clinton, Bob Geldof and Nelson Mandela have all made memorable speeches.

Elements of a Speech

- **Greeting:** Good morning/afternoon/evening, ladies and gentlemen…
- **Self introduction:** My name is _____ and my role is… / I am _____ and I'm here today to…
- **Aim of the speech:** I intend to inform you about/explain/discuss…
- **Main points:** I feel strongly about _____. The facts show that _____.
- **Conclusion/summary:** In conclusion I urge you to _____ / may I suggest _____.

Writing

Match the following speech with the audience. Write the columns below into your copy and use a pencil to connect the audience to the right speech.

Audience	Speech
Homeowners	New technology and autumn fashion
Businesspeople	Home-decorating tips
Teenagers	Upskilling and retraining to find the perfect job
College students-to-be	Best technology in business
Unemployed people	Choosing a course that suits you
Parents	New advances in antibiotics
Doctors	How to relate to teenagers

Assessing your Speech – Features of Quality

If you want to improve your speech-making skills, it is important to assess your speeches. The following table shows the features of a good speech and how they can be rated.

Content	Very interesting	Interesting	Dull	Uninteresting
Delivery	Very effective	Good	Fair	Poor
Introduction	Captivating	Good	Fair	Poor
Conclusion	Memorable	Good	Fair	Poor
Impact	Very strong	Strong	Fair	Poor
Confidence	Very good	Good	Fair	Poor
Voice	Varied	Interesting	Dull	Monotonous
Appearance	Very good	Good	Fair	Poor
Eye contact	Very good	Good	Fair	Poor
Use of gestures	Very good	Good	Fair	Poor

Sample Speech 1

This message, sent by Richard Mulcahy, Chief of Staff to the Volunteer Army during the Civil War, announces the death of Michael Collins on 22 August, 1922.

Read and imagine it being spoken by Richard Mulcahy.

TO THE MEN OF THE ARMY

Stand calmly by your posts. Bend bravely and undaunted to your task.

Let no cruel act of reprisal blemish your bright honour.

Every dark hour that Michael Collins met since 1916 seemed but to steel that bright strength of his and temper his brave gaiety.

You are left as inheritors of that strength and bravery.

To each of you falls his unfinished work.

No darkness in the hour: loss of comrades will daunt you in it.

Ireland! The Army serves – strengthened by its sorrow.

(signed)

R Ua Maolcatha, Chief of General Staff.

GLOSSARY

Reprisal: **Counterattack.**

Did you identify:

- The advice given to the men?
- The praise attributed to Michael Collins?
- The inspiration given to the men?
- The responsibility placed upon them?
- The positive, but bittersweet, ending?

 ## A. Reading

Rate this text for readability. Write the word/phrase of your choice into your copy.

VERY EASY ☐   **EASY** ☐   **OKAY** ☐   **HARD** ☐   **VERY HARD** ☐

 ## B. Research

Research some speeches made by celebrities – perhaps actors, musicians, singers or sports stars. Examine the speeches for any of the following elements:

- Sincerity of tone.
- Richness of language.
- Inspiration and hope.
- Instilling confidence.
- Clichés (overused, unoriginal phrases).
- Platitudes (banal, trite, commonplace statements).
- Expressing 'global' or 'safe' views.
- Making idealistic promises.
- Repetition of previous similar speeches which other celebrities/stars have made.
- Lack of originality.

Sample Speech 2

Breege O'Donoghue is a board director with Primark, which is known as Penneys in Ireland. In 2014, she won the inaugural Lifetime Achievement Award at the Image Business Awards. The following is an edited extract of the speech she gave at the event.

1. Growing up in rural Ireland in a loving family home with five special siblings, my earliest childhood memory was the Arctic freeze of blizzards which gripped Ireland for the first three months of 1947. Our farm was both idyllic and hard work: watching the cows being milked, feeding the calves, carrying water from the well, helping to make the hay, walking miles to and from school. My mother had great influence on the family. She was independent, strong-minded, and devoted to her family. There was no extravagance and money was always put aside for the rainy day. Christmas was magical, with all its preparations and waiting in anticipation of Santa.

2. My education, still bright in my mind, was grounded in the Catholic belief and practice. Career guidance was not a feature... the closest was Reverend Mother's visits to try and coax one to enter the order, to no avail. I can hear my chief executive at Primark, Paul Marchant, saying: "Thank God, the children had a lucky escape." Neither was a career choice in those days determined by ability, but by means. I didn't have the option to pursue a university degree at that stage, but I did have an ambition to do so. However, that foundation in education served me well, as did a work ethic which was modelled so well at home.

3. A career spread over 17 years included a three-year break from 1963 which I spent working in Switzerland and Germany. This provided me with a love of diversity, culture and language. In Switzerland, as you know, they speak four languages, and belong to four diverse culture groups which do not appear to display any particular affection for each other. On the final day of Pope John Paul II's historic 1979 visit to Ireland, I joined Penneys/Primark. I became a board member eight years later. There were then 17 stores;

now there are 285 in nine countries and 58,000 employees. This year's annual profit was €808m. We are now entering the US market. Primark's business directly contributes to the employment of more than 800,000 employees across three continents and we estimate that two million people are supported indirectly.

4. During my time there have been many positive advances for women and others – for example, implementation of equal pay, improvement in the status of women, equality recognised and discrimination on the base of sex, race or otherwise all unacceptable in principle. In fact, were it otherwise I might not be standing here, have not had this career and the same can be said for many other women. I salute the changes. For 21 years I was a member of the well-documented Primark 'gang of four' – the only female board member for 26 years, which was not without its challenges. I'm now one of two female members of a 'gang of seven', so the odds are moving in the right direction.

5. Over the years Primark's strategic vision, brand image and the estate has evolved in a dramatic fashion. In the year 2000, when Primark opened its 100th store after 31 years of trading, the entire estate was 1.4 million sq ft. Now, 14 years later, the estate is over seven times larger. Entering the UK market in the 1970s was a major deal, where we now enjoy number one volume share, as we do in Ireland, Spain and Portugal. Competing with world brands in Europe, we continue to roll out a business in major markets, including Germany and France, where our new store openings are often as reported as pop concerts. The authorities in Europe with whom we collaborate welcome Primark with open arms. The property developers seek us out, high street and shopping centre management view Primark as an important vehicle to deliver an exciting shopping environment, with greater choice and increased customer footfall to their locations.

6. But leadership in our business is the single most important element of our success and our orchestra is conducted by Paul Marchant, who understands how all the pieces come together, all of which we will need as we enter the exacting, exciting and challenging US market, a whole new experience – a foundation for Primark to be bigger and better. We will challenge and we are not afraid to be challenged. Innovation and talent are at the heart of our business.

7. I have been blessed with good health, energy and stamina. I have had an interesting, fulfilling and happy life so far and I look forward to continuing that way for a while longer. William Butler Yeats said: "Think where man's glory most begins and ends, and say my glory was I had such friends." Be true to oneself, show courage, independence, initiative, appreciate the need to recognise, respect and value differences. Know right from wrong, be ethically aware. Be satisfied only with the very best, do not be clothed in power and status, but generous in heart, mind and spirit and – yes, it is encouragement and love that inspire people to succeed and be happy the world over.

GLOSSARY

Idyllic: Peaceful or picturesque.

Extravagance: Lack of restraint spending money.

Pursue: Go after.

Diversity: Representation of different races, religions, sexual orientation and so on.

Implementation: The carrying out of a plan.

Strategic: Overall aims to be achieved.

A. Reading

Rate this text for readability. Write the word/phrase of your choice into your copy.

VERY EASY ☐   **EASY** ☐   **OKAY** ☐   **HARD** ☐   **VERY HARD** ☐

B. Group Work

Work in groups to find answers to the following questions and then write the answers into your copy.

1. Identify the specific audience Breege O'Donoghue is speaking to.
2. Is the speech organised in a logical, coherent way? Explain your answer.
3. Comment on the introduction. Why do you think Breege O'Donoghue used this information in her introduction?
4. Comment on the conclusion. What is the speaker's intention in the conclusion?
5. Do you think it is an effective speech? Explain your answer.
6. Imagine that you have been asked to edit the speech. What changes would you make to it? What would you add in or take out?

C. Writing

In a group, write a speech that you will deliver to parents and teachers on an open night in your school. Choose from the following list of topics. Each member of the group should write one paragraph.

- Our school has so much to offer.
- What education means to our age-group.
- The importance of extracurricular activities in a young person's life.
- It's all about balance.
- How to fit in at a new school.
- The challenges of First Year and how to survive them.

Use the steps below to help you.

Step 1: Use the RAFT strategy to organise your plan.

Role of the writer	Who are you writing as? A movie star? The president? A novelist?
Audience	To whom are you writing? Your fans? The public? A company?
Format	In what format are you writing? A diary entry? A newspaper? A blog? A speech?
Topic	What are you writing about?

Step 2: Choose your topic and brainstorm for points/ideas.
Label them in order of interest/suitability and delete the least relevant points.

Step 3: Each person takes a point and writes about it.
Each student must research their point and find facts to support it.

Step 4: Each person reads everyone else's paragraph and the group works together to put the speech together.

Step 5: Each person gets a turn to read their paragraph aloud while the listeners make suggestions for improving it.

D. Oral Language

Read your open night speech aloud to the class. Pretend they are your target audience.

E. Reflection

When you reflect on your reaction or response to material, you consider the impact (if any) that it had on you. On **page 66** of your **PORTFOLIO**, complete any of the following responses that apply to you as you react to material.

- What I already knew about the topic was _____

- Something new that I learned was _____

- I found _____ interesting.

- I never really thought about it like this before, but now I _____

- I was surprised to learn that _____

- It made me think about _____

- I now realise _____

- I really enjoyed _____

- I would have preferred _____

- It would have been better if _____

Abbreviations

Abbreviations are words or phrases that are shortened in a number of ways.

Simple Shortened Words

- Influenza – flu
- Advertisement – ad or advert
- Television – telly or TV
- Bicycle – bike
- Et cetera – etc.

Contractions

A contraction is a type of abbreviation. There are two forms: an abbreviation of more than one word or an omission of letters from a word.

Abbreviation of More Than One Word

Examples of this type of contraction include:

- He will – he'll
- We would – we'd
- Should not have – shouldn't've

Letter Omission

You do not need to use a full stop at the end of this type of contraction, because the last letter of the word is still present.

- Doctor – Dr
- Saint – St
- Limited – Ltd

Acronyms

These are abbreviations of a number of words, using the first letter in each word. For example:

- NATO – North Atlantic Treaty Organisation
- ATM – Automated Teller Machine
- DIY – Do It Yourself
- ICU – Intensive Care Unit

A full stop is optional for this type of abbreviation. American English often uses full stops. For example, U.S.A. can be written with full stops, but USA is also correct. Choose one format in your writing and stick to it.

Some acronyms are adopted as words in everyday language. For example:

- Awol – Absent Without Leave
- Laser – Light Amplification by Stimulated Emission of Radiation
- Radar – Radio Detection And Ranging
- Scuba – Self-Contained Underwater Breathing Apparatus

Apostrophes

Apostrophes are used to show possession. For example, in the phrase, 'The dog's collar is too tight', the apostrophe before the 's' shows that the collar belongs to the dog. Some other examples are:

- The elephant's trunk.
- The boy's feelings.
- The granny's bag.
- The band's manager.

Writing

Insert apostrophes into the following sentences:

1. Mauds ice-cream melted quickly and created such a mess.
2. The childs meal was served quickly but was too hot.
3. Martins car was brand new and looked fabulous.
4. Sheilas aunt flew to Boston for an operation.
5. The tigers paw healed very slowly.
6. The villains getaway car stalled and the guards caught her.
7. The hairdressers bag was overflowing with products.

Apostrophes and Plural Words

When making a plural word possessive, simply put the apostrophe after the 's'.
- All the boys' gear-bags were green.
- All the mothers' coats hung on the rail.

If the original word is already plural without an 's', such as women or media, then the apostrophe still goes before the 's' to make it plural:

- women's
- media's

Writing

Insert apostrophes in the following sentences.

1. All the elephants trunks were covered in sand after they slept on the beach.
2. The boys bags were filthy after training in the muck and rain.
3. The girls make-up melted in the scorching sun.
4. The dogs dishes were scoured clean.
5. 'Bring in the cats blankets,' shouted Tom.

Apostrophes and Words Ending in 'S'

When making words ending in 's' possessive, simply add 's.
- The Jones's house was new.
- Yeats's poetry is brilliant.
- Dr Seuss's books are hilarious.

Apostrophes: It's or Its?

'It's' with an apostrophe refers **only** to an abbreviation for 'it is'.

* It's a lovely day = It is a lovely day.

'Its' without an apostrophe refers to possession.

* The dog ate its dinner = The dinner belongs to the dog.

Writing

Insert apostrophes where necessary. Keep an eye out for capital letters too!

1. 'its a great day for the beach,' she exclaimed loudly.
2. 'Well I can't do anything about it, its too late,' he said.
3. 'its about time we left or else we'll be late,' they chorused.
4. 'its no laughing matter when the chicks come home to roost,' he mused.
5. The mechanic took the truck and fixed its broken exhaust.
6. 'Isn't its coat lovely and shiny after a bath?' squealed Sonia.
7. Its a foggy, cold day and its hard to drive with low visibility.
8. 'Its a beautiful day for a picnic,' said Jean.
9. 'Where's its paw hurting?' asked the vet.
10. Its not funny when its lashing rain, freezing cold and you've no coat.

Their/They're/There

These words sound the same and people often make mistakes when using them.

* 'Their' is used to show possession: their coats; their food; their money; their time.
* 'They're' is an abbreviation for 'they are': they're happy; they're busy; they're annoying.
* 'There' is used for location: he is over there; the car is there; let's go there.

Writing

Insert the correct word (their/they're/there) into the following sentences:

1. The family went to New York at Christmas. They went _____ to relax.
2. 'Whose money is this?' Sara asked. 'It's _____ money; it belongs to the twins,' Sam replied.
3. _____ are seven days in a week and _____ are 60 seconds in a minute.
4. 'Put the gearbags in the bus over _____ ,' shouted the coach.
5. Small children are so annoying when _____ whinging and squabbling.
6. 'Whose turn is it now?' she asked. 'It's _____ turn,' replied Mike.
7. ' _____ is only one thing to do now,' said the pilot 'and that is turn back.'
8. ' _____ a rotten bunch; you're worth the whole damn lot of them put together,' Nick said.
9. 'Put _____ coats over _____ and they'll know that _____ safe,' said George to Mildred.
10. _____ are 32 counties in Ireland.

Speeches for Debates

What is a Debate?

A debate is a formal argument between two teams or sides. One side argues in favour of the motion/topic and the other argues against it. Those in favour are the proposition, arguing for the proposed motion. Those opposing the motion are the opposition. There are points for and against the motion, called pros (from the Latin *pro*, meaning 'for' or 'on behalf of') and cons (from the Latin *contra*, meaning 'against').

Advantages of Debating

Debating helps us to develop many skills.

Preparation for the debate:

- Research skills
- Brainstorming
- Thinking

- Analysing
- Reflecting.

During the debate:

- Thinking on your feet, e.g. rebuttal
- Confidence
- Separating fact from fiction
- Questioning/cross-examining
- Identifying bias

- Time management
- Teamwork.

How to Write a Debate Speech

Top Tips

Consider your audience: Are they your peers, teachers, parents, the public? How can you tailor the content of the speech to appeal to each category of the audience?

Language: Formal language is usually punctuated with humour or occasional conversational language. In general, debates use the language of argument, persuasion and information.

Opening/Introduction

First impressions count. Work on a good opening. Use one of the following:

- A question
- A quotation
- A surprising statistic
- An anecdote
- A joke (if the topic permits it)
- An unexpected statement or stance to grab the attention of the audience.

Body of the Speech

- Have good content, well-researched information and correct, up-to-date facts and references.
- Organise your points logically.
- Use persuasive language to engage your audience.

Elements of Persuasive Language

- Inclusive language: Use 'we', 'we all', 'you all'. This language draws the audience in and makes them feel that they belong.
- Broad general statements: These may be deceptive, so look for facts to support them and question their validity.
- Triads: List things in threes.
- Repetition
- Rhetorical questions: Answers to these are usually obvious; for example, 'Is this what we all want for our children's future?'
- Good delivery is very persuasive. A person with confidence, charisma and charm is convincing. Some people are able to convince you that black is white!

Conclusion

A strong ending leaves an impression on the audience. Put power into the conclusion. Opt for:

- A quote.
- A brief, powerful, succinct summary.
- A thoughtful rhetorical question.
- An appeal for action or advice.

Rules for Debates

Each organisation has its own set of rules and guidelines for debates. Typical rules include:

- Age of participants.
- Numbers on a team.
- Timing.
- Role of chairperson/timekeeper/adjudicators.
- The order of speakers – the first speaker is from the proposition, then the opposition and so on.

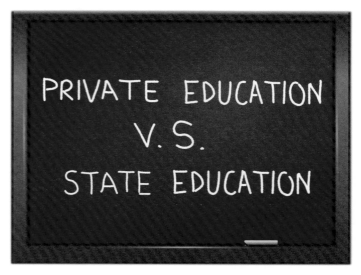

Usually in school debates, while the adjudicators add up marks, the motion is open to the audience to debate. This is known as the 'floor debate'. In more formal public debates, the floor debate occurs before the final speakers on each team deliver their summaries. In their summaries, they may deal with arguments raised in the floor debate. Then the audience, the debaters and the officials (collectively known as the 'house') are asked to vote on the motion.

Difference Between Public Speaking and a Debate

Public speaking requires a person to deliver a speech, whereas debating requires the person to argue, react and rebut, depending on what the previous speaker has said. Often debaters change their speeches as they react to what the other team says. Debaters have to think on their feet when faced with new or unexpected arguments.

Topics for Debate

Sport
- Abolition of contact sports
- Abolition of alcohol sponsorship.

Moral/Religious
- Vegetarianism
- Privacy of public figures
- Euthanasia
- Abolition of zoos
- Blood sports.

Health
- Alternative medicine
- Fast food.

Technology
- Censorship on the internet
- The health risks of mobile phones.

Sample Debate Speech

Motion: 'Tradition serves us better than innovation' or 'Old is better than modern'

1. Proposition

Traditions link us to the past, give us a sense of how life was lived and of what mattered to past generations. We see what previous generations valued, the morals and ethos they treasured, so that we can learn from their insight and wisdom.

Opposition

Traditions are old-fashioned, outdated, conservative and of no value. We live in a multicultural society, so we must embrace equality, innovative thinking and political correctness.

2. Proposition

The moral fabric of society is falling apart due to modernity. Families rarely have meals together, no one talks and everyone is too busy 'doing their own thing'. Real communication has vanished. It's all screens and messaging now. Capitalism and materialism are driving a culture of 'much wants more'. The future is bleak for today's children.

Opposition

Children have never had it so good. Full bellies, foreign holidays, a plethora of cultural, artistic and sporting hobbies to pursue, technology at their fingertips and the best that medicine can offer should they fall ill. Would you prefer that they walked two miles to school barefoot on an empty stomach? Stop romanticising the past. Embrace the modern and be grateful.

3. Proposition

Modern medicine is too intrusive. There are too many machines and too many drugs. How many of you in the audience, for example, have a grandparent taking about 20 different tablets a day – one for blood pressure, another to offset the effects of the blood pressure tablet on the heart? It's a money racket run by powerful pharmaceutical companies who are 'buying' doctors and 'buying' the IDA simply to sell pills we don't need. The traditional remedies from Mother Nature worked: a homemade poultice sorted out a skin infection, there was no need for antibiotics and chicken soup was the best medicine if you had the flu or a cold. Carrageen moss, seaweed and nettle soup cured a plethora of ailments. People ate natural food, worked hard and led healthy lives, unlike the modern, stress-filled rat-race we live in, with an overreliance on alcohol, drugs and expensive medicines.

Opposition

Billions of euro worth of funding in research is curbing cancer and heart disease, creating prosthetic limbs, providing CT and MRI scanners and saving millions of lives every year. Who in this audience tonight would prefer chicken broth or nettle soup to modern medicine? Innovation, not tradition, is the obvious and only way forward. Move out of your darkness, Proposition, and welcome the light.

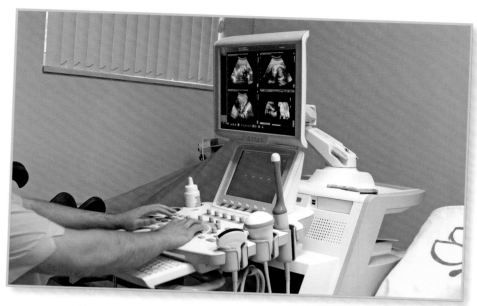

 # Group Work

The following headline appeared in *The Sunday Times* on 12 April, 2009:

'Facebook fans do worse in exams'

Research this topic and have a debate.

- Choose one side, for or against the motion.
- Find facts and statistics to support your argument.
- Find quotes from the media to support your argument.
- Do some research to strengthen your argument.
- Identify the emotional, persuasive elements of your argument.
- Have the debate.

How to Do a Presentation

What is a Presentation?

A presentation is an exercise in delivering information to an audience. A presentation can be given to inform, persuade, inspire curiosity and spark discussion. The presenter has control over what material to present.

How to Give a Presentation

Build on your experience of giving presentations. What skills do you think you need to improve or work on?

Use the RAFT Strategy:

R: Role – Your role is to speak and present information that will capture the interest of the audience.

A: Audience – Win them over, get them on your side, be entertaining, give them facts and questions to ponder.

F: Format – A presentation where you stand in front of the audience and deliver your message.

T: Topic – You choose your topic, you choose the details to present, you control the information.

Step 1

Set a precise aim/objective

What is the topic? What do you want to inform the audience about?

Set your precise aim in one sentence. Stick to this.

Step 2

Time: How much time have you got for the presentation? How much information can you relay in 3, 5 or 10 minutes?

Tools: What tools will you use?

Visuals: PowerPoint, pictures, photos, flipchart, audio clips, film clips, slide show or any other materials.

Step 3

Research the topic

Find information on your topic. Discard any unnecessary information. Keep asking yourself, 'Is this relevant to my main aim or topic?' Discard it if it is not.

You might categorise the information as follows:

- What is essential and central and must be included.
- What is interesting and worth saying if time allows.
- What is interesting but too detailed and wandering away from the main aim.
- What is not at all relevant to the main aim.

Retain the information that focuses on the topic.

Do not have too little or too much information. Too much may bore the audience; too little might leave the audience confused or uninformed.

Step 4

Order and sequencing

- In what order will you put your points/information?
- Organise the information in a logical sequence.
- Decide what to include based on what point it is making or how good it is.

Step 5

Rehearse then give the presentation

You may choose to use:

- cards with bullet point notes
- PowerPoint
- whiteboard/flipchart
- audio or film clips or a slideshow.

Team presentation

Each team member has a specific role. Each person must have a copy of the entire presentation and know their own part in it.

A. Listening

Listen to Newstalk's Henry McKean speaking to members of the public about cycling in Dublin. Make a list of the different opinions that you hear.

B. Group Work

Organise a vox pop.

- Choose an issue that your peers feel strongly about.

- Ask three questions about the issue; for example:

    1. What do you think about _____?

    2. Why does _____?

    3. Have you any suggestions/advice regarding _____?

- Record the responses.

- Ensure that you have a balance of responses.

- Replay a balance of responses to your class; for example, four in favour of and four against an idea.

Statistics

Statistics are numbers collected in large quantities. Data is gathered on a topic in order to analyse the results and reach a conclusion based on them. Once data is gathered, it is then orgranised and statistics are made available.

The following article, featured in the *Irish Independent* on 7 November, 2014, reveals statistics about Irish life.

The number of teenagers having babies has halved in the last six years with women waiting much longer to have babies and get married.

1. A new Central Statistics Office report paints a detailed picture of how Irish people live, die, shop, work, rest and play. *The Statistics Handbook 2013* draws together hundreds of reports to provide a comprehensive account of modern-day life and how it compares to decades past.

2. It shows that the number of weddings soared by nearly 20pc between 1994 and last year, when 20,680 couples tied the knot. However, while marriage is still in fashion, almost one in three couples now choose a civil ceremony compared to one in five in 2004, while Catholic weddings have fallen from 76pc of the total to 62.5pc in that period. Both men and women are now waiting five years longer to wed than they did two decades ago, with the average bride now aged 32.8 and the average groom 34.9.

3. We're also waiting much longer to have babies, with the number of teenage mums plummeting from 2,402 in 2008 to 1,218 last year. The early 30s are now the most common time to have a baby. Jack and Emily are well established as the most popular baby names, holding the top spots for several years. However, the baby boom is waning, with 68,930 births last year compared to 72,225 the year before.

4. The workforce has swollen by over 30,000 in the last year, with 1.87m people now working while the number of unemployed people fell by 23,000 to 300,700. People working in the hotel and restaurant sector earn just €316 a week, compared to over €1,000 a week for those working in computers.

5. Irish people made almost 6.6 million trips abroad last year, with 85pc of these to other EU countries, while most domestic trips were short breaks, averaging 3.3 nights or fewer if it involved staying with friends or relative. Hotel accommodation and travel accounted for over half our online purchases last year, with concert tickets a very popular purchase for teenagers and 20-somethings. Nearly half of businesses now use social media, such as Facebook, to try and reach consumers.

6. The report also shows that household disposable income fell by 3pc between 2011 and 2012 to €776 a week, and people are much less likely to get into hock than they used to be, ditching over 300,000 credit cards in the last five years and spending much more cautiously, the report shows.

7. There were 83 homicides last year, which is six less than in 2008, but the number of sexual offences soared by over 40pc to over 2,000. Public order and weapons offences have plummeted in the last five years, while burglaries fell back from over 28,000 in 2012 to 26,000 last year.

8. Farm animals far outnumber people in Ireland, with 6.9 million cattle, 5.1 million sheep and 1.6 million pigs. But Irish farmers are no longer sowing oats or potatoes at anything like the levels of yesteryear – just 11,000 hectares of potatoes were grown here last year, compared to 279,000 in 1853, while there were 27,000 hectares of oats grown, down from 639,000 in 1853.

 ## A. Reading

Rate this text for readability. Write the word/phrase of your choice into your copy.

VERY EASY ☐   **EASY** ☐   **OKAY** ☐   **HARD** ☐   **VERY HARD** ☐

 ## B. Literacy Questions

1. What do think about the headline in the article? Is it effective? Why was it chosen? Suggest a different headline.

2. Would you agree that the article uses the language of information? Explain your answer using quotes.

3. Do you think that the article is written in a logical, sequential style? Explain your answer using examples from the text.

4. Write a conclusion for the article.

 ## C. Numeracy

 'A picture paints a thousand words.' People take information quickly by looking at visuals. In groups, examine each of the statistics in the article and turn them into visuals.

You can use graphs, charts or pictures.

For example:

1. To show that farm animals exceed people, draw a picture of people and write 4.609 million beside it. Draw cattle and write 6.9 million beside it.

2. The number of weddings increased by almost 20 per cent between 1994 and 2013. How will you show this visually?

Letter Writing

Informal Letters

Informal letters are letters written to people you know, using informal, casual language. Today, emails are more common than informal letters.

Sample Informal Letter

4 Oak Lane,
Newtown,
Waterford

12/12/2015

Hi Sally,

How are you? Hope all's going well in Chicago for you. You're so lucky to have the dratted exams over you and to be spending your Transition Year abroad. I'm sick of it myself at this stage. Teachers and parents hassling me to study. Grrrrr!

I went to the annual school fashion show last night. It was brill as usual. Hilarious to see some of the weird, wacky outfits designed by our own TY students. You won't believe it but I won a spot prize! A hundred euro voucher for the new beauty salon in town. I was thrilled! You won't recognise me when you come home, I'll use the voucher for your homecoming night out!

Not much else happening. If you weren't abroad I wouldn't even be writing this snail mail but I know it's so nice to get a letter in the post... the novelty of it!!

Ok, gotta dash now, I'll Facebook you.

Lots of luv,

Isobel

 Writing

Surprise someone you know with a real letter. Write it in class and post it later. Then sit back and wait for the reply.

Formal Letters

Formal letters are written for a specific purpose and use formal, polite language. Examples include letters of enquiry, letters of complaint, cover letters for job applications and letters of praise.

Sample Formal Letter

4 Oak Lane,
Newtown,
Waterford

The Manager,
Hotel DeLuxe,
Ballybeg,
Donegal

12 February 2016

Dear Sir,

I write in order to express my gratitude to you and your excellent staff. My family and I had the pleasure of spending a week in your very fine establishment and we were most impressed and delighted with the service and the standards.

We had booked two adjoining double rooms but on arrival we were upgraded (at no extra cost) to two superior rooms simply because your hotel had the capacity to do this. The rooms were spotless, comfortable and had a most exquisite view of the bay.

The food at breakfast and dinner was simply delicious, fresh, tasty and filling. The waiters were very efficient and attentive, displaying patience and care with our two-year old twins as well as our wheelchair-using five-year-old.

The leisure centre was bright, clean and safe while the outdoor playground had swings, slides and a supervised bouncy castle.

Your hotel more than met the requirements of my family and I intend to speak highly of it and recommend it to my friends, neighbours and work colleagues.

Wishing you continued success.

Yours faithfully,

Thomas O'Donoghue

Thomas O'Donoghue

Writing

Think about a service, a product or a place that you were very happy with. Write a positive letter in praise of this. Include the recipient's name and address as well as your own. Follow the layout above.

Manifestos

A manifesto is a public statement that outlines the beliefs and intentions of a person or group. For example, a political party might release a manifesto explaining the policies they promise to put in place if they win the election. A manifesto is often written in persuasive language and then delivered orally to convince and inspire others.

Sometimes people write 'advice for life' pieces that are like manifestos. For example, the poem 'Warning' by Jenny Joseph is the poet's statement about what she is going to do when she gets old. Likewise, your Read and Enjoy piece in Chapter 3, 'Desiderata', offers advice to the reader such as 'enjoy your achievements as well as your plans', 'be yourself' and 'strive to be happy'.

A. Reading and Listening

Listen to the song 'Everybody's Free (to Wear Sunscreen)' on YouTube. Then read the creative modelling version of it below. Use it as inspiration for creating your own manifesto.

Everybody's Grand (in Ireland)

Ladies and gentlemen of Ireland,
it'll be grand.

If I could offer you only one tip for the future, relaxing would be it. The long-term benefits of relaxing have been proven by Frankie, whereas the rest of my advice has no basis more reliable than my own meandering experience. I will dispense this advice now.

Enjoy the power and beauty of your first car. Oh, never mind. You will not understand the power and beauty of your first car until its suspension has been ruined by Irish roads, but trust me, in 20 miles you'll look back and recall in a way you can't grasp now how many potholes lay before you and how harmless they really looked.

They don't spend motor tax like you imagine.

Don't worry about the future. Or know that worrying is about as useful as sunglasses in December. The real troubles in your life will be things you won't even expect, anyway. The kind of stuff that just lands in your lap on a random Thursday.

Do one thing every day that could end up on Joe Duffy.

Don't be reckless with other people's money. Don't put up with governments who are reckless with yours.

Vote.

Don't waste your time on Facebook. Sometimes you're happy, sometimes you're sad – the status is fleeting, and in the end, you can't fool yourself. Remember retweets you receive, forget the trolls. If you succeed in doing this, tell me how.

Keep your favourite texts, ignore your voicemails.

Delete.

Don't feel guilty if you don't know what you want to do with your day. The most interesting people I know don't know at ten to two what they want to do with their night. Some of the most interesting Instagrams I've seen were staged.

Get plenty of DVD boxsets.

Buy Creme Eggs, you'll miss them when they're out of season.

Maybe you'll get into running, maybe you won't. Maybe you'll take up piano, maybe you won't. Maybe you'll be the most popular kid, maybe you'll do something horribly embarrassing in front of everyone you know. Whatever you do, don't have too many notions or berate yourself either. Your selfies are boring at best, so are everybody else's.

Enjoy tea, drink it in every situation you can. Don't be afraid of what coffee people think of it. It's the greatest comfort you'll ever have.

Chat, even if you have nowhere to do it but in your own living room. Buy the paper even if you don't read it all. Do not read comments sections, they only make the internet seem ugly.

Take pictures with your mates, you never know when they'll be gone abroad. Be nice to your family, they're your best chance of getting pocket money. And the people most likely to stick up for you.

Understand that summers come and go, but a precious few that were really warm bridge the gap between September and April. The colder you get, the more you need to know that you were once warm.

Live abroad once but come home when you miss your mammy. Live with your friends but move on before it loses its shine.

Laugh.

Accept certain inalienable truths:

There's nothing on RTÉ, your Skybox didn't record, and you, too, will watch the *Late Late Show*. And when you do, you'll fantasise that when you were younger, guests were decent, VCRs were reliable and there was one for everybody in the audience.

Respect your liver.

Don't expect anyone else to buy you things. Maybe you have generous grandparents, maybe your pocket money is ridiculous. Either one could run out.

Don't check-in too much online. We get that you're fun, we know you're alive.

Be careful whose number you take and be patient with those who supply them. Texting is a minefield of misunderstood messages, taking things up the wrong way and worrying about things for far longer than they're worth.

But trust me it'll be grand.

 B. Group Work

In groups, create a Best Friend Manifesto. It might include statements like 'Secrets are taken to the grave' and 'Best friends swap homework'.

The Media and You

The media is the general term used for TV, radio, the internet and newspapers, magazines and all mediums of communication that inform the public. It is divided into:

- Print media: newspapers, magazines and a wide range of printed material.
- Broadcast media: television and radio.
- Digital media: the internet.

Stereotyping in the media

What is stereotyping? A stereotype is a widely held, oversimplified view or idea of a person or thing. For example, men are macho and don't cry; women are motherly and are carers; girls play with dolls; boys play with trucks and cars.

A. Oral Language

In pairs, discuss the following:

1. How the media portrays people. Consider characters in TV shows and people in advertisements. Are they portrayed in a stereotypical way? Find examples. Are there any characters/presenters who go against the stereotype?

2. Are media reports/articles objective or subjective? Is there bias/prejudice in them?

3. Can television teach? What role does it play in your life?

4. Do you question and critique the media or do you accept everything it tells you?

Let's look at some of the types of text we find in newspapers and magazines and on online media sites.

Newspapers

Front Page

The front page of a newspaper contains headline national and/or world news stories.

What's Inside?

- National news
- World news
- Features on health, technology and lifestyle
- Business pages
- Letters to the editor
- Comment – articles from writers/politicians/ public figures on particular issues
- Personal notices
- Advertisements
- Classified advertisements
- Announcements – death notices, in memoriam notices, marriage and birth notices
- TV and radio listings
- Weather
- Horoscopes
- Puzzles: crosswords and sudoku.

Headlines

Tabloid headlines usually exaggerate and are sensational.

Wedding Slaughter at Shotgun Wedding

Aston Villa Axe No-Goals Boss

JEDWARD TO BE WIZ OF OZ

Corrie Beauty in Fiancé Love Split

Bounce Your Way to Total Fitness
– Tramp-o-Lean

BRITAIN'S TOT TALENT
– Simon Cowell's tot (son Eric) turned one on Valentine's Day 2015

Broadsheet headlines are less sensational and more factual and restrained.

Guest shot dead and two men injured in wedding day attack

Keane in running as Villa axe Lambert

Teenager alleged to have thrown brick released by Gardai

Thieves steal McGinley's Ryder Cup mementos

Four Held As Gardaí Catch €1M Jewellery Heist Suspects

Headlines often use puns and alliteration.

Puns are a play on words, where there's a double meaning.

British Airways bulldog revelling in the chase

No plane sailing in Aer Lingus bid

BRIAN BOWLED OVER BY CRICKET

Alliteration is the repetition of a letter or sound at the start of words in a phrase.

WILL TO WIN IT

Hammers halt Saints march after Adrian sees red

Research

Look at some recent newspapers and list any interesting headlines you find. Look out for sensational wording, puns and alliteration.

Newspaper Reports

Formal Language

by Emile Laurac

THE body of a train driver has been found in the wreckage following a head-on train crash in Switzerland that left at least 35 passengers injured. The driver was pulled from the debris after two trains collided on the same track having travelled towards each other near Granges-Marnand station in the west of the country. Dozens of passengers were hurt, four of them seriously, in the crash. Desperate passengers aboard the carriage swaying in the sky were forced to crawl up the carriageway in a bid to shift the weight in the wagon and prevent it from plunging over the edge. Steven Bueller, one passenger aboard, told Swiss radio: "We all went to the back to shift the weight, to try to stop it from pitching into the ravine. It was a nightmare scene with many terrified people aboard." The derailment occurred near the Swiss resort of St Moritz, with carriages veering off into a ravine.

The ravine is in a mountainous region of south-eastern Switzerland. Swiss police said yesterday the accident happened after the train encountered a mudslide on the tracks. At least three train carriages came off the tracks near Tiefencastel. Up to 200 people were on board the trains at the time of the accident, which followed heavy rain in the region. The train is operated by Rhaetische Bahn, which runs a network of narrow-gauge routes in Switzerland's mountainous south-eastern corner. The line where the crash occurred is not near to a road – helicopters with an air rescue service helped with the recovery efforts. By mid-afternoon, everyone had been evacuated from the train cars, with uninjured passengers taken to Tiefencastel and put on buses. One of the trains had set off from St Moritz on a line that leads north to Chur, the Graubuenden region's administrative capital.

 Writing

1. Write a headline for the above report. Is your headline suitable for a tabloid or broadsheet newspaper?

2. Identify the paragraphs. Write a number beside the sentence you think should be the start of a new paragraph.

3. Answer the following: What happened? When? Where? To whom? Why? How?

Mix of Formal and Informal Language

Report 1

By Anne Penketh

IT was the night of the 'supermoon' and Clemence Lapeyre slipped out of the beach-side house, where she was staying with relatives, to enjoy the moonlit night from the sea on an old paddle board. It was after 10.30pm when she set out from the beach in Morsalines, on the Cherbourg peninsula, on Sunday. Forty hours later, after losing her paddle and her glasses in rough seas and pushed by strong westerly winds, she was found more than 68 miles away, drifting off the cliffs of Etretat, just up the coast from Le Havre. Rescuers have called her survival a "miracle". Yesterday the 24-year-old from Paris was in hospital in Fecamp, suffering from dehydration, sunburn and exhaustion. "It was a beautiful night with a very beautiful moon and she apparently decided to go paddling by moonlight without letting us know," her uncle, Christophe Remy-Nerys, said yesterday. "It was only late the next day that we realised she had disappeared." After a fruitless search on land, the family realised that the board was missing and lifeguards began looking for her in the waters around Morsaline. "We were watching the helicopter circling overhead, we were on the shore trying to find a sign, anything suspicious," Mr Remy-Nerys told the BFM TV news channel. A launch and an inflatable boat assisted the helicopter search.

Writing

1. Write a headline for the above report. Is your headline suitable for a tabloid or broadsheet newspaper?

2. Identify and number the paragraphs.

3. Answer the following: What happened? When? Where? To whom? Why? How?

Report 2

By Henry Samuel

FIVE French climbers and their guide slid to their deaths on Mont Blanc yesterday, in one of the worst disasters on Europe's highest mountain in recent years. The accident brings the death toll on the notoriously dangerous massif, which has been plagued by bad weather this summer, to 14 in the past month. Four men and one woman, aged between 27 and 45, set out with their 42-year old guide on Tuesday morning for an expedition organised by France's national association for outdoor sports, UCPA.

The group intended to reach the Aiguille d'Argentiere peak on the Mont Blanc massif, which stands at 12,802ft. They had left during a "break" in bad weather on a relatively easy ascent via the Fleche Rousse ridge. But poor conditions set in and the climbers, all at a "good technical level", were reported missing after failing to arrive at their shelter. The caretaker of the Argen-tiere refuge, Fred Laurenzio, said the group and the guide had left at 4am "in very good weather conditions". By 5pm, he alerted mountain rescue workers in Chamonix, who were unable to reach the missing climbers that night, as the summit was shrouded in snowfall and mist.

They finally located five bodies yesterday morning at between 11,482ft and 12,139ft. Gendarmes said they had fallen 820ft down a slope. The guide's body was found in a crevasse, according to the Haute-Savoie state prefect. The mountain rescue gendarmes of Chamonix said the group had died after slipping and making a "violent fall" on to a glacial rock bar where several previous accidents have occurred. "We don't know what their problem was here, but it forced them to try to descend by night," a spokesman said. Seventy-four deaths were recorded on the mountain between 1990 and 2011.

A. Writing

1. Write a headline for the above report. Is your headline suitable for a tabloid or broadsheet newspaper?

2. Identify and number the paragraphs.

3. Answer the following: What happened? When? Where? To whom? Why? How?

B. Group Work

In groups, imagine you work for a tabloid newspaper. Each member of your news team has to write a news report. Choose from one of the following:

- Child Mauled by Savage Bear in Zoo
- Armed Raiders Botch Bank Robbery
- Out of Control Blaze Reduces Hotel to Ashes
- Typhoon Rips Town to Tatters

Your reports must include:

- A headline (as above or your own headline).
- Answers to: What happened? When? Where? To whom? Why? How?
- Suitable paragraphs.

Peer Assessment

Swap reports to proofread and edit each other's work.

Special Reports

In a special report, the journalist chooses a topic that is in the news and talks to experts to find out what is really going on.

The following is a special report that featured in the *Irish Independent* in January 2015.

Why the Health Experts Are Souring on Sugar

Experts are still hugely divided on whether sugar is addictive.

1. IRISH and international experts are divided on whether sugar is addictive or the main culprit in the spiralling obesity crisis. In a bid to combat tooth decay and excessive weight gain the World Health Organisation (WHO) is about to recommend a drastic reduction in the amount of added sugar we eat. WHO is set to recommend a maximum daily intake of 10pc of calories from sugar – around 12 teaspoons. But it will state that ideally consumers should aim for half that – just six teaspoons a day – for greater health benefits.

2. Dr Donal O'Shea, an endocrinologist and head of the Obesity Management Clinic in Loughlinstown Hospital, said he believed sugar was addictive. "The pattern of consumption of sugar in Ireland is highly abnormal, and the parts of the brain that light up when it's eaten fit in with the theory that it is addictive," he said. The extreme difficulty people had cutting back on sugar – and the cravings many experienced after years of habitual overconsumption – also backed up the addiction argument. Dr O'Shea welcomed the new WHO guidelines as hugely "impressive and ambitious". He said that while they might seem drastic, added sugar hadn't existed in our diets until 400 years ago, but it was now ubiquitous in everything from breakfast cereals to chocolate milk and sweetened drinks. He predicted a "societal revolt" within 15 years against the harmful effects of sugar and tough regulation in the form of taxes and bans on sales of products such as sweetened drinks to under-16s.

3. However, Dr Mary Flynn, chief nutrition specialist in the Food Safety Authority of Ireland (FSAI), strongly disagreed that sugar was addictive or the biggest cause of Ireland's obesity crisis. She said it was vital "not to let fat off the hook" for its contribution to weight gain. "The biggest problem in our diet is fatty foods – and sugary, fatty foods are probably the worst of all," she said. Sugar was not the problem in isolation but the difficulty was that it made nearly everything more palatable, particularly high-fat foods like doughnuts, that you wouldn't eat much of unless they were sweet.

How to Write a Formal Article/Report

Examine the report on sugar. Notice the features of a good report:

Paragraph 1   Clear introduction to the topic: is our sugar intake harmful?

Paragraph 2   An expert's opinion: sugar is addictive.

Paragraph 3   Another expert disagrees that sugar is addictive.

Paragraph 4   Think about a conclusion for this article. In pairs suggest a brief conclusion.

 Group Work

Break up into groups of four. Imagine that your group works for a broadsheet newspaper. You have to write a formal, factual report on one of the following topics:

• Serious injuries are on the increase in schools' rugby.

• Using iPads in the classroom: good or bad?

• Regular reading improves your skills in English.

Each person in the group must write one paragraph on one particular point.

One person writes the introduction. This is Paragraph 1.

You will need three more paragraphs.

Find expert opinions and facts to support each viewpoint, for and against.

Editorial

An editorial is the comment/opinion of the editor of the newspaper. Usually the editor comments on important topical issues that have been reported in the newspaper.

The following article is an editorial from the *Irish Independent*, 10 January 2015.

A Spoonful of Sugar is Killing Us Slowly

Most of us regard sugar as a pile of white granules that we stir into tea and coffee, a substance that is not only visible but adds to the enjoyment of things we might eat every day, like a bowl of porridge.

But it is the sugar that you don't see that is silently driving more and more Irish people into health problems such as obesity, diabetes and general ill health. Health experts are increasingly concerned about the sugar intake of the population, and the fact that babies and young children are bombarded by sugary foods from the moment they get up in the morning until they go to bed.

There is no doubt that sugar in soft drinks, processed foods and almost everything we ingest is becoming a major national health epidemic.

Some commentators may have scoffed at a sugar tax – and it is something that the food industry will resist – but we have to recognise that sugar consumption has now reached dangerous levels in our ordinary lives and it needs to be curtailed, officially or unofficially, if it is not to become the major health hazard of the 21st century.

Reviews

A review is an assessment of something, such as a new film, book, drama, musical, game or television programme. The person writing the review usually weighs up the good and the weak points of what they are reviewing and gives a recommendation.

A reviewer is often a person who has a lot of experience with the thing they are talking about, but their recommendation is still only their opinion. Reviewing is often about taste, so what one person loves another person might hate!

Elements in a review

- Introduction
- Development
- Evaluation
- Recommendation.

Reviews do not have to include each of the four elements above, nor do they have to follow the order given. Some reviews begin with a recommendation: 'It's a fantastic film; rush to your nearest cinema right now to see it!'

Sample Reviews

Best Young Adult Books *by Justine Carbery*

The following is an edited extract from a review by Justine Carbery of the best young adult books published in 2013.

For the younger teen there are many hotly anticipated sequels to savour: Jeff Kinney's *Diary of a Wimpy Kid: Hard Luck* (Harry N. Abrams) which sees our favourite hero Greg Heffley struggling to find a new pal after his best friend Rowley Jefferson ditches him. David Walliams (some say a successor to Roald Dahl) is back with two hilarious instalments: *Gangsta Granny* (HarperCollins) which sets an 11-year-old boy up as an aide to his jewel-thieving granny, and *Demon Dentist* (HarperCollins), where Alfie comes face to face with an evil new dentist who gives out sweets to all the children...

Fans of Charlie Higson will be delighted with his latest page-turner to hit the shelves. *The Fallen* (Penguin) is fast-paced and full of action, a sure hit with younger teens. Darren Shan's *Zom-B Baby* (Simon & Schuster Children's Books), Robert Muchamore's *Scorched Earth* (Hodder Children's Books), and Rick Riordan's *The Lost Hero* (Disney-Hyperion) will also appeal to fans of these series.

Michael Grant's *Light* (Electric Monkey) is an edgy, dark book, a satisfying conclusion to a nail-biting *Gone* series. Filled with action, suspense and shocking revelations, *Light*, and the rest of the series represents dystopian thrillers at their best.

Russian Roulette (Walker) is a thought-provoking prequel to the best-selling Alex Rider spy series, which focuses on the Russian assassin Yassen Gregorovich. Well-written and fast-paced, it could be read as a stand-alone or in conjunction with the rest of the series… Anthony Horowitz delivers every time. A sure hit for Christmas.

Review of Pauline McLynn's Jenny Q

The following review originally appeared in the Children's Books Ireland magazine, *Inis*.

Best known as an actress and comedian, Pauline McLynn has tried her hand at writing for the teenage market with her debut young adult novel *Jenny Q*.

In it, Jennifer Quinn deals with the teenage trials of having a really embarrassing family and somehow navigating the emotional minefield of liking boys for the first time.

Realistic from the outset, the novel, set in the fictional Dublin suburb of Oakdale, makes mention of the recession and the central characters spend much of their time knitting Christmas presents. Jenny and her 'Bestests' Dixie and Ugg (Eugene) make up the 'Knit and Knatter' club, which meets in Jenny's bedroom to stitch and knit as they discuss pregnancy (Jenny's mum's), the Slinkies (school popular kids) and Stevie Lee (obligatory crush). Notably, McLynn seems to have a knack for teenage dialogue, with their OTT take on everything captured just so, down to the misspelled txt msgs.

Showing insight into the minutiae of the teenage thought process, McLynn lists 'being left alone' among Jenny Q's likes, while her hair is 'strawberry blonde NOT ginger'.

Jenny is a good-head-on-her-shoulders character who isn't afraid to follow her own sense of right and wrong and stand up to bullies.

Funny and well-paced, *Jenny Q* is a confident debut and will make a welcome addition to the shelves of Louise Rennison and Lois Lowry fans.

A. Reading

Rate these texts for readability. Write the word/phrase of your choice into your copy.

VERY EASY ☐   **EASY** ☐   **OKAY** ☐   **HARD** ☐   **VERY HARD** ☐

B. Writing

Write a review of one of the following:

- A book
- An album
- A game

- A radio programme
- A TV programme
- A new technology gadget.

Look up reviews online to get ideas for writing interesting, clever reviews.

C. Group work

In a group, figure out what the class Top 5 is for any of the following:
- Albums
- Games

- Books
- Television programmes.

Cover Stories

A cover story is an article that is featured on the front cover of the newspaper or magazine it appears in. The headline that advertises a cover story is often accompanied by an image of the subject of the article.

Cover stories are chosen because they will be of the greatest interest to the publication's readers, and will therefore help to sell more copies of the newspaper or magazine.

The following article about pop star Taylor Swift appeared in *Stellar* magazine in March 2015.

8 Times Taylor Swift Rocked Our World

Taylor Swift is the superstar we all love to, well, love – and it's a testimony to Taylor (autobiography title, anyone?) that the only negative stories the internet snarks can come up with all focus on her "out-of-control" love life. If that's what a messy love life looks like, heck, we'll have one in each colour…

To her credit, Taylor takes it in her stride. Love-life gossips? Thanks, you inspired 'Blank Space', the second single from her fifth studio album, 1989, a song that immediately went to number one on the Billboard Hot 100, bumping 'Shake It Off' from the top spot. That'd be, you guessed it, the first single from 1989 – meaning that Taylor is the first woman in history to succeed herself to first place. In terms of record-breaking, though, Taylor's got more to shout about than anyone else; 1989 went platinum in the US during its first week of sales, making it the first solo album in the whole year to do so, and the highest selling release week since 2002. Now that's what we call crazy. But when it comes to why we heart Taylor, her musical success is just one of the reasons we admire her – sure, we all love a good dance-along to 'Shake It Off' (or 'Love Story', '22', 'You Belong With Me' or 'We Are Never Ever Getting Back Together', the best breakup anthem of all time), but our adoration for Taylor runs way, way deeper than that.

1. If you follow Taylor on Instagram, you'll already know that she's all about her girlfriends. Last year, she and supermodel Karlie Kloss went on a road trip up the California coast and Instagrammed every minute; at this year's Golden Globes, she partied with Lorde and Selena Gomez. In an interview for *ASOS Magazine* late last year, she admitted that girls are her number one priority, especially where fashion is concerned. "When it comes to getting dressed, it's always based on what my friends will think. The opinions of girls are more important to me at this point in my life!" Preach.

2. You know those stars who are always talking about rolling in the door at 7am and swilling whiskey for breakfast? Taylor couldn't be further from the angst-ridden, rebellious celebs of yore. A fan of keeping things neat 'n' tidy, she likes nothing more than baking cookies with her mates. But don't get it twisted – she's still the best friend you'll (likely) never have. "When you say 'control freak' and 'OCD' and 'organised', that suggests someone who's cold in nature, and I'm just not. But I like my house to be neat, and I don't like to make big messes that would hurt people." Can we be bessies, please?

3. In Taylor's penthouse apartment in Nashville (to be clear, she owns four homes – the aforementioned Nashville condo, a cottage-style house in Beverly Hills, another penthouse in Tribeca, NYC, and a beachside mansion in Rhode Island) she has an enormous, human-

It's probably too easy to be pessimistic, but it does seem increasingly that what is real is being replaced by the fake and inauthentic. The things we're endlessly commemorating didn't happen quite like that: we didn't look quite like that: we didn't feel quite like that. But with enough editing and tweaking, carefully selecting the words and pictures that make our lives look most enviable, we present the world with an idealised version of ourselves which is: almost by definition, contrary to reality.

6. Does it matter? Centuries ago, nostalgia was recognised as being closely related to melancholia. That the world is now awash both with Instagram-induced instant nostalgia and unprecedented levels of depression, at least in the consumerist West, is surely no coincidence. We're only able to live fully in retrospect, once an experience has been given an official existence through being commemorated, and then, once it has been immortalised, we either compare our current lives unfavourably with that now-idealised past or else compare it unfavourably to someone else's, either way leading to dissatisfaction.

If it's not too pretentious, we could even say that we have all chosen to exist in the state that Sartre called "bad faith", except that the French philosopher thought it consisted in not living authentically whereas the awful truth may be that we no longer know what authenticity is so couldn't embrace it even if we wanted to. All we have instead are catchphrases and kitsch.

Still, everything happens for a reason, right? I think I'll make my own flipogram to illustrate the point. I know just the right heart-rending ballad to accompany it too. Loving the feels.

 ## A. Reading

Rate this text for readability. Write the word/phrase of your choice into your copy.

VERY EASY ☐   **EASY** ☐   **OKAY** ☐   **HARD** ☐   **VERY HARD** ☐

 ## B. Oral Language

'With enough editing and tweaking, carefully selecting the words and pictures that make our lives look most enviable, we present the world with an idealised version of ourselves which is: almost by definition, contrary to reality.'

Do you agree or disagree with Eilis O'Hanlon's comment? Have a debate about it. Find out more about how to debate on **page 238**.

Feature Articles

Feature articles are written about specific subjects and topics. There is no end to the subjects that might be written about.

Read the following feature article about crosswords from the *Irish Independent* and think about the kinds of topics you would like to write an article about.

One Hundred Years of Crosswords

by Darragh McManus

1. Invented by Arthur Wynne, the crossword was originally intended as nothing more than a new twist on the existing puzzle pages in the *New York World*. Yet it became a phenomenon that conquered the world, has just celebrated its 100th birthday – and remains an essential element of newspapers. Almost everyone does the crossword from time to time: some are obsessive about it. There are crossword societies and competitions. Whole magazines are devoted to it. The deaths of cryptic crossword-setters, such as the *Guardian*'s Rev John Graham in November, are treated as major events.

2. So, to the casual dabbler, what's the appeal of this simple, black-and-white word-puzzle? Brian Head is editor of the UK-based Crossword Club's magazine, simply called *Crossword*, which runs clue-writing competitions and breaks new ground with themed puzzles. "For me, it's mainly the beauty of some cryptic clues, and the way that one solution leads to another," he says. "Cryptics are superior artistically, but simple crosswords also have their place. "Crosswords take up very little space in newspapers and magazines, so are easily and cheaply disseminated. The level of difficulty can be adjusted from the trivial to almost impossible, so can appeal to all tastes. Special interests can be catered for. And they're possible in any language – I've even seen Chinese versions – though most non-English seem to be definition only."

3. Moving across the Atlantic, Elizabeth Gorski is a crossword constructor for *The New York Times*, *Wall Street Journal* and others, and edits *Crossword Nation,* a nationally syndicated puzzle provider. Her crosswords were commissioned for the Sandra Bullock comedy *All About Steve*.

Elizabeth describes crosswords as "a fun, irresistible challenge that can be quantified. It's like playing violin: no matter how proficient you become, there's always room for improvement. And puns, especially the worst ones, keep me coming back for more.

"You can complete some simple crosswords during a 20-minute subway ride. But a cryptic is like a box of rich marzipan: a little goes a long way, and the puzzle lasts for days, sometimes weeks. Cryptics sometimes send chills up one's spine, especially when the answer – which may take days to crack – is staring you in the face." Elizabeth adds: "I solve only one per day, if that. For me, it's more rewarding to construct a crossword, which, really, is akin to solving a complex puzzle. 'Can I make this puzzle that will rack solvers' brains in an entertaining way?'" She got into designing puzzles because of music: "I've studied music since I was eight, and play the viola in orchestras and chamber groups. Musical study, which instilled the daily discipline of practice and learning, inspired me to start making puzzles.

"My favourite part of it is hearing from solvers who say, "your puzzle drove me crazy. You're a horrible, awful, evil woman!' I love when that happens."

4. Will the crossword survive for another hundred years? It seems unlikely, as the world becomes increasingly besotted with electronic gadgets. Yet other "simple" pleasures abide, and indeed are enjoying a resurgence in popularity: sales of print books, for example, have risen, while those of e-readers appear to have flat-lined. Brian isn't sure about how the crossword will fare from now to 2113: "They are, up to a point, adaptable to new technology: many are available and can be solved online.

"Even so, I rather think that they have less appeal to the young: membership of the Crossword Club is certainly ageing. And I do just wonder whether they will still be flourishing in another hundred years." Elizabeth is more optimistic about the future, though. The proof of crosswords' lasting appeal, she says, is "in the behaviour of solvers – they keep coming back to the grid, day after day. And the dimensions are just right as a gaming surface. The crossword's rules and grid layout create a fair playing-field for everyone. They're perfect, in the same way a football field or tennis court are perfect."

 ## A. Reading

Rate this text for readability. Write the word/phrase of your choice into your copy.

VERY EASY ☐   EASY ☐   OKAY ☐   HARD ☐   VERY HARD ☐

 ## B. Writing

Imagine you write for a popular teenage magazine. You have been asked to write a feature article on a topic of particular interest to you.

1. Fill in the template on **page 68** of your **PORTFOLIO**, which will help you to understand the structure of a feature article.
2. Write your article into your **PORTFOLIO**.

Interviews

Journalists conduct interviews with people in order to find out exactly what their experiences, opinions and hopes are. People in the public eye are often interviewed about their latest projects or successes. You may have read an interview between a journalist and a sports star, an author, an actor or a musician.

The Athlone Ranger *by Stuart Clark*

The following is an edited extract of an interview with Robbie Henshaw, taken from *Hot Press* magazine's February 2015 issue.

Heads don't so much turn as spin 360° *Exorcist*-style as Robbie Henshaw walks through the Athlone Shopping Centre. It's obvious from all the waves and shouts of "Howaya, Robbie!" that the whole town is rooting for the local lad who still lives at home with his parents, and commutes daily to Galway where he's been having another outstanding season with Connacht who are in the unusual position come February of still being in both the Pro12 and Rugby Challenge Cup running.

The 21-year-old has also been hitting the M6 quite a bit recently (February 2015) in order to meet up with his Ireland teammates at The Aviva and Carton House where they've been preparing this past fortnight for the Six Nations and the Rugby World Cup that follows.

Following eye-catching Autumn International performances against South Africa and Australia, which resulted in two Southern Hemisphere scalps being claimed, Henshaw has been hailed by everyone from Alan Quinlan and Will Greenwood to Andy Ward and BOD himself as the natural inheritor of Brian O'Driscoll's number 13 shirt.

"Robbie's a very quick learner," O'Driscoll enthused after the Springboks victory. "He's taken a lot on board. Reads situations very well. Good basic skills. Nice feet. Powerful. He's a huge man – and an unbelievably nice fella!"

Henshaw, as low key and self-effacing off the pitch as he is aggressive and confident on it, sensibly refuses to get caught up in all the hype.

"I used to think, 'Oh no, cliché!' when sports people said, 'I'm taking it one game at a time' but that's absolutely what you have to do," he proffers. "Dave Kearney making his Six Nations debut last season and then playing every minute of every game gives myself and the other new lads something to aspire to, but you could be out training tomorrow and injure yourself. As well as the Autumn Internationals went I'm not a guaranteed starter and need, when I do get the opportunity, to keep proving myself."

His first full 80 minutes in a green shirt being full of intelligent runs, deft kicking and bone-crunching hits against an almost freakishly large Springboks side didn't come as any surprise to Connacht fans who'd known for the last two seasons that the lad's a bit special. It was no surprise to his peers either, with Robbie the first person to win back-to-back IRUPA Young Player of the Year Awards.

"I'd never thought of myself as being small until I ran out onto the pitch against South Africa," laughs Henshaw who at 6' 3' and 100kg is a bit of a man mountain himself. "They're probably the most physically dominant team in the world. Those first few hits felt like running into a train. I like to throw myself into tackles, not be fearful and stick my body on the line for the team too, but Tendai Mtawarira and the du Plessis brothers charging at you is terrifying! You know their coach has said to them, 'Go in hard on that young guy, he could be a weak link', so it's absolutely essential that you hang on in there and not let them intimidate you."

Robbie reckons his rugby education "doubled, maybe tripled" playing against the Springboks.

"You can train and talk tactics until the cows come home, but you don't really know what it's like to come up against a Southern Hemisphere team until they're in your face," he resumes. "It gives you a taster of how experienced and skilful they are compared to European players. They've direct runners and a good kicking game from the number 9. Hougaard, Willie le Roux and their number 13, Jan Serfontein, are real handfuls so the fact we were able to contain them for large parts of the game was a huge confidence booster, especially with a World Cup coming up.

"Australia weren't as big as South Africa, but they're probably more agile, skilful and difficult to defend against. It was surreal being on the same pitch as Israel Folau who I've been following for a few years. That fandom, if you like, goes out the window at kick-off. One of the things Joe Schmidt kept stressing was, 'You're here on merit. Just because they've more caps doesn't mean that they're better than you. Play your natural game; intimidate them.' He's really encouraging."

The first thing Robbie learned to play proficiently as a kid wasn't rugby or GAA, but the box-accordion.

"Traditional Irish music has always been a big craze in my family," he enthuses. "When I was about eight my granddad taught me this listening technique; he'd whistle into my ear and I'd play back what I'd heard. 'Ships in Full Sail', a jig, and 'Sally Gardens', a reel, were two of the first things I learned. I still get to take part in the odd session in Sean's Bar and my local in Coosan Point."

Indeed there's evidence of this on YouTube.

"Er, yeah, from a couple of years ago," he winces slightly. "I got to see Mumford & Sons in the Phoenix Park, which was great, and I'd be a big fan of Ben Howard as well. Christy Moore's a bit of an idol; I was at Oxegen with my dad when he sung 'Ride On' with Coldplay."

I'm sure if we asked nicely Christy would participate in an Irish Rugby World Cup song – we'd probably get his pal Damo Dempsey, too – with Robbie on accordion, naturally.

"That'd be amazing," he smiles. "My girlfriend's from Mullingar and knows Niall Horan – I've met him and he's a great guy – so perhaps he'd do it as well?"

Rugby and music industry people, let's make it happen! Is there a Connacht ghetto-blaster?

"There's actually a big sound system in the dressing-room on which you'd get everything from Sam Smith to Avicii, it's very varied. Ronan Loughney would put on a few easy listening songs; he plays the guitar himself."

The Henshaw household was also a sporting one with his dad playing rugby and his sister big into her Gaelic.

"I played soccer, rugby and Gaelic; I was a Westmeath minor footballer and at 17 had serious aspirations to make the step up to the seniors. Eventually though I had to decide 'Which sport?', and I chose rugby."

Did that have anything to do with the fact you get paid for playing one and not the other?

"Honestly, no," Robbie insists. "At the time I was enjoying my rugby that little bit more because of the physical aspect. If I retire from rugby and my body's still able I'd like to go back and have a stab at playing Gaelic for the county. That'd be a goal for me."

Henshaw was just 18 and barely out of school when he signed for Connacht. Did he have to bulk up to withstand the rigours of pro rugby?

"Yeah, the first thing they did was stick me on a programme. It was done gradually so as not to put on too much body fat, but I'm 15 kilos heavier than I was then which is a massive jump in weight. I do an hour in the gym twice a week, with an optional third session. It's quite short and sharp, but they're keeping an eye on you all the time to make sure you're not slacking."

If you'd been bold and scoffed a tikka masala and naan bread from the local curry house the night before, would they know?

"Yeah, you have to be sneaky about it if you're going to be naughty! You have to eat what's put out in front of you. Sometimes you might get a little treat for yourself after a game – you'd have your hood up hoping no one sees you – but there's not much that gets past our nutritionist, Ruth Martin, who keeps hammering the positive eating message home."

Asked to recall his full Connacht debut, Robbie sighs a little and says: "I had my school graduation the night beforehand – I got 435 points in my Leaving, which was way more than my parents expected! – and had to get up at five o'clock to fly to London, so there were no celebratory bubbles! It was against Harlequins at The Stoop and I managed to score a try, which was pretty cool. The step up in physicality was huge; I took a couple of hits that day which really hurt!"

Was there a Plan B in terms of what he'd have done if he hadn't made it as a professional sportsman?

"I was thinking P.E. teacher or sports surgeon, I've always been interested in the lower-limbs, so something in the podiatry field maybe."

Whilst you get the impression Henshaw is slightly embarrassed about the rave reviews he's been receiving – he visibly reddens when I tell him how big a fan former Ireland international Alan Quinlan is – it must be nice having Brian O'Driscoll in one's corner.

"Yeah, I really appreciate him backing me; it gives you that little extra bit of confidence, I've been lucky in terms of mentors; at my first Connacht training-session, Dan Parks, the Scotland international, came over and said, 'Don't worry, you're alright, you've got this.' From then on he was always talking to me on the pitch, helping me with what to do, where to go, whether to run or kick it back. He was really, really helpful in my development as a player...

Does he find it hard to switch-off after a defeat?

"Yes, I'm really bad at it," Robbie admits. "I can't let it go sometimes. You'll be reflecting in your head and going through what went wrong. I've been told by my parents, 'You need to try and ease off.' That's just the hold the game has on you though; you just want to win all the time and improve and do well."

 ## A. Reading

Rate this text for readability. Write the word/phrase of your choice into your copy.

VERY EASY ☐   **EASY** ☐   **OKAY** ☐   **HARD** ☐   **VERY HARD** ☐

B. Group Work

1. Your group are the editors. Figure out where to put the following sub-headlines.
   - Why Choose Rugby?
   - Jigs and Reels
   - Praise from BOD and Others
   - Little or Large Against South Africa
   - Introduction
   - Bulking Up
   - Australia
   - Plan B

2. Read the article again. Identify the questions that Robbie Henshaw was asked. Some are obvious and are printed in the text. Other questions are not shown in the article. Figure them all out and list them in order from the beginning to the end of the text.

3. Write two more questions that you would like to ask Robbie Henshaw if you were interviewing him.

TV and Radio Interviews

A TV interview is a conversation between a presenter and a person of interest that is broadcast on television.

Radio interviews are broadcast on the radio and are often available to listen to later online.

Although interviews on TV and radio often seem casual, they require a lot of preparation. Before they take place, researchers find out details about the interviewee and the questions are written based on that information.

A. Listening

Listen to the following interview with internet star Zoella on *This Morning*. As you listen, write down the questions she is being asked.

1. Do you think there is a logical order to the questions Zoella was asked? Explain your answer.

2. Suggest three other opening questions that you feel are necessary to allow Zoella to 'introduce' herself to the audience. Remember, some of the audience may never have heard of Zoella.

3. Imagine you are interviewing Zoella. Suggest three more questions you would like to ask her.

B. Listening

Listen to the poet Sarah Clancy talking to Rick O'Shea and reading her poem 'Solutions to Homelessness' on RTÉ Radio 1's *Poetry Programme*. If you were interviewing Sarah, what questions would you ask her?

Obituaries

An obituary is written about a person after they have died. It contains information on the kind of person they were, their career and other biographical details. In national newspapers, obituaries are written about famous or well-known people from all walks of life, such as novelists, politicians, film directors, poets and sports stars. In local newspapers, obituaries are often written about people who made a contribution to the local community.

The following obituary of Desmond O'Grady, a Limerick-born poet who died in August 2013, was published in the *Sunday Independent* shortly after his death.

Obituary: Desmond O'Grady, Poet and Translator

by Emer O'Kelly

1. Desmond O'Grady, the poet and translator who has died after a heart attack at the age of 78, was arguably, with the exception of Yeats, the most international of twentieth-century Irish poets. Indeed, to re-read just one of his collections in the knowledge that he is gone is to realise again the breathtaking compass, awe-inspiringly rigorous scholarship, and searingly sophisticated simplicity of his work.

2. *The Wandering Celt,* published by Dedalus in 2001 is the essence of internationalism and Europeanism. It traces our roots across Europe and through history: the legend of the wandering Jew transposed to Celtic Ireland through the ages on a trail which O'Grady himself followed when he left the country in the 1950s. He went on to live his life as an interrogation of language and learning, and to encounter "the reality of experience."

   In 'The Library', from that millennium collection, he writes:

   Greeks called it a receptacle of books,
   Romans a book place, Hindus
   the Treasure of the Goddess of Speech.
   Private libraries may achieve imperial reach.
   To evaluate people look at their libraries.

   That exposition lies at the heart of O'Grady's reality of experience: European culture meticulously defined. (A new and exquisitely beautiful translation of 'The Song of Songs' is part of the collection.)

3. Born in Limerick and educated in Roscrea, Co. Tipperary, Desmond O'Grady became inflamed by literature in his teens, much of it found and read "under the counter" as was necessary in Ireland then, including the works of Verlaine, Baudelaire and Rimbaud as well as Eliot, and of course Joyce. But he didn't wait as long as the Master to flee: he was still in his teens when he headed for Paris, and got a job in the bookshop Shakespeare and Company.

He soon made friends with Sartre, de Beauvoir, Picasso, and of course, Beckett, who, he recalled in later life, regarded him as "an acolyte".

He, on the other hand, regarded Beckett, who had recently published *Waiting for Godot*, as a high priest. Soon, the young Irishman was part of literary Paris.

4. When he married an exiled Iraqi Catholic they moved to Rome; O'Grady taught English there... and was the voice of Pope Pius XII on Vatican radio. He organised the 1966 Spoleto International Poetry Festival, and worked as secretary to Ezra Pound, who had become an admirer while in hospital in Washington, and the young O'Grady had sent him his work. O'Grady also worked as the European editor of the *The Transatlantic Review*.

5. When he and his wife separated (there were to be many more loves), he went to teach at Harvard, where he became friendly with Robert Lowell, and continued the links he had forged in Europe with the Beat writers Kerouac and Ginsberg. He took his doctorate at Harvard before returning to his spiritual home on mainland Europe and from there to Egypt and its ancient culture. And all the time he was absorbing, distilling and writing, while teaching at the American University in Cairo and at the University of Alexandria.

6. Desmond O'Grady published seventeen volumes of poetry as well as his numerous translations, all of which brought him acclaim and recognition throughout the poetic world. And while he returned to live in Ireland, settling in Kinsale for the last 20 years of his life, his monumental sense of the breadth of literature and broader culture never deserted him.

   In 'Millennium Elegy' (2001), he wrote:

   > Those reflected perspectives that face myself shock me dumb.
   > The Bang that made us all will suck us back to 0.
   > All life began, will end in naught.
   > Physics theory in three letters spells that.

7. It is a cosmic vision. Yet the tributes to him this week in Ireland have concentrated on the award of the Patrick and Katherine Kavanagh Fellowship in 2004, his membership of Aosdána, and the fact that the late Seamus Heaney admired his work. The great European sophisticate and scholar poet, renowned for his sense of humour, might have smiled wryly at the parochialism.

   Desmond O'Grady is survived by his daughters Deirdre and Giselle, his son Leonardo, his brother Tom and his sister Betty.

Letters to the Editor

Readers can write or email their views on an issue to the editor. The editor publishes some of these on the 'Letters to the Editor' page. This allows the public to express their views. Often other readers respond to letters in this section, agreeing or disagreeing with views expressed.

Examples of Letters to the Editor

Screenitis is the next big health scare. Avoid becoming a victim. Get a balance between 'screening' and normal, old-fashioned things like reading an actual newspaper and an actual book.
Melanie, Gweedore, Donegal

The government needs to stop wasting money on state cars, plush offices, travel junkets and instead use it where it's needed such as building more houses and alleviating the problem of homelessness.
Jason Daly, Dublin 4

It's appalling to read about farmer cruelty to animals. Keep convicting the heartless wretches and publicise their names.
Pablo Spears, Macroom, Cork

Format of Letters to the Editor

The way letters to the editor are presented in a newspaper varies. Some national newspapers begin the letter with 'Sir' if the editor is male or 'Madam' if the editor is female. Some put a heading on the letter and omit 'Sir'/'Madam'. The author's name and brief address is often given at the end of the letter. If the author prefers, this can be withheld and replaced with 'Name and address with editor'.

Letter from Virginia to *The New York Sun* About Santa

Read this short letter written in 1897 by an eight-year-old girl in New York, who wondered if there really was a Santa. Then read the reply that the newspaper wrote to her.

In 1897, Francis P. Church wrote the following response to a letter in *The New York Sun*.

We take pleasure in answering thus prominently the communication below, expressing at the same time our great gratification that its faithful author is numbered among the friends of *The Sun*:

Dear Editor—

I am 8 years old. Some of my little friends say there is no Santa Claus. Papa says, "If you see it in *The Sun*, it's so." Please tell me the truth, is there a Santa Claus?

Virginia O'Hanlon

Virginia, your little friends are wrong. They have been affected by the skepticism of a skeptical age. They do not believe except they see. They think that nothing can be which is not comprehensible by their little minds. All minds, Virginia, whether they be men's or children's, are little. In this great universe of ours, man is a mere insect, an ant, in his intellect as compared with the boundless world about him, as measured by the intelligence capable of grasping the whole of truth and knowledge.

Yes, Virginia, there is a Santa Claus. He exists as certainly as love and generosity and devotion exist, and you know that they abound and give to your life its highest beauty and joy. Alas! How dreary would be the world if there were no Santa Claus! It would be as dreary as if there were no Virginias. There would be no childlike faith then, no poetry, no romance to make tolerable this existence.

We should have no enjoyment, except in sense and sight. The eternal light with which childhood fills the world would be extinguished.

Not believe in Santa Claus! You might as well not believe in fairies. You might get your papa to hire men to watch in all the chimneys on Christmas Eve to catch Santa Claus, but even if you did not see Santa Claus coming down, what would that prove?

Nobody sees Santa Claus, but that is no sign that there is no Santa Claus. The most real things in the world are those that neither children nor men can see. Did you ever see fairies dancing on the lawn? Of course not, but that's no proof that they are not there. Nobody can conceive or imagine all the wonders there are unseen and unseeable in the world.

You tear apart the baby's rattle and see what makes the noise inside, but there is a veil covering the unseen world which not the strongest man, nor even the united strength of all the strongest men that ever lived could tear apart. Only faith, poetry, love, romance, can push aside that curtain and view and picture the supernatural beauty and glory beyond. Is it all real? Ah, Virginia, in all this world there is nothing else real and abiding.

No Santa Claus! Thank God! He lives and lives forever. A thousand years from now, Virginia, nay 10 times, 10,000 years from now, he will continue to make glad the heart of childhood.

 ## Group Work

In groups, answer the following questions on the reply to Virginia's letter.

1. Figure out the meaning of words you are not familiar with.
2. Figure out the argument the writer makes in support of the view that there is a Santa.
3. List the author's arguments for believing in Santa, using brief points/summaries.
4. What impression do you get of the author of the reply?

Online Journalism

Nowadays, many people get their news and entertainment from online news sites, such as *TheJournal.ie* and irishtimes.com, rather than from printed newspapers.

Blogs, and 'microblogs' like Twitter, are also a useful source of up-to-date information about what is happening in the world.

 ## Group Work

1. What are the pros and cons of getting your news online instead of from printed publications?

2. Why do you think people write blogs about their hobbies, such as fashion or sports?

3. Is someone who writes a blog about politics or sports the same as a journalist who writes about these topics for a newspaper?

4. Do you think online journalism will ever completely replace printed news?

Advertising

Advertising aims to persuade you to buy a product or service. The language of persuasion is used in text and in visuals. Notice how people in advertisements are usually good-looking and flawless! Advertising often tries to persuade us to like and want particular brands or products by encouraging us to think that they will make our lives easier or better.

 ## Writing

List the types of media used to advertise. Search until you think you have identified as many sources as possible for advertising. Compare your list with the person beside you.

Internet Advertisements

Internet advertisements are visual, colourful and often animated. They are designed to be difficult to ignore.

Banner advertisements appear at the top of the internet browser page. You might have noticed ads in the sidebar if you are on Facebook, or how YouTube often plays a few minutes of advertising just before you watch a clip.

Pop-up ads literally pop up on the web page you are visiting or in a new page or browser. These ads often flash to grab your attention while you are accessing your social media or emails.

Television Advertisements

Television advertisements are visual and aural and have an instant impact on the viewer. Some are enjoyable, funny, clever and entertaining, while others are simply boring or ineffective. Think about television ads that you like and ones that you dislike.

A. Group Work

Carry out a simple survey to find out your class group's three favourite television ads. List the features of these ads that make them enjoyable or effective.

Identify the features of quality:

- What makes the ads effective? Consider music, storyline, use of child/animal/drama/dance, emotional appeal, etc.

- Who is the target audience?

- To what extent are the ads convincing or successful? Try scoring them out of 10.

You could make a table like the one below to record the features you observe. The 2014 John Lewis Christmas ad is given as an example. You can watch it on YouTube.

Advertisement: John Lewis Christmas 2014	Features
Plot: beginning	Boy plays with penguin, imaginary friend (snow/painting)
Plot: middle	Boy realises penguin seeks love and companionship
Plot: end	Boy gives penguin a partner as a Christmas present
Music	Emotive, sad, uplifting – 'Real Love' by John Lennon, covered by Tom Odell
Visual appeal	Lots of blue tones, Christmassy (lights, tree, snow, etc.)
Target audience	Christmas shoppers and children
Audience response	Happiness, tears
Overall impact	Warm, feel-good ad
Other features/comments	

 ## B. Group Work

On **page 72** of your **PORTFOLIO**:

1. Use the above example to analyse two more 2014 Christmas ads, such as Sainsbury's or Burberry, available on YouTube.

2. If possible, create an ad for television.

   What will you need?

   - A product or service you wish to advertise.
   - A device to film the ad and capture the sounds and visuals effectively (your phone would do fine!).
   - Actors, costumes, props, lighting, etc.
   - Technical knowledge to edit the advertisement.

Print Advertisements

Print ads can be different sizes, such as a full page, a half page and so on. The more space required in a newspaper or magazine, the more it costs the company placing the ad.

Content of an Advertisement

- **Words:** The words in an ad are called 'copy'.
- **Visuals:** The images or pictures.

Copy

There may be any of the following copy in a print advertisement:

- Name of product/company
- Caption
- Slogan
- Details about the product or service
- A form to fill in
- A coupon or token to cut out
- Terms and conditions (known as 'T&Cs')

- Text in tiny print giving extra information
- Rules (if it's a competition)
- Price
- Call to action (for example, 'call now')
- A comparision to a competing product
- A logo
- A quote from a satisfied customer or maybe even a celebrity.

Techniques used to make an advertisement effective include:

- Original idea in terms of visuals
- Text
- Slogan
- Layout
- Colour
- Price
- Special offers.

Factors to Consider When Designing a Print Advertisement

- Who the target audience is and how the advertisement will best appeal to them.
- Visuals, i.e. whether or not to include an image of the product.
- What text to use and how much.
- What colours to use and where.
- Which fonts to use.
- How to lay out the visuals and the text.
- How to maximise visual impact.
- Whether to use puns (a clever play on words, using double meanings) or parodies (a funny imitation of something else).

Sometimes a picture paints a thousand words. Look up ads that rely on visuals more than copy; for example, the advertisement for Nike which was simply a page, coloured black with a white tick (the Nike logo) on it and a tiny piece of text.

Study the following adverts and identify the strengths and weaknesses in them.

 A. Literacy Questions

1. In your opinion, what is the most striking feature of the advertisement below? Explain your answer.

2. Who is the target audience/market? Explain your answer.

3. Imagine you work for an advertising agency. You have been asked to improve the advertisement. Suggest at least two improvements that might make the advertisement more effective.

64th Festival | **21 October – 1 November 2015**

Koanga
DELIUS
21, 24, 27, 30 OCT

Guglielmo Ratcliff
MASCAGNI
22, 25, 28, 31 OCT

Le Pré aux clercs
HÉROLD
23, 26, 29 OCT, 1 NOV

ShortWorks

The Portrait of Manon
MASSENET
22, 25, 28 OCT

Hansel and Gretel
HUMPERDINCK
23, 26, 29, 31 OCT

Tosca
PUCCINI
24, 27, 30 OCT, 1 NOV

Plus recitals, concerts, talks, lectures.

TICKETS NOW ON SALE
Online: **Wexfordopera.com**   Phone: **1850 4 OPERA**

Winners of the Best Opera Production and Audience Choice Awards at the 2015 Irish Times Irish Theatre Awards

Join the Conversation
#WexfordOpera

B. Literacy Questions

1. In your opinion, what is the most striking feature of the advertisement below? Explain your answer.

2. Who is the target audience/market? Explain your answer.

3. Imagine you work for an advertising agency. You have been asked to improve the advertisement. Suggest at least two improvements that might make the advertisement more effective.

C. Literacy Questions

1. In your opinion, what is the most striking feature of the advertisement below? Explain your answer.

2. Who is the target audience/market? Explain your answer.

3. Imagine you work for an advertising agency. You have been asked to improve the advertisement. Suggest at least two improvements that might make the advertisement more effective.

Branding

A brand is a name, logo or design that clearly identifies a company or product. Companies use colour to encourage the consumer to remember their product. For example, mobile phone companies: Vodafone uses red and Meteor uses orange.

Many other companies also work colour into their branding. For example, Aer Lingus uses green and Lidl uses a yellow circle against a blue background.

Logos are used for instant recognition.

Slogans are easy to remember. They are purposely 'catchy' and give immediate brand recognition:

- McDonald's – 'I'm lovin' it'
- Tesco – 'Every little helps'
- Centra – 'Brighten up your day'
- Dunnes Stores – 'Always better value'
- Spar – 'Under the tree at Spar'
- Toyota – 'Best built cars in the world'

Endorsements are when companies use celebrities to promote their product. Celebrities get paid for endorsing products or services. For example, Cheryl Fernandez-Versini endorses L'Oréal; George Clooney endorses Nespresso; Amy Huberman endorses Newbridge Silverware; and Imelda May endorses the Credit Union. Can you think of other examples?

Classified Advertisements

These are small advertisements in the classifieds section of the newspaper. They are classified (organised) according to whether they advertise cars for sale, business opportunities, jobs available, holiday homes for rent or public notices. Each advertisement is listed in alphabetical order in each category.

 A. **Research**

Research the following:

1. The cost of placing a classified advertisement in your local newspaper. Find out the cost of placing an advertisement for one week only or for a series of weeks.

2. The cost of full- and half-page advertisements in a popular Sunday newspaper.

3. The cost of quarter- and half-page advertisements in a national daily newspaper.

 B. **Writing**

Imagine that you need to place classified advertisements in the local newspaper to advertise the following:

- Four-bedroom detached holiday home in Rosslare Strand, available to rent in the summer. All bedrooms ensuite. June €600 per week. July €700 per week. August €800 per week. All mod cons. Sleeps 8. No pets allowed. 5 minutes from the beach. Enquiries to Kaleb 080-5566777.

- Audi 6 car for sale. Only one previous owner. 2015. 30,000 km. 6-speed. Manual. Diesel. Saloon. Isofix, CD player, Servotronic steering, Bluetooth. Alloy wheels. Mint condition. Beautiful dark brown leather upholstery. Genuine reason for sale: emigrating to Australia. Bargain price. Taxed until end of the year. Tel. Lisa 080-9996669.

- Rapidly expanding business requires driver urgently to drive buses and trucks in Ireland and Europe for travel and for commercial purposes. Full, clean driving licence essential. Minimum experience required of three years. Must be willing to work unsocial hours and be away from home for long periods of time. Excellent remuneration and benefits for suitable applicants. Tel. Bob immediately 080-09090987.

Write out the text of each advertisement. Reduce the number of words used above. Keep the text concise but include the most necessary details. Advertisements are charged based on the word count. More words take up more column inches in the newspaper and these inches cost!

Compare your ads with your friends'. Count the words and work out the cost of placing your ads in a local or national newspaper.

Radio Advertising

Radio advertisements have many of the same features as print advertisements but must appeal to the sense of sound only, so they use dialogue and music to grab listeners' attention.

A. Listening

Listen to the following ad from the Irish Epilepsy Association.

1. What details have you learned from the ad?
2. What features of a good ad can you identify?
3. What type of ad is this? Is it selling a product?

B. Listening

Listen to the following ad from the GAA.

1. What is the ad about?
2. What features of a good ad can you identify?
3. What kinds of radio stations and programmes do you think this ad would play on?

C. Writing

Write a script for your own radio ad. You can inform your audience about an important topic or talk about a product that they should buy.

Remember to use the RAFT strategy: Who are you? Who are your audience? What is your format? What is your topic or message?

D. Oral Language

With a partner, plan and record the ad you have written. See what sounds you can use in the ad to make it appealing for listeners.

Travel Writing

Travel articles are written about a person's experiences and opinions of a place they have visited. They are the written version of the holiday programmes on television. A well-written travel article allows the reader to imagine themselves in the location – they can almost see the sights, hear the sounds and experience the local smells. Travel articles also offer advice on hotels, restaurants, tourist attractions, shopping and the cost of travelling to an area.

Wild West Arizona – Bucket List Perfection

by Constance Harris

1. All my life I have wanted to visit Arizona, see the Grand Canyon and experience the desert.

   I attribute this passion to a life-long love of Westerns: John Ford's epic, *The Searchers*, TV's *Rawhide* and *The Lone Ranger*. Good versus evil, little guy versus big guy, innocence over exploitation, are always compulsive themes.

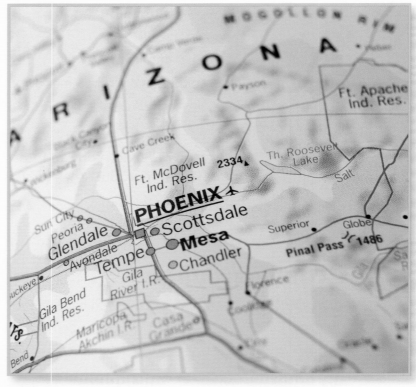

2. Arizona is a state with a fantastic history of frontiersmen and women, be it Native American, the preservation of heritage, the development of the railroad and hotels, photography, art, architecture and more.

   Arizona was founded after the end of the Civil War in the 1880s. Physically, it is made up of vast expanses of dry plain, dramatic, rocky, mountains and lush desert plant life. There is very little water above ground, although the Native Americans did build a system of canals around Phoenix, the capital of Arizona, to irrigate their fields that are still used today.

3. It's impossible not to fall in love with this desert landscape with its prickly, sometimes painful, but entirely beguiling, plant life, rattlers (yes, the snakes) and scorpions.

   Thankfully, I didn't see the latter two on my wanders, but the land does now live in my dreams and I definitely want to return.

The moment you get off the plane in Phoenix, the gorgeous, warm, sweet, dry air fills your lungs and relieves them of the damp oppression of Irish weather. I now understand why so many northern Americans (Arizonians call them Snow Swallows) holiday in the state from autumn through to spring. It's a fast-growing city of only about sixty years of age and the people are friendly and open.

4. We stayed in the Pointe Hilton Tapatio Cliffs Resort, a four-star, family-friendly hotel (also loved by golfers), built in the Spanish Hacienda style. It has several pools, a lovely terrace restaurant and they do a fabulous breakfast.

   A great introduction to this unique land is the Desert Botanical Gardens, which we visited on our first day. After an hour of not too strenuous walking and learning, you can then feel entitled to enjoy a pretty excellent nosh up in their restaurant, Gertrude's.

   A nice dovetail then would be to visit the Heard Museum, the best Native American history and culture museum I have visited in America so far and well worth a visit. I recommend you start from the first floor and work your way down to best understand the Native American experience since the white man came.

5. Arizona is Indian country – Apache, Hopi, Navaho, Pino – but the only one I met on my trip was the tour guide at the Heard. Did you know the Choctaw tribe raised and sent money to Ireland to buy us food during the Great Famine, because they saw us as their brothers?

   The more time you spend in Arizona, the more tribes you learn of and of the division between Native American culture and mainstream America. There are plenty of reservations (some with casinos) and you can seek permission from the relevant tribe to visit them. Our plan was to visit the Grand Canyon and do some nice treks along the way.

6. As you leave Phoenix, the Sonorian desert landscape opens up to you – high-ridged mountains in a dusty, sunny, haze surround, seemingly only populated by the Saguaro, the state's iconic, very tall cacti.

   We drove along route 87 to Flagstaff and the Grand Canyon National Park. Passing through little towns like Pine, Bishop and Strawberry, we got a feel for small community life here. Some were very rural, dirt track type towns with general stores and little street markets of local crafts and food and where men sold dogs. It was all so far away from the 'super' retail park reality of urban America...

Flagstaff, on route 66, is a lovely and interesting town to stop in and rest a while. It's a college town, full of young people, hip, vintage and designer clothing, niche sweets, candles and spiritual stores, Native American art galleries and some cool restaurants such as Pasto Cucina Italiana.

It also has a fantastic observation centre, The Lowell Observatory, which I highly recommend as the night sky is stunning.

We stayed at the Little America Hotel, a friendly relaxed place that does a great breakfast. Around here, it is too cold for snakes and scorpions: the wildlife is more likely to be brown bear, elk and squirrels, due to the lush Ponderosa forest.

Between Flagstaff and the Grand Canyon south rim are vast plains, land you imagine buffalo once roamed, now stands empty except for a daisy chain of pylons. It's all blue sky and dried out golden grass. Then, in the distance, a kind of great wall appears to rise up before you in subtle hues of pink, earthy red, blue and purple. It's the Grand Canyon.

7. There is much to do in the Grand Canyon National Park so I recommend you decide up front how much time you want to spend. We walked a few short trails and visited some key sites such as the Watch Tower, at Desert View, designed by Mary Colter, and El Tovar, an historic hotel which has a local museum of the area and an excellent restaurant. If you want to experience the Canyon in depth, you can hire horses, ride down into it and stay in lodges on the canyon bed.

But the highpoint of the trip for this philistine and train junkie, was a three-hour train trip on the Grand Canyon Railway to Williams, on a mid 20th-century Pullman. Order the best tickets you can get – the carriages are amazing and diverse. The most expensive ticket buys you entry to the last carriage, luxuriously upholstered, with its own private bartender and you can stand outside, at the end of the train, like in *North by Northwest* and make like it is the end of the world. The train was even held up by bandits. I have never been happier.

Williams looks like a quiet kind of place. Actually, it was a lot of fun as it has some mad bars and cafes. We rested in the Grand Canyon Railway Hotel and enjoyed the nightlife.

8. Next day we drove to Scottsdale (which is conjoined with Phoenix as the two cities have expanded so much). Scottsdale was built in the days of the Wild West so it has older buildings and with it comes an old town attitude of feeling a little superior.

The main street is brimming with upscale art galleries, jewellery stores and restaurants. Chic cuisine is a big deal. We enjoyed a sublime lunch of Argentine tapas in The House Brasserie, which had just been nominated by the chefs in Arizona as their most rated restaurant.

On our last morning, we tried some kayaking and saw an American Bald Eagle. After, we went on to visit Frank Lloyd Wright's self-sufficient, planned, home Taliesin West. For the last night of any holiday, it would be hard to beat the romantic and luxurious experience of the Four Seasons Resort Scottsdale at Troon North. Fabulously set, nestling in a truly rugged, desert mountain landscape in what is fast becoming the new 'celeb' rural escape (Oprah has a house here), with its luxury spa, several restaurants, bars and pools, it was the perfect end to a trip of a lifetime.

GLOSSARY

North by Northwest: An American spy, thriller film directed by Alfred Hitchcock in 1959.

Frank Lloyd Wright: Famous architect from Phoenix. He believed in organic architecture.

How to Write a Travel Article

Notice the structure and format in the 'Wild West Arizona' article:

Paragraph 1	Personal aim/ambition: 'All my life I have wanted to…'
Paragraph 2	History of Arizona: we get the background and context.
Paragraph 3	Personal opinion: '… fall in love with… I definitely want to return'.
Paragraph 4	Phoenix: hotel details and what to visit.
Paragraph 5	Indian tribes.
Paragraph 6	Journey to the Grand Canyon: Flagstaff.
Paragraph 7	The Grand Canyon and Williams.
Paragraph 8	Scottsdale and conclusion.

 ## A. Reading

Rate this text for readability. Write the word/phrase of your choice into your copy.

VERY EASY ☐   **EASY** ☐   **OKAY** ☐   **HARD** ☐   **VERY HARD** ☐

 ## B. Writing

Choose a location that you know and like. Write a travel article on it, using the template on **page 74** of your **PORTFOLIO**. Use the Arizona article above as a guide. Aim to write one page.

St Lucia: Once More Unto the Beach

by Barry Egan

After approximately my second spiced rum, I'm slowly starting to feel like a local in St Lucia. (I'm possibly even picking up a bit of the French-Creole Patois, mon.) Equally as slowly, but surely, the sun is beginning to set and I'm standing at the counter of a beautifully ramshackle bar in Soufrière, discussing the music of Burning Spear with a Rastafarian fisherman. Back-lit with the golden glow of sunset, my new Rasta friend is more interested in Ireland, 6,366 kilometres away. He wants to know about Bono and U2. More often than not in life, it appears my pockets have more holes in them than money but here, tonight, you don't need much to have a few drinks in the golden sun in a little fishing village with rainforest behind you and a volcano rising out of the sea in front.

I can see my wife walking out of the aforesaid sea in her itsy-bitsy bikini – like a County Dublin version of Ursula Andress in *Dr. No.* I say goodbye to my Rasta mate and join my wife for a quick dip. The sea twinkles like jewels. It is also like a bath and the colour of pure turquoise. (For the record: courtesy of the sun, I'm the colour of pure pink. I look like a prawn in shorts with ginger hair. For the record: She Who Must Be Obeyed is already in possession of a rich suntan, despite this being only our third day.)

When wifey and I look up from the warm waters, we can see the towering twin peaks of the Pitons – the national symbol of the country, these two volcanic spires, 770 and 743 metres high respectively, jut straight out of the ocean floor as if put there by magic. You'd be hard pressed to find a better view anywhere else in the world. That said, exhilarating views are *de rigeur* in St Lucia.

An hour later, in the ultra-fabulous Ladera hotel high up in the mountains we are looking down on the sea and eating fresh fish (Cajun-marinated snapper and tuna with flavours to die for) in the hotel's world-famous, three-level, open-air restaurant Dasheen. (St Lucia is full of sublime restaurants offering field-to-fork, or sea-to-fork, menus. Everything in the Caribbean is natural – apart from maybe the occasional surgically enhanced Californian glamour puss lying on a beach near to you.) After dinner, we go for a midnight stroll through Ladera's sumptuous property. There are a million stars in the Caribbean sky. It is like a giant spaceship overhead with all its lights on in the otherwise pitch-dark sky. It is impossible not to feel in some way entranced by the astrological wonder of it all. We've just embarked on the adventure of a lifetime, even the tropical adventure of a lifetime, here in the unspoilt beauty of St Lucia.

The surreal nature of what greets us the next morning at dawn is something to write home about: our suite (which we called home for six incredible days) has three walls – so the sun seems to rise directly in your open-air room. We open our eyes to see the Pitons in front of us and the sea 1,800 feet below us. What adds to the near-spiritual magic of the experience is that there is a very large plunge pool in our suite that we can recline in and look out on the dramatic views across this utterly enchanted paradise.

That said, everywhere you go, you see something that is visually or sensorily extraordinary on this most mountainous, and green, of the Caribbean islands. (We visited Castries, the anything-but-green capital of St Lucia, one afternoon and maybe it was our jet-lag but the place didn't particularly endear itself to us.)

New York, New Dream *by Maeve Higgins*

Maeve Higgins is an Irish comedian and writer. In this article for *The Irish Times*, she talks about her youthful expectations of New York City, the 'Big Apple', and how she felt about it when she finally moved there.

The dream was a fuzzy thrilled mess I'd created out of films and books. Back then, New York was no more real than any idea, an **abstract** place in a glowing future where I'd have ambition, adventures, a bunch of **sardonic** friends, a series of tragic romances and bagels, lots of bagels.

When I moved here, I began trying to figure out what New York truly is, deciding what to believe, learning how to actually be here. My first clue came from "Grand Central", a Billy Collins poem printed small on the back of my subway ticket. It begins "The city orbits around eight million centers of the universe." I think – that's it! New York is people.

I wander around Battery Park, looking out at the ferries crossing the Hudson to New Jersey. The Statue of Liberty has her back to me but I don't take it personally. I see One World Trade Centre, still under construction and obscured by a heavy mist, but still **formidable**, gigantic.

I look at all the people on the street and am about to get into a condition I call "Maudlin Maeve" when I suddenly see an old school friend, walking down Murray Street with her brand new baby.

Delighted by the coincidence, (I'm speaking for myself, Gemma seemed ... confused? Dismayed?) we have tea in her apartment and I admire the baby. She's an extremely cute baby, in fact the only way she could be cuter is if she had had big gold hoop earrings on.

I leave Gemma's building and realise that my phone is dead and I don't know how to get to my show. I start to panic, until I remember an old trick my forefathers used – they would take their headphones off and ask other humans the way.

I bundle onto a bus that says "Crosstown" and find a seat beside an old lady who is all wrapped up in a huge pink scarf, **chenille**. I ask her if the bus will take me to the Village. Her reply is muffled and musical. "It sure will, Baby." I wish I was her baby – I'd follow her everywhere and make her cuddle me non-stop.

The bus is warm and travels slowly along 8th Avenue, rocking slightly, making me drowsy. I look out the window as rickety noodle bars give way to solemn court buildings and think about the last time I was on a bus, back home in Ireland. Not in a misty eyed way, it was only three weeks ago.

It was the bus from Cork to Castletownbere, except it was Tuesday so the bus only went as far as Glengarriff. I'd asked the driver if there was another bus that would take me the last 30 miles to Castletownbere. That's when he said, Zen like, "I am the bus". Then he recommended hitchhiking the rest of the way, which I did.

After the show, I go for dinner with people and we get talking about who is from where. On my right there's a man who looks like he's from Carlow (1990s clothes, baffled face) but is actually a Russian Jew. On my left, a charmingly drunk woman who says she's definitely half-Korean and possibly part Native American. Opposite us sits a man from Guyana who's married to a woman from Trinidad, via Japan.

I think about where I'm from, Cobh via Carrigtwohill, and I can't help myself from saying: "This is so cool." As the words hit the air, I realise how obnoxious I'm being – collecting and commenting on my companions' **ethnicity** like they are an interesting new coffee blend...

Yesterday I was walking in the Upper West Side and heard a seven-year-old zinging a grown up. They were just ahead, carefully picking their way through the icy puddles, the man was carrying the boy's schoolbag and a small violin case. Waiting to cross at the lights, the ear-muffed boy said he didn't feel like practising that day. The man said: "Well, Jacob, if you wanna be great at something, you have to do it everyday." Jacob didn't miss a beat. "So you wanna be great at babysitting?" The man inhaled through his nose and said: "I guess so, Jacob, I guess so..."

I go to Grand Central Station to the Whispering Gallery – an arch that you whisper into and the sound travels right across the concourse to the person listening at the corresponding pillars – but I can't properly test it out because I'm on my own. I consider stopping one of the commuters racing by, but I don't know if they'd appreciate my revelations.

I've been ignoring my credit card debt for six years. I don't actually like bagels. I'm never quite sure what is real. Instead I look at my ticket again, at the last lines of the poem. "Lift up your eyes from the moving hive and you will see time circling under a vault of stars and know just when and where you are." That's exactly right, you know, because when I look up I see with total clarity that I'm not dreaming, it is now and I am in New York.

GLOSSARY

Zinging: Criticising sharply or attacking.

 ## A. Reading

Rate this text for readability. Write the word/phrase of your choice into your copy.

VERY EASY ☐   EASY ☐   OKAY ☐   HARD ☐   VERY HARD ☐

 ## B. Literacy Questions

1. What kind of a person is the narrator, Maeve Higgins? Use the information in the extract to support your answer.

2. Of all the locations and places mentioned in the extract, which one appeals to you the most? Explain your answer.

3. Identify and comment on one piece of descriptive writing that you like in the article.

4. Use a dictionary to find the meaning of the words in **bold**.

  ## C. Writing

Imagine you have been asked to write an article for your local newspaper about your experiences of a new place. It can be in Ireland or abroad. Model your article on Maeve's and write it on **page 76** of your **PORTFOLIO**.

- Begin with the sense of anticipation, hope and expectation before you go there.
- Include your first impressions/experiences when you arrive.
- Describe the place itself: parks, buildings, etc.
- Comment on the people.
- Describe an experience/trip/event/activity that you did there.
- Bring your own personality, sense of humour and opinion into the article.
- Think about a clever conclusion – Maeve brings hers back to the poem again.

An Astronaut's Guide to Life on Earth

by Chris Hadfield

Canadian astronaut Chris Hadfield was commander of the International Space Station (ISS) from December 2012 until May 2013. Here, in an extract from his book, he writes about journeying from Earth to the ISS.

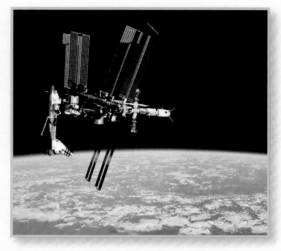

Getting up to the ISS really doesn't take that long: you could make it there from Earth in less than three hours if you had to, and recently, several crews have done so, in the interests of **efficiency**. But we were **allotted** more than two days, as Soyuz crews usually have been, and I was glad of that time to ramp down from the adrenaline of launch and get used to the reality of being in space. On Station, we'd be conducting and monitoring scientific experiments, maintaining and repairing the spaceship itself, communicating constantly with Mission Control—the schedule would be packed.

A full day in limbo, before all that started, gave us a chance to adapt and reflect, almost undisturbed. On the Soyuz, unless you're directly over Russia, you don't have communication with the ground. A few times a day, then, we'd give Mission Control in Korolev a summary of the status of the vehicle, and they'd give us any data we needed for rendezvous and docking. Otherwise: peace and quiet. We were alone.

I woke at 5:30 DMT (Decreed Moscow Time) and quickly calculated: seven hours of sleep. I felt rested, though puffy-faced and congested—typical **adaptation** symptoms. My joints ached somewhat after being motionless for so many hours during launch and I had a bit of a headache, but the main thing I was aware of was a quiet sense of joy.

The night before, digging through the storage locker by his seat in the re-entry capsule, Tom had discovered cards from our spouses. I'd saved mine, tucking it away in my left leg pocket. Now, while the sun was coming up, I wanted to read it. As I opened the envelope, two small paper hearts floated out, turning slowly and catching the sun's rays. I trapped them carefully in my hand and held them as I read Helene's words. I decided those hearts would keep me company in my small sleeping pod on the ISS over the next five months, delicate and vivid reminders of my life on Earth.

By this point Tom was waking too, so we rooted around for nasal spray and anti-nausea pills in the large toolbox-sized metal box called, prosaically enough, container #1. Roman was also stirring. We took turns peeing, then retrieved breakfast: canned cheese bread, dried fruit and a juice box. Coffee would have been nice, we agreed, but we'd have it soon enough, in pouches, on the ISS.

Roman was already moving quickly and energetically, smoothly efficient, as if his last long stay in space had been only yesterday. This Soyuz was his, and he treated it with **proprietary** care and respect. He soon settled down to watch the old Soviet comedies from the 1960s that Energia had loaded on his iPod. Tom was unobtrusive, solicitous and clearly happy to be back in space. He moved more deliberately and patiently, ever helpful. I felt relaxed and lazy, like a bubble in a languid stream. I took off my Omega Speedmaster watch to play with it in weightlessness. With a little push it became a metal jellyfish, the strap pulsing in and out like a living thing.

My body was starting to remember zero gravity, which, when you get used to it, is like being on the best ride at the fair, only it never stops. You can flip and tumble and float things across the spaceship, and it never gets old. It's just a constant, entertaining change of rules.

And as my vestibular system adapted during our day of downtime, I started to be able to look out the window for longer and longer periods of time. The world was rolling by underneath, every place I'd ever read about or dreamed of visiting streaming past. There was the Sahara, there was Lake Victoria and the Nile, snaking all the way up to the Mediterranean. Explorers gave their lives trying to find the source of the Nile, but I could detect it with a casual glance, no effort at all.

The night sky was beautiful, too: fine-spun necklaces of countless tiny lights dressed up the jet-black cloak covering Earth. Looking out on the second day of our mission, I became aware that in the far distance, there was a distinctive-looking star. It stood out because, while all the other stars stayed exactly the same size and shape, this one got bigger and bigger as we got closer to it. At some point it stopped being a point of light and started becoming something three-dimensional, **morphing** into a strange bug-like thing with all kinds of appendages. And then, isolated against this inky background, it started to look like a small town.

Which is in fact what it is: an outpost that humans have built, far from Earth. The International Space Station. It's every science fiction book come true, every little kid's dream realised: a large, capable, fully human creation orbiting up in the universe.

And it felt miraculous that soon we'd be docked there, and the next phase of our expedition would begin.

GLOSSARY

Soyuz: The name of the space shuttle they are travelling in.

Rendezvous: French for meeting at an agreed time and place.

Prosaically: Unimaginatively, something ordinary and commonplace.

Retrieved: Brought back from somewhere.

Unobtrusive: Not attracting attention, not conspicuous.

Solicitous: Showing interest or concern.

Languid: Relaxed, perhaps lazy, very little movement or effort made.

Vestibular: In the inner ear, related to sense of balance.

Appendages: Things added to or attached to something bigger or more important.

 ## A. Reading

Rate this text for readability. Write the word/phrase of your choice into your copy.

VERY EASY ☐   **EASY** ☐   **OKAY** ☐   **HARD** ☐   **VERY HARD** ☐

 ## B. Literacy Questions

1. Where exactly was Chris Hadfield travelling to? Use quotes to support your answer.
2. Explain why the astronaut had 'a packed schedule'.
3. List the adaptation symptoms Chris experienced.
4. Explain how Chris felt about 'the world rolling by underneath'.
5. Identify two examples of good descriptive writing in the extract that appealed to you. Explain why you like them.
6. Find the meaning of the words in **bold**. Write down the meaning that most suits the context it is used in the extract.

Read and Enjoy

Buen Camino! *by Natasha Murtagh and Peter Murtagh*

The Camino de Santiago is a pilgrim trail in Europe that many people walk in order to spend some time reflecting on their life or their faith. In this extract from *Buen Camino!*, Natasha, a girl from County Wicklow who is walking with her father, talks about how the pilgrimage is starting to change how she thinks about her life and home.

Finally, after about two hours of nothing along the way, and nothing in my stomach, I smelt meat, and heard Beyoncé. I looked up, and there, perched on the side of the road was a beautiful sight. A large white van opened up into a café, with a man beside it, cooking burgers and hot dogs on a BBQ and playing Beyoncé music. If I hadn't been dehydrated, I probably would have cried with happiness. But before I could even celebrate, I see Dad in the distance walking straight by. I would have happily dined without him except he had all the money. I didn't. And he was too far ahead to shout at. Trying not to look in, or breathe, I walked by. I tried to cheer myself up by thinking of a couple of fainting goats, but it didn't work.

Eventually, I began thinking of other things. I began thinking of home. And I started to realise something for the first time. The urge to sign onto Facebook, and see what I was missing, had died. The yearning for a juicy gossip text from Andrea, or one of my other friends, had disappeared. It no longer interested me. I was feeling something different about home. I didn't know whether it was fear of change, or fear of reality. On the Camino I've been surrounded by such selfless, good-hearted, and good-intentioned people for so long, that some things about my life back home don't seem appealing. My life is filled with brilliant people whom I couldn't love more, and I wouldn't change any of them. But my life is also filled with things like *The Hills,* MTV and *Big Brother*. And there are also people in my life at home I encounter that are selfish, greedy and unkind. I was feeling for the first time that I had escaped something. And the fact I didn't realise this earlier, meant to me that I was slipping into a world where this was accepted by me.

When I ask people why they are doing the Camino, many of them say to escape the bad things at home. This hadn't been a main reason for me, and now I'm thinking, maybe it should be. My thoughts along the way have changed. They are less materialistic, and I'm finding I get more lost in my surroundings, rather than my thoughts. The littlest things are making me happy and I notice small things more than ever. I'm not saying I don't enjoy hearing from home, I'm just saying I can feel the Camino is changing me. And it's changing me in a positive way. I'm really happy.

After the longest 17 kilometres of my life, I came crawling into a small café in a town, where I found Dad, happily perched at the bar, with a *bocadillo*, a *café con leche* and a very large cognac. "I've earned this," he said with a big smile as a laughing Swedish woman took his picture. I had a cup of tea and a Coke. We sat there for nearly an hour, and then moved on, with Charlie, a 31-year-old Englishman, who looks creepily like Ralph Fiennes.

In the next town, we came to a bar where we found Andrew, Gary, Reece, Steve and Jesús, the usuals. I also saw an internet connection, where I immediately Googled Ralph Fiennes so I could show Charlie. I was content for the rest of the day after my proud Doppelganger find. It was only three kilometres until we reached the place we planned to stay. Unfortunately it wasn't such a great 'town'. To put it in a nutshell, aside from the *albergue* the most that was on offer was a post box.

ASSESSMENT

Complete this assessment on **page 78** of your **PORTFOLIO**.

Written Assessment

A. Their/There/They're

Write in the correct word in each sentence.

1. _____ coats were soaking wet after the unexpected shower.

2. The chocolate cake is over _____ on the shelf.

3. _____ are nine million bicycles in Beijing.

4. _____ are six numbers in the Irish Lotto.

5. 'Where are _____ shoes?' asked George.

6. _____ going to Spain on holiday.   (6 marks)

B. Review

Write an interesting review of one of the following: film/book/CD/TV show/concert.

Peer Assessment
Compare your paragraphs and corrections with your partner.

C. Statistics

Present the following statistics visually. Use pictures and images, pie charts, bar graphs or percentages to present the information.

Junior Certificate Exam 2014:

- Total Number of students who sat the Junior Certificate exam in 2014: 60,327.
- 29,277 of these were female and 31,050 male.
- Leitrim had a total of 473 candidates sitting the exam, while Dublin had 15,078.
- In total, 44,688 Students sat English at Higher Level.
- 23,195 were female and 21,493 male.   (15 marks)

D. Advertising

1. Explain the following terms as they are used in advertising:

Target audience _____

Endorsement _____

Visuals _____

Copy _____

Slogan _____

ASSESSMENT

Logo _____

Caption _____

Pun _____

(2 marks each)

2. List two effective features in a print advertisement (magazine/newspaper advertisement). (2 marks each)

E. Newspapers

1. List two differences between tabloid and broadsheet newspapers. (2 marks each)

2. Newspapers print articles on topics that are newsworthy and of interest to readers. List six topics/subjects which feature on the front page and the inside pages of newspapers. (6 marks)

3. Suggest two things that newspapers could include if they wanted to attract teenage readers and encourage them to read the newspaper regularly. (2 marks each)

Oral Language Assessment Practice (60 marks)

Choose **one** of the following oral language tasks. Write out the text then deliver it orally. Your teacher will listen and complete an assessment sheet.

1. Introduction for a guest speaker to the class
Imagine that any person of your choice is visiting your class to talk about a particular topic. Give a two-minute introduction.

2. A short personal talk
Choose one of the following topics: My favourite hobby/book/film/concert/singer/group. Deliver the talk.

3. A persuasive speech
Choose from one of the following:
'Smartphones are a person's best friend' or 'The wonders of YouTube'. Deliver the speech.

4. An interview
Imagine you are being interviewed for admission to Transition Year. List three reasons why you wish to do Transition Year and convince the listener of how suitable you are for it and how good a contribution you can make.

5. A presentation
Give a three-minute presentation on your favourite celebrity, YouTube personality, TV or radio presenter, sports star, etc.

CHAPTER 5

Drama

❧ *My Learning Expectations* ❧

In this chapter I will:

- Learn to **understand** how drama tells a story
- See how **gestures, dialogue** and **live action work** in telling a story
- **Take part** in a play and **act**
- **Understand characters** by **analysing** what they say and do

Drama

Even when it is tragic, storytelling is always beautiful. It tells us that all fates can be ours, it wraps up our lives with the magic which we only see long afterwards. Storytelling reconnects us to the great sea of human destiny.

from *A Way of Being Free* by Ben Okri

In the Preface to his *Collected Plays*, Arthur Miller described how he felt watching an audience's reaction to a performance of his first successful play, *All My Sons*:

It made it possible to dream of daring more and risking more. The audience sat in silence before the unwinding of All My Sons *and gasped when they should have, and I tasted that power which is reserved, I imagine, for playwrights, which is to know that by one's invention a mass of strangers has been publicly transfixed.*

In many ways, studying drama is similar to studying fiction – we must pay attention to plot, characterisation and setting. However, we must also consider the staging of a play. Drama tells a story through performance. It uses many of the following features:

- dialogue
- action
- mime
- gesture
- lighting
- costumes
- props
- sound effects
- voiceovers.

When you attend a performance, you are participating and engaging in a live experience. The actors are performing in front of you. This may be considered a more real and tangible experience than watching a film. If an actor forgets their lines or trips and falls or drops something, it cannot be undone and usually the show must go on.

Drama is a very engaging way of telling a story. Before printing was invented, stories were passed down orally. Exceptional storytellers engaged their audiences with dramatic gestures, expressions and actions. Drama has evolved from the ancient classical Greek and Roman plays through to Shakespeare and to today's modern drama. Genres in drama include tragedy, comedy and tragicomedy. Shakespeare's well-known tragedies include *Macbeth*, *King Lear*, *Othello* and *Hamlet*. His comedies include *Henry IV, Part 1* and *Twelfth Night*, while *The Merchant of Venice* can be viewed as a tragicomedy.

Features of Drama

As you may remember from *Great Expectations 1*, drama uses a number of features to tell the story. Drama is a performance. The written script comes to life on stage in order to tell the story.

On the Page

- **Scripts** are generally written in acts and scene. The scenes move the story forward through its introduction/beginning and conflict/middle to its resolution/ending.
- **Stage directions** tell the actors the tone they should say their lines in ('sadly', etc.), where they should move to on the stage and what props they should use. They also give information about the sound effects and lighting.
- **Plot** is what happens in the play. It is the story.
- **Characters** are the people who feature in the story of the play. Sometimes a character is unseen, only spoken about by other characters.
- **Dialogue** is the words spoken by the characters.
- **Ensemble** plays include a cast of characters that are given roughly equal amounts of dialogue.
- **Narrators** tell the audience more about the story.
- **Conflict** occurs when characters disagree or deceive each other. This causes tension in the story.
- **Climax** is the highest point of tension in the story. It usually happens before the resolution/ending of the play.

On the Stage

- **Costumes** are the clothes actors wear on stage. They can tell us a lot about the setting and characters, such as what period the story is set in and which class a character is from.
- **Sets** show where each scene of the play is set. A play might use painted backdrops to show a countryside exterior or a cottage interior, for example.
- **Props** are the objects used by the actors during a performance, such as chairs, tables, drinking glasses and so on.
- **Lighting** is the lights used during a performance. It can help to show the setting of a scene or add to the atmosphere.
- **Sound** is the actors' voices and any other music or sound effects needed in a performance, such as an angry crowd outside.
- **Atmosphere** is crucial in a live performance in order to captivate the audience.

Extracts from Drama on the Prescribed List

In the following extracts from dramas on your prescribed list of texts, we will explore some of the different features of drama we have just revised.

Focus on Stage Direction

Pay attention to the stage directions in this extract from Seán O'Casey's 1923 play *The Shadow of a Gunman*.

 # The Shadow of a Gunman *by Seán O'Casey*

Seán O'Casey was born in Dublin in 1880, one of 13 children. His father died when he was six and he left school at 14. He joined the Gaelic League, learned Irish and supported the nationalist cause. Following unsettled years in Irish history from 1913 to 1922, O'Casey was inspired to write plays. Without formal training, he wrote *The Shadow of a Gunman* in 1923, followed by *Juno and the Paycock* (about the Civil War) in 1924 and *The Plough and the Stars* (about the Easter Rising) in 1926. In 1926, he won the Hawthornden Prize for *Juno and the Paycock*. The play was later turned into a film, directed by Alfred Hitchcock.

L-Left, C-Centre, R-Right

Room in a tenement house in Hilljoy Square. Upstage, L. wall, a small window. On the R. a door. C. back, a large window curtained with shabby lace curtains. To R. of window a washhand-stand with basin; in basin a jug containing water, a dirty towel over jug. To L. of window a dresser, with crockery. On the L. wall is the fireplace. In room are two beds, one to the R. of window having its head towards C. of stage; the other L. of window with its head to back of stage. L.C. downstage is a table. On the table are a vase containing wild flowers, a few books, writing materials and a typewriter charged for work. Beside table a chair facing typewriter. Another chair in front of bed R. on which clothes are hanging over back. At the head of this bed a large suitcase filled with bundles of knives, forks, spoons, braces, etc. On mantelpiece, above fireplace, is a statue of the Sacred Heart, and a small crucifix and a candle in candlestick

Davoren *is sitting at the table typing. He is about 30. There is in his face an expression that seems to indicate an eternal war between weakness and strength; there is in the lines of the brow and chin an indication of a desire for activity, while in his eyes there is visible an unquenchable tendency towards rest. His struggle through life has been a hard one, and his efforts have been handicapped by an inherited and self-developed devotion to "the might of design, the mystery of colour and the belief in the redemption of all things by beauty everlasting." His life would drive him mad were it not for the fact that he never knew any other. He bears upon his body the marks of the struggle for existence and the efforts towards self-expression*

Seumas *Shields, who is in the bed to the right, is a heavily built man of 35; he is dark-haired and sallow-complexioned. In him is frequently manifested the superstition, the fear and malignity[1] of primitive man.*

1. Evilness badness.

D. Pairwork

Figure out the plot/action. Chart it in sequence from the beginning to the end of the extract. For example:

First, Donal is writing at the table. Seumas wakes up late, around noon and…

E. Research

Imagine that you have been asked to write a paragraph/page for the theatre programme for *The Shadow of a Gunman*. The programme will be sold to audiences in New York during the play's two-week run. Your task is to explain the background and the context of the play to an audience who may not be very familiar with Irish history. They may also be unfamiliar with the colloquial (conversational) manner of speech that the Irish people had in the 1920s. Use the guide on **page 86** of your **PORTFOLIO** to help you to complete the task.

F. Oral Language

1. Act it out

Casting roles: Donal Davoren, poet; Seumas Shields, pedlar, disillusioned nationalist; Maguire, secret rebel, pedlar; Mr Mulligan, landlord; Woman who shouts to wake up Seumas.

Props: Two tables, typewriter, two chairs, large jug, basin, vase of flowers, small jug.

Costumes: Old-fashioned clothes to suit the 1920s. Make a list of what you need.

Soundtrack: What sounds will you need to make the action more real and credible?

2. Reflect on your experience

1. List any difficulties that your group had organising and performing the scene.
2. Briefly explain what worked well.
3. List any new skill or information that you learned from acting out the scene.

Focus on Conflict

Pay attention to how the opening scene of Nikolai Gogol's *The Government Inspector* introduces the conflict that the rest of the play will revolve around. Notice how the rapid dialogue adds excitement and sets up the story.

The Government Inspector *by Nikolai Gogol*

Nikolai Gogol was a dramatist, novelist and short story writer. Born in Ukraine in 1809, he enjoyed writing while in school and was influenced by his father, who wrote poetry and plays. Gogol's early poems were unsuccessful, so he turned to writing drama. In 1836, *The Government Inspector* was published and its success convinced him of his literary talent. His most famous short story is *The Overcoat*.

In the **Mayor's** *house. On stage are assembled the* **Charity Commissioner**, *the* **Schools Superintendent**, **Judge**, *the* **District Physician** *and the* **Mayor**.

Mayor	Well, gentlemen! I've asked you all here today because I've got some very nasty news for you. It looks as if there's a Government Inspector on his way to see us.
Judge	On his way . . . *here*?
Charity Commissioner	A Government Inspector?
Mayor	A Government Inspector from Petersburg. Under secret orders. And travelling – incognito[1]!
Judge	That's terrible!
Charity Commissioner	Dear God, what'll become of us!
Schools Superintendent	And under secret orders too.
Mayor	I knew something horrible was going to happen. I was warned. I had this dream, last night, about these rats. Huge black fellers, they were, I never seen such rats in my life. In they come, two of them, very slow . . . creeping closer and closer all night through. Then they give a horrifying sniff – and turn tail and walk off. And this morning, there was this letter from Chmikhov – *(To the* **Charity Commissioner***)* – you know him, Artemy Philipovich. Listen to this, now. 'Dear Friend and Benefactor' *(He mumbles, skipping through it.)* '. . . want to . . . tell you . . . five hundred roubles[2] . . . hasten to . .' Ah! here we are, 'and hasten to warn you that a Government official is on his way to inspect the province, and our district in particular. I have this from an absolutely reliable source. This Inspector is travelling incognito

1. Concealing one's identity.

2. Russian money.

. . . *(He looks up.)* – in-cog-nito-o d'you see? – *(He reads.)* – and introduces himself under a different name in each district. I know that you, like everyone else, have your little weaknesses, you're much too sensible to say no to the perquisites[3] of your office . . .'

(He coughs and looks around.) Yes, well, we're all friends here.

. . . 'so I advise you to take every precaution[4] you can, as he may turn up at any moment – if, indeed, he isn't already living among you – incognito! My sister Anna Kirilovna and her husband are staying with us. Ivan Kirilovich has put on a lot of weight and never stops playing the fiddle . . .' Yes well, the rest of it's just family matters, d'you see . . . There you are. Now you know.

Judge	This is incredible! What's it all about?
Schools Superintendent	Yes, Anton Antonovich, Why should they want to inspect *us*?
Mayor	It's the whim of fate, my friends. So far it's always been other districts, but our luck's changed now!
Judge	Anton Antonovich, it's my belief there's more to it than that. It's a political move, that is. It's my belief there's going to be a war, and they're sending an Inspector round to look for traitors!
Mayor	War? Traitors? What are you talking about? This isn't a frontier town, is it? You could gallop for three years without reaching a foreign country.
Judge	You're wrong, Anton Antonovich. The authorities in Petersburg and Moscow are cleverer than you think. They may be a long way away, but they know everything, let me tell you, *everything*!
	They are all terrified.
Mayor	Well, that's as may be, we shall soon find out; at least you've been warned. I've taken certain precautions myself, you'd best do the same, all of you. 'Specially you, Arte: Philipovich! *(To the **Charity Commissioner**.)* The Inspector, he's sure to visit your hospital, you'd best see it tidied up a bit. Give those patients of yours some clean night-caps, clean sheets, give them a good wash, last time I saw them they all looked like chimney sweeps!
Charity Commissioner	We haven't got any sheets.
Mayor	Well, buy some, you've been charging for them for the last twenty years, haven't you? And label your patients, put a notice over their beds in some foreign language – Latin, if you can – with a list of dates and diseases, that sort of thing. And stop them smoking that foul tobacco, a civilised man can't breathe in the place. You'd best throw half of them out anyway, you've got far too many, the Inspector'll think the doctor doesn't know his business.

3. Something that is required as a prior condition.

4. An action taken to stop something from happening.

Charity Commissioner	He's a splendid doctor, we've got everything nicely organised. Leave it to nature, that's what we say. There's no point in spending a fortune on expensive medicines. Man's a simple creature, if he's going to get well, he'll get well and if he's going to die, then he'll die. Anyway, the doctor's a German, he doesn't understand a word anyone says.
District Physician	*(beaming)* Ja. Onderstand everyt'ing!
Mayor	Ha! And you, Amos Fyodorovich, you'd best do something about that courthouse of yours, the place is like a farmyard. Tell the porter to move his geese out of the vestibule⁵ for a start, the petitioners have to sit there and have their feet pecked at for hours on end. Of course the porter should be encouraged to keep poultry, but couldn't you persuade him to keep them somewhere else? It's not the thing in a magistrate's court, d'you see. I've been meaning to speak to you about it for a long time.
Judge	Don't worry about that, I'll see he kills them today. Perhaps you'd come to dinner tonight, Anton Antonovich?
Mayor	*(ignoring the invitation)* Your courtroom, Amos Fyodorovich, it's full of rubbish! All your hunting gear lying about, riding crops in the dossier cupboard, boots up on the bench, it's a terrible sight. I know you're fond of hunting, but you clear all that away until this Inspector's been and gone, you can put it all back later. And that clerk of yours! Very clever man, I daresay, but he stinks of vodka day and night! It's not the thing for an officer of the law. That's another thing I've been wanting to speak to you about, only I keep forgetting. He ought to do something about it, eat garlic or onions or get Doctor Christian to give him some medicine.
District Physician	Ja, garlick. Gut! *(He beams.)*
Judge	He says it's his natural smell. He says his nurse dropped him when he was a baby, and he's smelt of vodka ever since.
Mayor	Well, if it can't be helped, it can't. I just thought I'd mention it, that's all. As for what Chmikhov calls 'our little weaknesses', that's not for me to talk about. No man is without sin, because that's the way the good Lord made us. Voltaire⁶ can say what he likes, but he's a sinner just the same.
Judge	Depends what you mean by 'sin', Anton Antonovich. There are sins and sins. I don't mind admitting I take bribes – but only thoroughbred puppies, you can't call that a sin.
Mayor	Thoroughbred puppies are still bribes.
Judge	But not sinful bribes, Anton, there's the difference. Now if a man accepts a fur coat worth five hundred roubles, or a shawl for his wife . . .

5. A hall or lobby or antechamber next to the outer door.

6. An eighteenth-century philosopher who criticised the establishment.

326

and came back to try and get the knife, risking being caught by the police. Maybe all those things are so. But maybe they're not. I think there's enough doubt to make us wonder whether he was there at all during the time the murder took place.

10th Juror   What d'ya mean doubt? What are you talking about? Didn't the old man see him running out of the house? He's twisting the facts. I'm telling you! *(To the 11th Juror)* Did or didn't the old man see the kid running out of the house at twelve ten? Well, did he or didn't he?

11th Juror   He says he did.

10th Juror   Says he did! *(To the others)* Boy-oh-boy! How do you like that? *(To the 11th Juror)* Well, did or didn't the woman across the street see the kid kill his father? She says she did. You're makin' out like it don't matter what people say. What you want to believe, you believe, and what you don't want to believe, so you don't. What kind of way is that? What d'ya think these people get up on the witness stand for — their health? I'm telling you men the facts are being changed around here. Witnesses are being doubted and there's no reason for it.

5th Juror   Witnesses can make mistakes.

10th Juror   Sure, when you want 'em to, they do! Know what I mean?

Foreman   OK. Let's hold the yelling down.

10th Juror   You keep saying that. Maybe what we need is a little yelling in here. These guys are going off every which way. Did hear the scream, didn't hear the scream. What's the difference? They're just little details. You're forgetting the important stuff. I mean, all of a sudden here everybody...

8th Juror   I'd like to call for another vote.

10th Juror   Listen, I'm talking here.

Foreman   There's another vote called for. How about taking seats?

Jurors *who are standing move towards their seats*

3rd Juror   What are we gonna gain by voting again?

Foreman   I don't know. The gentleman asked...

3rd Juror   I never saw so much time spent on nothing.

2nd Juror   *(mildly)* It only takes a second.

Foreman   OK. I guess the fastest way is to find out who's voting not guilty. All those in favour of "not guilty" raise their hands.

The 5th, 8th and 9th Jurors raise their hands

Still the same. One, two, three "not guiltys". Nine "guiltys".

7th Juror	So now where are we? I'm telling you, we can yakety-yak until next Tuesday here. Where's it getting us?
11th Juror	Pardon. *(He slowly raises his hand)* I vote "not guilty".
7th Juror	Oh, brother!
3rd Juror	Oh, now listen! What are you talking about? I mean, we're all going crazy in here or something! This kid is guilty. Why don'tcha pay attention to the facts. *(To the 4th Juror)* Listen, tell him, will ya? This is getting to be a goddamn joke!
Foreman	The vote is eight to four, favour of "guilty".
3rd Juror	I mean, everybody's heart is starting to bleed for this punk little kid like the President just declared it "Love Your Underprivileged Brother Week" or something. *(To the **11th Juror**)* Listen, I'd like you to tell me why you changed your vote. Come on, give me reasons.
11th Juror	I don't have to defend my decision to you. I have a reasonable doubt in my mind.
3rd Juror	What reasonable doubt? That's nothing but words. *(He pulls out the switch-knife from the table and holds it up)* Here, look at this. The kid you just decided isn't guilty was seen ramming this thing into his father. Well, look at it, Mr Reasonable Doubt.
9th Juror	That's not the knife. Don't you remember?
3rd Juror	Brilliant! *(He sticks the knife into the table)*
7th Juror	I'm tellin' ya, this is the craziest. *(To the **8th Juror**)* I mean, you're sittin' in here pulling stories outa thin air. What're we supposed to believe? *(To the others)* I'm telling you, if this guy was sitting ringside at the Dempsey–Firpo fight[3], he'd be tryin' to tell us Firpo won. *(To the **8th Juror**)* Look, what about the old man? Are we supposed to believe that he didn't get up and run to his door and see the kid tearing down the stairs fifteen seconds after the killing? He's only saying he did to be important. I mean, what's the point of the whole — —?
5th Juror	Hold it a second.
7th Juror	And the Milwaukee rooter[4] is heard from.
5th Juror	Did the old man say he ran to the door?
7th Juror	Ran. Walked. What's the difference? He got there.
6th Juror	He said he ran to the door. At least, I think he did.
5th Juror	I don't remember what he said. But I don't see how he could run.
4th Juror	He said he went from his bedroom to the front door. That's enough, isn't it?
8th Juror	Wait a minute. Where was his bedroom, again?

3. A famous fight in 1923 between World Heavyweight boxing champion Jack Dempsey and Argentinian boxer Luis Ángel Firpo.

4. A fan of the Milwaukee baseball team.

10th Juror	Down the hall somewhere. I thought you remembered everything. Don't you remember that?
8th Juror	No. Mr Foreman, I'd like to take a look at the diagram of the apartment.
7th Juror	Why don't we have them run the trial over just so you can get everything straight?
8th Juror	Mr Foreman...
Foreman	I heard you.

The **Foreman** *goes to the door and knocks*
The **Guard** *unlocks the door and enters*
The **Foreman** *confers briefly with him*
The **Guard** *exits and locks the door after him*

3rd Juror	All right, what's this for? How come you're the only one in the room who wants to see exhibits all the time?
5th Juror	I want to see this one too.
3rd Juror	And I want to stop wasting time.
4th Juror	If we're going to start wading through all that business about where the body was found...
8th Juror	We're not. Not unless someone else wants to. I'd like to see if a very old man who drags one leg when he walks because he had a stroke last year can get from his bed to his front door in fifteen seconds.
3rd Juror	He said twenty seconds.
8th Juror	He said fifteen.
3rd Juror	Now I'm telling you he said twenty. What're you trying to distort...
11th Juror	He said fifteen.
3rd Juror	How does he know how long fifteen seconds is? You can't judge that kind of thing.
9th Juror	He said fifteen seconds. He was very positive about it.
3rd Juror	He's an old man. You saw him. Half the time he was confused. How could he be positive about anything?

The **Guard** *unlocks the door and enters, carrying a large diagram of the apartment*
The diagram is a layout of a railroad flat. A bedroom faces the el tracks. Behind it is a series of rooms off a long hall. In the front room is an X marking the spot where the body was found. At the back of the apartment we see the entrance into the apartment hall from the building hall. We see a flight of stairs in the building's hall. Each room is labelled and the dimensions of each room are shown. The **Foreman** *takes the diagram*

*The **Guard** exits and locks the door*

12th Juror   I don't see what we're going to prove here. The man said he saw the boy running out.

8th Juror   Well, let's see if the details bear him out. As soon as the body fell to the floor, he said, he heard footsteps upstairs running towards the front door. He heard the upstairs door open and the footsteps start down the stairs. He got to his front door as soon as he could. He swore that it couldn't have been more than fifteen seconds. Now, if the killer began running immediately — —

12th Juror   Well, maybe he didn't.

8th Juror   The old man said he did.

7th Juror   You know, you ought to be down in Atlantic City at that hair-splitters' convention.

6th Juror   Listen, baseball, why don't you stop making smart remarks all the time?

7th Juror   My friend, for your three dollars a day you've gotta listen to everything.

10th Juror   *(to the **8th Juror**)* Well, now that you've got that thing in here, what about it?

8th Juror   *(to the **Foreman**)* May I? *(He takes the plan and puts it on a chair)* This is the apartment in which the killing took place. The old man's apartment is directly beneath it and exactly the same. Here are the el tracks. The bedroom. Another bedroom. Bathroom. Living-room. Kitchen. And this is the hall. Here's the front door to the apartment. And here are the stairs. Now, the old man was in bed in this room. *(He indicates the front bedroom)* He says he got up, went out into the hall, down the hall to the front door, opened it and looked out just in time to see the boy racing down the stairs. Am I right so far?

3rd Juror   That's the story, for the nineteenth time.

3rd Juror	Come on, willya! Let's get this kid stuff over with.

*They watch as the **8th Juror** reaches the last chair. He pretends to open an imaginary chain-lock and then opens the imaginary door*

8th Juror	Stop!
2nd Juror	Right.
8th Juror	What's the time?
2nd Juror	Fifteen — twenty — thirty — thirty-five — forty — forty-two seconds exactly.
6th Juror	Forty-two seconds!
8th Juror	I think this is what happened. The old man heard the fight between the boy and his father a few hours earlier. Then, while lying in bed, he heard a body hit the floor in the boy's apartment, and he heard the woman scream from across the street. He got up, tried to get to the door, heard someone racing down the stairs, and assumed it was the boy.
6th Juror	I think that's possible.
3rd Juror	Assumed? Now listen to me, you people. I've seen all kinds of dishonesty in my day — but this little display takes the cake. You come in here with your sanctimonious[5] talk about slum kids and injustice, and you make up some wild stories, and all of a sudden you start getting through to some of these old ladies in here. Well, you're not getting through to me. I've had enough. What's the matter with you people? Every one of you knows this kid is guilty. He's got to burn. We're letting him slip through our fingers here.
8th Juror	Slip through our fingers? Are you his executioner?
3rd Juror	I'm one of 'em.
8th Juror	Maybe you'd like to pull the switch.
3rd Juror	For this kid? You bet I'd like to pull the switch.
8th Juror	I'm sorry for you.
3rd Juror	Don't start with me now.
8th Juror	Ever since we walked into this room you've been behaving like a self-appointed public avenger.
3rd Juror	I'm telling you now! Shut up!
8th Juror	You want to see this boy die because you personally want it, not because of the facts.
3rd Juror	Shut up!
8th Juror	You're a sadist[6]!

5. Self-righteous.

6. A person who enjoys inflicting pain on others.

| 3rd Juror | Shut up, you son of a bitch! |

The 3rd Juror lunges wildly at the 8th Juror

The 8th Juror holds his ground. The 5th and 6th Jurors grab the 3rd Juror from behind. He strains against the hands, his face dark with rage

Let go of me, God damn it! I'll kill him! I'll kill him!

| 8th Juror | *(calmly)* You don't really mean you'll kill me, do you? |

The 3rd Juror breaks from the 5th and 6th Jurors, stops struggling and stares bitterly at the 8th Juror as the curtain falls

A. Reading

Rate this text for readability. Write the word/phrase of your choice into your copy.

VERY EASY ☐   **EASY** ☐   **OKAY** ☐   **HARD** ☐   **VERY HARD** ☐

B. Literacy Questions

1. Do you agree that people often say 'I'll kill you' but do not mean it? Give examples from your own experiences.

2. Having read the extract, what genre do you think the play fits into?

3. Use bullet points to list the events of the murder in the order in which they took place.

4. Make two lists. List one: the jurors who think the boy is guilty. List two: the jurors who have 'reasonable doubt'.

5. Find one aspect of the story that the 8th Juror is unconvinced about. Do you agree with him about this? Explain your answer and then discuss it with the class.

6. What kinds of attitudes do the jurors have? What do these attitudes suggest about their personalities? Try to describe each juror based on their words and actions.

   For example: The 8th Juror is determined to seek justice and wants to be convinced about the facts and details of the case. He is willing to work hard to give the boy a fair chance. He asks questions, he queries things, and he remains calm. The 10th Juror appears brash, loud and rash. He also has poor grammar: 'He don't even speak good English.'

C. Oral Language

In groups, dramatise the above scene.

Checklist

- ✓ How many characters are there?
- ✓ Do you need a narrator?
- ✓ Do you need a director?
- ✓ What can be used for props?
- ✓ Consider the costumes that might be worn in a production of this play.
- ✓ What do you need for sound and lighting?

| **Kipps** | Thank you, Mr Bunce! (*He clicks his fingers to the back of the theatre*) |

Instantly come the sound effects of a London street: cars, horses, shouts from street vendors, etc. The Actor is momentarily amazed. He listens for a while, then...

Actor	Recorded sound!
Kipps	Precisely. A remarkable invention, is it not?
Actor	Extraordinarily true to life! I could swear I was in a London street, attempting to negotiate the thundering traffic!
Kipps	And so, Mr Kipps, will our audience. No need to speak of cars and trams and horses, smoke and grime. No need in fact, for words. Just let the recorded sound be heard and they are there. Transported.
Actor	But the scene is to be in an office, is it not? Why do we have London's traffic flowing through an office?
Kipps	Why indeed? Mr Bunce! (*He clicks his fingers again*)

At once the traffic sound begins to fade and dissolves into the sonorous ticking of a long-case clock

| **Actor** | (*listening with a certain amount of awe*) Remarkable. |

The clock fades out. The street sounds return

| **Kipps** | (*with a superior smile*) The miracle of science, the hands of Bunce. He is particularly good at this sort of thing. And so to work. I am you, you are your clerk. I enter briskly, you are already at work. |

A. Reading

Rate this text for readability. Write the word/phrase of your choice into your copy.

VERY EASY ☐   **EASY** ☐   **OKAY** ☐   **HARD** ☐   **VERY HARD** ☐

B. Group Work

1. The real actor takes on the part of Mr Kipps. His reading of the manuscript brings the scene to life. Identify two examples of description from the text which help to bring the scene to life.

2. Research the extract from Shakespeare's *Hamlet* mentioned in this scene. Which act and scene is it from? Figure out why the real actor thinks it is suitable to include it in this story.

3. What does Mr Kipps hope to achieve by telling his story? Quote from the extract to support your answer.

4. Explain in detail how the real actor makes the office scene realistic. What devices does he use?

Section B

Actor   *(preparing to perform)* You must forgive me, this is not—

Kipps   —your forte. Quite. And it won't become so unless you attempt it. Begin. Just as we went through it all last night. (Calling to the back of the theatre) I thank you!

The London street sound gives way to the sonorous clock

Kipps *exits*

*The **Actor**, alias Tomes the clerk, stands working at a ledger. His desk might be the stool, or a pile of boxes. Whatever, it suggests discomfort*

Kipps *enters briskly. He tosses his briefcase on to the desk and sits*

Kipps *has learnt his part. The **Actor** struggles manfully, reading from the manuscript. The conceit is that although the **Actor** is unaccomplished, his enthusiasm for the task will grow through the early part of the enactment, in spite of his protestations*

	A foul day, Tomes.
Tomes	Yes, Mr Kipps. *(He sniffs)*
Kipps	November. The drearest month of the year. Lowering to the spirits.
Tomes	Yes, Mr Kipps. *(He sniffs)* This fog don't help.
Kipps	*(looking up from his desk to address the audience)* The thickest of London pea-soupers. A yellow fog. A filthy, evil-smelling fog, a fog that choked and blinded, smeared and stained. I worked at some dull details of the conveyancing[1] of property leases, forgetful for the moment of it pressing against the window like a furred beast at my back.

> 1. In law, preparing property documents.

Tomes *leaves his ledger, moves to **Kipps's** desk and knocks on it. **Kipps** looks up*

Tomes	Mr Bentley wishes to see you, sir.
Kipps	Straight away?
Tomes	Straight away, sir, if you would. *(He sniffs)*
Kipps	*(addressing the audience)* That sniff, incidentally, occurred every twenty seconds, for which reason Tomes was confined, in general, to a cubbyhole in an outer lobby.

Kipps *stands*

Actor	What now?
Kipps	Now you become Bentley.
Actor	Oh yes, of course. *(A beat)* Do I do all right? Will it pass?
Kipps	Excellent. We'll make an Irving of—
Actor	*(angrily)* Will you be quiet about Irving!
Kipps	Apologies. Carry on.

*The **Actor** sits the other side of the desk from **Kipps**, becoming **Mr Bentley** as he does so. He polishes his glasses*

Bentley	Sit ye down, Arthur, sit ye down.

Kipps *sits. **Bentley** spreads himself in a relaxed way, taking his time before he speaks*

	I don't think I ever told you about the extraordinary Mrs Drablow?

Kipps *shakes his head*

	Mrs Drablow. *(He takes out her will and waves it at* **Kipps***)* Mrs Alice Drablow of Eel Marsh House. Dead, don't you know.
Kipps	Ah.
Bentley	Yes. I inherited Mrs Drablow from my father. The family has had their business with this firm for... oh... *(He waves his hand, signifying ages)*
Kipps	Oh yes?
Bentley	A good age. Eighty-seven.
Kipps	And it's her will you have there, I take it?
Bentley	Mrs Drablow was, as they say, a rum 'un. Have you ever heard of the Nine Lives Causeway?
Kipps	No, never.
Bentley	Nor ever of Eel Marsh in _____shire?
	That the written convention of "_____shire" might be vocalised, I suggest that the actor mumbles and coughs through the "_____"
Kipps	No, sir.
Bentley	Nor, I suppose, ever visited that county at all?
Kipps	I'm afraid not.
Bentley	Living there, anyone might become rum.
Kipps	I've only a hazy idea of where it is.
Bentley	Then, my boy, go home and pack your bags, and take the afternoon train from King's Cross, changing at Crewe and again at Homerby. From Homerby you take the branch line to the little market town of Crythin Gifford. After that, it's a wait for the tide!
Kipps	The tide!
Bentley	You can only cross the causeway at low tide. That takes you on to Eel Marsh and the house.
Kipps	Mrs Drablow's?
Bentley	When the tide comes in you're cut off until it's low again. Remarkable place. *(He stands to look out of the window)* Years since I went there, of course. My father took me. She didn't greatly care for visitors.
Kipps	Was she a widow?
Bentley	Since quite early in her marriage.
Kipps	Children?

Bentley	Children. *(He rubs at the window panes as a church bell tolls in the distance. He turns)* According to everything we've been told about Mrs Drablow, no, there were no children.
Kipps	Did she have a great deal of money or land?
Bentley	She owned her house, of course, and a few properties in Crythin Gifford—shops with tenants, that sort of thing; there's a poor sort of farm, half under water. And there are the usual small trusts and investments.
Kipps	Then it all sounds pretty straightforward.
Bentley	It does, does it not?
Kipps	May I ask why I'm to go there?
Bentley	To represent this firm at our client's funeral.
Kipps	Oh yes, of course. I'll be very glad to go up to Mrs Drablow's funeral, naturally.
Bentley	There's a bit more to it than that.
Kipps	The will?
Bentley	I'll let you have the details to read on your journey. But, principally, you're to go through Mrs Drablow's documents — her private papers... whatever they may be. Wherever they may be... and to bring them to this office.
Kipps	I see.
Bentley	Mrs Drablow was—somewhat... disorganised, shall I say? It may take you a while.
Kipps	A day or two?
Bentley	At least a day or two, Arthur.
Kipps	Will there be anyone there to help me?
Bentley	I've made arrangements. There's a local man dealing with it all — he'll be in touch with you.
Kipps	But presumably she had friends... or even neighbours?
Bentley	Eel Marsh House is far from any neighbour.
Kipps	And being a rum 'un she never made friends, I suppose?
Bentley	*(chuckling)* Come, Arthur, look on the bright side. Treat the whole thing as a jaunt.

Kipps *stands*

(Waving his hand towards the window) At least it'll take you out of all this for a day or two. You'll reach Crythin Gifford by late this evening, and there's a small hotel you can put up at for tonight. The funeral is tomorrow morning at eleven.

Bentley *stands up and moves away from the desk*

A. Reading

Rate this text for readability. Write the word/phrase of your choice into your copy.

VERY EASY ☐   EASY ☐   OKAY ☐   HARD ☐   VERY HARD ☐

B. Literacy Questions

1. The Actor (Kipps) plays the minor roles of Tomes, the clerk, and the solicitor, Mr Bentley. Describe the character of Tomes. Use quotes from the extract to support your answer.

2. Give an example of effective description of the London fog.

3. Write a paragraph describing Mrs Drablow and her situation. Use all of the information given in the extract to write an accurate, informative paragraph.

4. Imagine and draw the location of Crythin Gifford, Eel Marsh and Nine Lives Causeway. Include Mrs Drablow's house, shops and houses in the village, the tide, the causeway, the small hotel and so on.

5. What impression do you get of Mrs Drablow and of the village? What creates this impression?

6. In your group, speculate on what might happen next in the story. The young solicitor travels to Mrs Drablow's village, attends the funeral and…

C. Writing

Fill in the following table on **page 90** of your **PORTFOLIO**.

Name of play	
Acts and scenes	
Genre	
Dialogue	
Stage directions	
Setting	
Characters	
Plot	
Atmosphere/mood	
Narrator/voiceover	
Beginning/opening scene	
Roles	
Sound	
Lighting	
Sets/backdrops/scenes	
Costumes	
Props	

D. Oral Language

1. Act it out

In groups, act out any section of the play. Organise your cast, props, costumes, lighting, sound and so on.

2. Reflect on your experience

1. List any difficulties that your group had organising and performing the scene.

2. Briefly explain what went well.

3. List any new skill or information that you learned from acting out the scene.

Focus on the Narrator

Blood Brothers by Willy Russell is an example of a play that uses a narrator to help tell the story. The story is told through music and song. Consider the impact that using music to tell a story can have – think back to what you learned about in Chapter 3 about the power that words and music together can have.

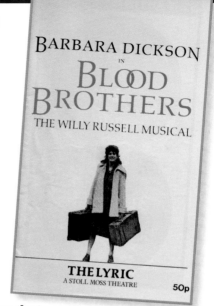

Blood Brothers *by Willy Russell*

Blood Brothers is set in Liverpool between the 1960s and 1980s and tells the story of brothers Mickey and Edward, who are separated shortly after birth and grow up in completely different families and environments. Their paths cross when they are about eight and they make a pact to become blood brothers, not realising that they are actually related by blood. At about 14, they both fall in love with the same girl. The musical is loosely based on a story that Russell read as a child about two brothers switched at birth. It was written and performed first as a school play in 1982, before Russell wrote the musical score, and it was first performed as a musical in 1983 in the West End. It is the third longest-running musical in West End history.

The overture comes to a close.

Mrs Johnstone   *(singing)* Tell me it's not true. Say it's just a story.

*The **Narrator** steps forward.*

Narrator   *(speaking)*
So did y' hear the story of the Johnstone twins?
As like each other as two new pins,
Of one womb born, on the selfsame day,
How one was kept and one given away?
An' did you never hear how the Johnstones died,
Never knowing that they shared one name,
Till the day they died, when a mother cried
My own dear sons lie slain?

*The lights come up to show a re-enactment of the final moments of the play – the deaths of **Mickey** and **Edward**. The scene fades.*

Mrs Johnstone *enters with her back to the audience.*

Narrator   An' did y' never hear of the mother, so cruel,
There's a stone in place of her heart?
Then bring her on and come judge for yourselves
How she came to play this part.

*The **Narrator** exits.*

*Music is heard as **Mrs Johnstone** turns and walks towards us. She is aged thirty but looks more like fifty.*

Mrs Johnstone (singing)

Once I had a husband,
You know the sort of chap,
I met him at a dance and how he came on with the chat.
He said my eyes were deep blue pools,
My skin as soft as snow,
He told me I was sexier than Marilyn Monroe.
And we went dancing,
We went dancing.

Then, of course, I found
That I was six weeks overdue.
We got married at the registry an' then we had a 'do'.
We all had curly salmon sandwiches,
An' how the ale did flow,
They said the bride was lovelier than Marilyn Monroe.

And we went dancing,
Yes, we went dancing.

Then the baby came along,
We called him Darren Wayne,
Then three months on I found that I was in the club again.
An' though I still fancied dancing,
My husband wouldn't go,
With a wife he said was twice the size of Marilyn Monroe.

No more dancing
No more dancing.

By the time I was twenty-five,
I looked like forty-two,
With seven hungry mouths to feed and one more nearly due.
Me husband, he'd walked out on me,
A month or two ago,
For a girl they say who looks a bit like Marilyn Monroe.

And they go dancing
They go dancing

Yes they go dancing
They go . . .

An irate **Milkman** *(the* **Narrator***) rushes in to rudely interrupt the song.*

Milkman Listen, love, I'm up to here with hard-luck stories; you own me three pounds, seventeen and fourpence an' either you pay up today, like now, or I'll be forced to cut off your deliveries.

Mrs Johnstone I said, I said, look, next week I'll pay y' –

Milkman Next week, next week! Next week never arrives around here. I'd be a rich man if next week ever came.

Mrs Johnstone	But look, look, I start a job next week. I'll have money comin' in an' I'll be able to pay y'. Y' can't stop the milk. I need the milk. I'm pregnant.
Milkman	Well, don't look at me, love. I might be a milkman but it's got nothin' to do with me. Now you've been told, no money, no milk.

The **Milkman** *exits.*

Mrs Johnstone *stands alone and we hear some other kids, off.*

Kid One	*(off)* Mam, Mam, the baby's cryin'. He wants his bottle. Where's the milk?
Kid Two	*(off)* 'Ey, Mam, how come I'm on free dinners? All the other kids laugh at me.
Kid Three	*(off)* 'Ey, Mother, I'm starvin' an' there's nothin' in. There never bloody well is.
Mrs Johnstone	*(perfunctorily)* Don't swear, I've told y'.
Kid Four	*(off)* Mum, I can't sleep, I'm hungry, I'm starvin'...
Kids	*(off)* An' me, Mam. An' me. An' me.

Mrs Johnstone	*(singing)* I know it's hard on all you kids, But try and get some sleep. Next week I'll be earnin', We'll have loads of things to eat, We'll have ham, an' jam, an' spam an' *(Speaking)* Roast Beef, Yorkshire Puddin', Battenberg Cake, Chicken an' Chips, Corned Beef, Sausages, Treacle Tart, Mince an' Spuds, Milk Shake for the Baby.

There is a chorus of groaning ecstasy from the **Kids**.

Mrs Johnstone	*(picks up the tune again)* When I bring home the dough, We'll live like kings, like bright young things, Like Marilyn Monroe. And we'll go dancing . . .

Mrs Johnstone *hums a few bars of the song, and dances a few steps as she makes her way to her place of work – **Mrs Lyons's** house. During the dance she acquires a brush, dusters and a mop bucket.*

Mrs Lyons's *house, where **Mrs Johnstone** is working. **Mrs Lyons** enters carrying a parcel.*

Mrs Lyons	Hello, Mrs Johnstone, how are you? Is the job working out all right for you?
Mrs Johnstone	It's, erm, great. Thank you. It's such a lovely house it's a pleasure to clean it.
Mrs Lyons	It's a pretty house, isn't it? It's a pity it's so big. I'm finding it rather large at present.
Mrs Johnstone	Oh. Yeh. With Mr Lyons being away an' that? When does he come back, Mrs Lyons?
Mrs Lyons	Oh, it seems such a long time. The Company sent him out there for nine months, so, what's that, he'll be back in about five months' time.
Mrs Johnstone	Ah, you'll be glad when he's back, won't you? The house won't feel so empty then, will it?

Mrs Lyons *begins to unwrap her parcel.*

Mrs Lyons	Actually, Mrs J, we bought such a large house for the – for the children – we thought children would come along.
Mrs Johnstone	Well, y' might still be able to . . .
Mrs Lyons	No, I'm afraid . . . We've been trying for such a long time now ... I wanted to adopt but. . . Mr Lyons is . . . well, he says he wanted his own son, not someone else's. Myself, I believe that an adopted child can become one's own.
Mrs Johnstone	Ah yeh . . . yeh. 'Ey, it's weird though, isn't it? Here's you can't have kids, an' me, I can't stop havin' them. Me husband used to say that all we had to do was shake hands and I'd be in the club. He must have shook hands with me before he left. I'm havin' another one, y' know.
Mrs Lyons	Oh, I see . . .
Mrs Johnstone	Oh but look, look, it's all right, Mrs Lyons, I'll still be able to do me work. Havin' babies, it's like clockwork to me. I'm back on me feet an' workin' the next day, y' know.

If I have this one at the weekend I won't even need to take one day off. I love this job, y' know. We can just manage to get by now –

She is stopped by **Mrs Lyons** *putting the contents of the package, a pair of new shoes, on to the table.*

Mrs Johnstone	Jesus Christ, Mrs Lyons, what are y' trying to do?
Mrs Lyons	My God, what's wrong?
Mrs Johnstone	The shoes . . . the shoes . . .
Mrs Lyons	Pardon?
Mrs Johnstone	New shoes on the table, take them off . . .

Mrs Lyons *does so.*

Mrs Johnstone	*(relieved)* Oh God, Mrs Lyons, never put new shoes on a table . . . You never know what'll happen.
Mrs Lyons	*(twigging it; laughing)* Oh . . . you mean you're superstitious?
Mrs Johnstone	No, but you never put new shoes on the table.
Mrs Lyons	Oh, go on with you. Look, if it will make you any happier I'll put them away.

She exits with the shoes.

Music is heard as **Mrs Johnstone** *warily approaches the table and the* **Narrator** *enters.*

Narrator	There's shoes upon the table an' a joker in the pack. The salt's been spilled and a looking glass cracked. There's one lone magpie overhead.
Mrs Johnstone	I'm not superstitious.
Narrator	The Mother said.
Mrs Johnstone	I'm not superstitious.
Narrator	The Mother said.

The **Narrator** *exits to re-enter as a* **Gynaecologist**[1].

Mrs Johnstone	What are you doin' here? The milk bill's not due till Thursday.
Gynaecologist	*(producing a listening funnel)* Actually I've given up the milk round and gone into medicine. I'm your gynaecologist. *(He begins to examine her.)* OK, Mummy, let's have a little listen to the baby's ticker, shall we?
Mrs Johnstone	I was dead worried about havin' another baby, you know, Doctor. I didn't see how we were gonna manage with another mouth to feed. But now I've got me a little job we'll be OK. If I'm careful we can just scrape by, even with another mouth to feed.

1. Doctor specialising in women's reproductive health.

The **Gynaecologist** *completes his examination.*

Gynaecologist   Mouths, Mummy.

Mrs Johnstone   What?

Gynaecologist   Plural, Mrs Johnstone. Mouths to feed. You're expecting twins. Congratulations. And the next one please, Nurse.

The **Gynaecologist** *exits.*

Mrs Johnstone, *numbed by the news, moves back to her work, dusting the table upon which the shoes had been placed.*

Mrs Lyons *enters.*

Mrs Lyons   Hello, Mrs J. How are you?

There is no reply.

(Registering the silence.) Mrs J? Anything wrong?

Mrs Johnstone   I had it all worked out.

Mrs Lyons   What's the matter?

Mrs Johnstone   We were just getting straight.

Mrs Lyons   Why don't you sit down.

Mrs Johnstone   With one more baby we could have managed. But not with two. The welfare have already been on to me. They say I'm incapable of controllin' the kids I've already got. They say I should put some of them into care.

But I won't. I love the bones of every one of them. I'll even love these two when they come along. But like they say at the welfare, kids can't live on love alone.

Mrs Lyons   Twins? You're expecting twins?

The **Narrator** *enters.*

Narrator   How quickly an idea, planted, can
Take root and grow into a plan.
The thought conceived in this very room
Grew as surely as a seed, in a mother's womb.

The **Narrator** *exits.*

Mrs Lyons   *(almost inaudibly)* Give one to me.

Mrs Johnstone   What?

Mrs Lyons   *(containing her excitement)* Give one of them to me.

Mrs Johnstone   Give one to you?

Mrs Lyons   Yes. . . yes.

Mrs Johnstone   *(taking it almost as a joke)* But y' can't just. . .

Mrs Lyons	When are you due?
Mrs Johnstone	Erm, well, about. . . Oh, but Mrs . . .
Mrs Lyons	Quickly, quickly, tell me . . . when are you due?
Mrs Johnstone	July he said, the beginning of . . .
Mrs Lyons	July . . . and my husband doesn't get back until the middle of July. He need never guess . . .
Mrs Johnstone	*(amused)* Oh, it's mad . . .
Mrs Lyons	I know, it is. It's mad . . . but it's wonderful, it's perfect. Look, look, you're what, four months pregnant, but you're only just beginning to show ... so, so I'm four months pregnant and I'm only just beginning to show. *(She grabs a cushion and arranges it beneath her dress.)* Look, look. I could have got pregnant just before he went away. But I didn't tell him in case I miscarried, I didn't want to worry him whilst he was away. But when he arrives home I tell him we were wrong, the doctors were wrong. I have a baby, our baby. Mrs Johnstone, it will work, it will if only you'll . . .

Mrs Johnstone	Oh, Mrs Lyons, you can't be serious.
Mrs Lyons	You said yourself, you said you had too many children already.
Mrs Johnstone	Yeh, but I don't know if I wanna give one away.
Mrs Lyons	Already you're being threatened by the welfare people. Mrs Johnstone, with two more children how can you possibly avoid some of them being put into care? Surely, it's better to give one child to me. Look, at least if the child was with me you'd be able to see him every day, as you came to work.

She stares at **Mrs Johnstone**, *willing her to agree.*

Mrs Lyons	Please, Mrs Johnstone. Please.
Mrs Johnstone	Are y' . . . are y' that desperate to have a baby?
Mrs Lyons	*(singing)* Each day I look out from this window, I see him with his friends, I hear him call, I rush down but as I fold my arms around him, He's gone. Was he ever there at all? I've dreamed of all the places I would take him, The games we'd play, the stories I would tell The jokes we'd share, the clothing I would make him, I reach out. But as I do. He fades away.

The melody shifts into that of **Mrs Johnstone** *who is looking at* **Mrs Lyons**, *feeling for her.* **Mrs Lyons** *gives her a half-smile and a shrug, perhaps slightly embarrassed at what she has revealed.* **Mrs Johnstone** *turns and looks at the room she is in. Looking up in awe at the comparative opulence and ease of the place. Tentatively and wondering she sings:*

Mrs Johnstone	If my child was raised In a palace like this one, (He) wouldn't have to worry where His next meal was comin' from. His clothing would be (supplied by) George Henry Lee.

Mrs Lyons *sees that* **Mrs Johnstone** *might be persuaded.*

Mrs Lyons	*(singing)* He'd have all his own toys And a garden to play in.
Mrs Johnstone	He could make too much noise Without the neighbours complainin'.
Mrs Lyons	Silver trays to take meals on.
Mrs Johnstone	A bike with *both* wheels on?

Mrs Lyons *nods enthusiastically.*

Mrs Lyons	And he'd sleep every night In a bed of his own. Mrs Johnstone He wouldn't get into fights He'd leave matches alone. And you'd never find him Effin' and blindin'. And when he grew up He could never be told To stand and queue up For hours on end at the dole He'd grow up to be

Mrs Lyons
and
Mrs Johnstone   *(together)* A credit to me.

Mrs Johnstone   To you.

I would still be able to see him every day, wouldn't I?

Mrs Lyons   Of course.

Mrs Johnstone   An' . . . an' you would look after him, wouldn't y'?

Mrs Lyons   *(singing)*
I'd keep him warm in the winter
And cool when it shines.
I'd pull out his splinters
Without making him cry.
I'd always be there
If his dream was a nightmare.
My child.
My child.

There is a pause before **Mrs Johnstone** *nods.* **Mrs Lyons** *goes across and kisses her, hugs her.* **Mrs Johnstone** *is slightly embarrassed.*

Mrs Lyons   Oh. Now you must help me. There's so much ... I'll have to ...
(She takes out the cushion.) We'll do this properly so that it's
thoroughly convincing, and I'll need to see you walk, and baby
clothes, I'll have to knit and buy bottles and suffer from piles.

Mrs Johnstone   What?

Mrs Lyons   Doesn't one get piles when one's pregnant? And buy a cot and . . .
Oh, help me with this, Mrs J. Is it in the right place? *(She puts the
cushion back again.)* I want it to look right before I go shopping.

Mrs Johnstone   *(helping her with the false pregnancy)* What you goin' the shops
for? I do the shopping.

Mrs Lyons   Oh no, from now on I do the shopping. I want everyone to know
about my baby. *(She suddenly reaches for the Bible.)*

     Music.

Mrs J, we must make this a, erm,
a binding agreement.

Mrs Lyons *shows the Bible to* **Mrs Johnstone**,
who is at first reluctant and then lays her hand on it.

The **Narrator** *enters. A bass note, repeated as a heartbeat.*

Narrator   In the name of Jesus, the thing was done,
                  Now there's no going back, for anyone.
                  It's too late now, for feeling torn
                  There's a pact been sealed, there's a deal been born.

Mrs Lyons *puts the Bible away.* **Mrs Johnstone** *stands and stares as* **Mrs Lyons,** *grabs shopping bags and takes a last satisfied glance at herself in the mirror.*

Mrs Johnstone   Why . . . why did we have to do that?

Mrs Lyons   Mrs J, nobody must ever know. Therefore we have to have an agreement.

Mrs Johnstone *nods but is still uncomfortable.*

Mrs Lyons   Right, I shan't be long. Bye.

Mrs Lyons *exits.*

Mrs Johnstone *stands alone, afraid.*

The heartbeat grows in intensity.

 ## A. Reading

Rate this text for readability. Write the word/phrase of your choice into your copy.

VERY EASY ☐   **EASY** ☐   **OKAY** ☐   **HARD** ☐   **VERY HARD** ☐

 ## B. Literacy Questions

1. What impression do you get of Mrs Johnstone from the extract? Use quotes to support your answer.
2. Do you have any sympathy for Mrs Lyons? Explain your answer using quotes to support your view.
3. What private arrangement have Mrs Johnstone and Mrs Lyons come to in this act?
4. How does Mrs Johnstone feel about the secret deal? Use quotes to support your answer.

 ## C. Oral Language

 In groups, dramatise the above scene.

Checklist

✓ How many characters are there?
✓ Do you need a narrator?
✓ Do you need a director?
✓ What can be used for props?
✓ Consider the costumes that might be worn in a production of this play.
✓ What do you need for sound and lighting?

Shakespearean Drama

The next two extracts, from *Romeo and Juliet* and *The Merchant of Venice*, were written by William Shakespeare.

Shakespeare was an English poet, playwright and actor. He was born in Stratford-upon-Avon in the sixteenth century and wrote 37 plays and numerous sonnets. His work has been translated into every major living language.

Shakespeare's plays are popular because they entertain, they focus on what it means to be human, they expose human flaws and encourage reflection. Shakespeare's early plays in the 1590s were comedies featuring witty dialogue, romantic action, deceit, disguises, mistaken identity and exotic settings. From 1599 onwards, he wrote tragedies which focused on people in power; leaders, kings and princes who had serious human flaws like greed for power, lust, egoism and pride.

Some passages in Shakespeare's plays are written in prose, others are written in verse called iambic pentameter and often he ends a speech using a rhyming couplet.

Romeo and Juliet *by William Shakespeare*

Romeo and Juliet is one of Shakespeare's most famous tragedies. It tells the story of two 'star-crossed lovers', Romeo and Juliet. Their families, the Montagues and the Capulets, have been feuding and fighting for years, so their love will not be accepted. In this scene, after their secret wedding night, Romeo and Juliet prepare to part, as daylight is dawning and they cannot be seen together.

Enter **Romeo** *and* **Juliet** *aloft at the window*

Juliet	Wilt thou be gone? It is not yet near day.
	It was the nightingale and not the lark
	That pierc'd the fearful hollow of thine ear.
	Nightly she sings on yon pomegranate tree.
	Believe me, love, it was the nightingale.

Romeo	It was the lark, the herald of the morn,
	No nightingale. Look, love, what envious streaks
	Do lace the severing[1] clouds in yonder east.
	Night's candles are burnt out, and jocund[2] day
	Stands tiptoe on the misty mountain tops.
	I must be gone and live, or stay and die.

Juliet	Yond light is not daylight, I know it, I.
	It is some meteor that the sun exhales
	To be to thee this night a torchbearer
	And light thee on thy way to Mantua.
	Therefore stay yet: thou need'st not to be gone.

1. Parting.
2. Cheerful, light-hearted.

3. Captured.

4. Reflection of the moon (Cynthia was another name for Artemis, the Greek goddess of the moon).

5. Vault-like, arching.

6. Hurry away.

7. High notes.

8. Music.

9. Frighten.

10. Morning music.

Romeo Let me be ta'en[3], let me be put to death,
I am content, so thou wilt have it so.
I'll say yon grey is not the morning's eye,
'Tis but the pale reflex of Cynthia's brow[4].
Nor that is not the lark whose notes do beat
The vaulty[5] heaven so high above our heads.
I have more care to stay than will to go.
Come death, and welcome! Juliet wills it so.
How is't, my soul? Let's talk. It is not day.

Juliet It is, it is! Hie hence[6], be gone, away!
It is the lark that sings so out of tune,
Straining harsh discords and unpleasing sharps[7].
Some say the lark makes sweet division[8].
This doth not so, for she divideth us.
Some say the lark and loathed toad change eyes.
O, now I would they had chang'd voices too,
Since arm from arm that voice doth us affray[9],
Hunting thee hence with hunt's-up[10] to the day.
O now be gone, more light and light it grows.

Romeo More light and light: more dark and dark our woes!

Enter **Nurse** *hastily*

Nurse Madam!

Juliet Nurse?

Nurse Your lady mother is coming to your chamber!
The day is broke, be wary, look about!

Exit **Nurse**

Juliet Then, window, let day in and let life out.

Romeo Farewell, farewell! One kiss and I'll descend.

He goes down

Juliet Art thou gone so? Love, lord, ay husband, friend!
I must hear from thee every day in the hour,
For in a minute there are many days.
O, by this count I shall be much in years
Ere I again behold my Romeo!

Romeo	Farewell! I will omit no opportunity That may convey my greetings, love, to thee.
Juliet	O think'st thou we shall ever meet again?
Romeo	I doubt it not, and all these woes shall serve For sweet discourses[11] in our times to come.
Juliet	O God, I have an ill-divining soul[12]! Methinks I see thee, now thou art so low, As one dead in the bottom of a tomb. Either my eyesight fails, or thou look'st pale.
Romeo	And trust me, love, in my eye so do you. Dry sorrow drinks our blood.[13] Adieu, adieu. *Exit*
Juliet	O Fortune, Fortune! All men call thee fickle[14]; If thou art fickle, what dost thou with him That is renown'd for faith? Be fickle, Fortune, For then I hope thou wilt not keep him long, But send him back.

11. Conversations.

12. Uneasy, bad feeling.

13. Sadness drains their health.

14. Changeable, unstable.

A. Reading

Rate this text for readability. Write the word/phrase of your choice into your copy.

VERY EASY ☐   **EASY** ☐   **OKAY** ☐   **HARD** ☐   **VERY HARD** ☐

B. Literacy Questions

1. What is your impression of Romeo in this scene?
2. List two things that prove that daylight is dawning.
3. Identify two examples of personification in the scene.
4. Do you think this is a tense scene? Explain your answer.

C. Oral Language

In groups, dramatise the above scene.

Checklist

✓ How many characters are there?
✓ Do you need a narrator?
✓ Do you need a director?
✓ What can be used for props?
✓ Consider the costumes that might be worn in a production of this play.
✓ What do you need for sound and lighting?

The Merchant of Venice *by William Shakespeare*

The main plot of *The Merchant of Venice* centres on the hatred between Antonio, a wealthy merchant, and Shylock, a Jewish moneylender. Antonio is a Christian who despises Shylock because of his religion and because of his occupation as a moneylender who charges interest on loans. When Antonio's best friend Bassanio needs cash quickly, they are forced to borrow from Shylock, providing Shylock with an opportunity to exact revenge. In this scene, Bassanio has just asked Shylock for a loan of 3,000 ducats. Antonio acts as a guarantor for Bassanio, promising to repay the loan to Shylock within three months of the money being borrowed.

Enter **Antonio**

Bassanio　　This is Signior Antonio.

Shylock　　[*Aside*] How like a fawning publican he looks!
　　　　　　　I hate him for he is a Christian;
　　　　　　　But more, for that in low simplicity
　　　　　　　He lends out money gratis[1], and brings down
　　　　　　　The rate of usance[2] here with us in Venice.
　　　　　　　If I can catch him once upon the hip[3],
　　　　　　　I will feed fat the ancient grudge I bear him.
　　　　　　　He hates our sacred nation, and he rails[4],
　　　　　　　Even there where merchants most do congregate,
　　　　　　　On me, my bargains, and my well-won thrift,
　　　　　　　Which he calls interest: cursed be my tribe
　　　　　　　If I forgive him!

1. Without interest.
2. Interest rates.
3. Get the better of him.
4. Complains.

Bassanio	Shylock, do you hear?
Shylock	I am debating of my present store[5] And by the near guess of my memory, I cannot instantly raise up the gross Of full three thousand ducats: what of that? Tubal, a wealthy Hebrew of my tribe, Will furnish[6] me; but soft! how many months Do you desire? [*To ANTONIO*] Rest you fair good signior, Your worship was the last man in our mouths.
Antonio	Shylock, albeit[7] I neither lend nor borrow By taking nor by giving of excess, Yet to supply the ripe[8] wants of my friend, I'll break a custom: [*To BASSANIO*] is he yet possess'd[9] How much ye would?
Shylock	Ay, ay, three thousand ducats.
Antonio	And for three months.
Shylock	I had forgot,—three months—[*To BASSANIO*] you told me so. Well then, your bond, and let me see,—but hear you, Methought, you said you neither lend nor borrow Upon advantage[10].
Antonio	I do never use it.
Shylock	When Jacob graz'd his uncle Laban's sheep[11],— This Jacob from our holy Abram was (As his wise mother wrought in his behalf) The third possessor: ay, he was the third.
Antonio	And what of him? did he take interest?
Shylock	No, not take interest, not, as you would say, Directly int'rest,—mark what Jacob did,— When Laban and himself were compromis'd[12] That all the eanlings[13] which were streak'd and pied Should fall as Jacob's hire[14], the ewes being rank[15] In the end of autumn turned to the rams, And when the work of generation was Between these woolly breeders in the act, The skilful shepherd pill'd[16] me certain wands, And in the doing of the deed of kind He stuck them up before the fulsome[17] ewes, Who then conceiving, did in eaning[18] time Fall parti-colour'd[19] lambs, and those were Jacob's. This was a way to thrive, and he was blest: And thrift is blessing if men steal it not.

5. Money.

6. Supply.

7. Although.

8. Urgent.
9. Informed of.

10. When interest is charged.

11. A Bible story in Genesis.

12. Agreed.
13. Lambs.
14. Jacob's wages.
15. Ready to mate.

16. Peeled.

17. Mating.
18. Lambing.
19. Spotted.

	Antonio	This was a venture, sir, that Jacob serv'd for;

Antonio

This was a venture, sir, that Jacob serv'd for;
A thing not in his power to bring to pass,
But sway'd and fashion'd by the hand of heaven.
Was this inserted to make interest good?
Or is your gold and silver ewes and rams?

Shylock

I cannot tell, I make it breed as fast,—
But note me, signior.

Antonio

Mark you this Bassanio,
The devil can cite Scripture for his purpose,—
An evil soul producing holy witness
Is like a villain with a smiling cheek,
A goodly apple rotten at the heart.
O what a goodly outside falsehood hath!

Shylock

Three thousand ducats, 'tis a good round sum.
Three months from twelve, then let me see; the rate.

20. Bound.

Antonio

Well Shylock, shall we be beholding[20] to you?

Shylock

21. Judged.
22. Rates of interest.

23. Loose robes.

Signior Antonio, many a time and oft
In the Rialto you have rated[21] me
About my moneys and my usances[22]:
Still have I borne it with a patient shrug,
For suff'rance is the badge of all our tribe,
You call me misbeliever, cut-throat dog,
And spit upon my Jewish gaberdine[23],
And all for use of that which is mine own.
Well then, it now appears you need my help:
Go to then, you come to me, and you say,
'Shylock, we would have moneys,' you say so:

24. Spit.
25. Kick me like you kick a stray dog.
26. Money is what you want.

You that did void your rheum[24] upon my beard,
And foot me as you spurn a stranger cur[25]
Over your threshold, moneys is your suit[26].
What should I say to you? Should I not say
'Hath a dog money? Is it possible
A cur can lend three thousand ducats?' Or

27. In a low voice.

Shall I bend low, and in a bondman's key[27]
With bated breath and whisp'ring humbleness
Say this:
'Fair sir, you spat on me on Wednesday last;
You spurn'd me such a day; another time
You call'd me dog: and for these courtesies
I'll lend you thus much moneys'?

Antonio

I am as like to call thee so again,
To spit on thee again, to spurn thee too.
If thou wilt lend this money, lend it not
As to thy friends, for when did friendship take

28. When did friends charge interest?

A breed for barren metal of his friend?[28]

> But lend it rather to thine enemy,
> Who if he break, thou may'st with better face
> Exact the penalty.

Shylock Why look you how you storm!
I would be friends with you, and have your love,
Forget the shames that you have stain'd me with,
Supply your present wants, and take no doit[29]
Of usance for my moneys, and you'll not hear me,—
This is kind I offer.

29. A tiny sum.

Bassanio This were kindness.

Shylock This kindness will I show,
Go with me to a notary[30], seal me there
Your single bond, and, in a merry sport,
If you repay me not on such a day,
In such a place, such sum or sums as are
Express'd in the condition, let the forfeit[31]
Be nominated for an equal pound
Of your fair flesh, to be cut off and taken
In what part of your body pleaseth me.

30. A legal clerk.

31. Penalty.

Antonio Content in faith, I'll seal to such a bond,
And say there is much kindness in the Jew.

Bassanio You shall not seal to such a bond for me.
I'll rather dwell in my necessity.

Antonio Why fear not man, I will not forfeit it,—
Within these two months, that's a month before
This bond expires, I do expect return
Of thrice three times the value of this bond.

Shylock O father Abram, what these Christians are,
Whose own hard dealings teaches them suspect
The thoughts of others! Pray you tell me this,—
If he should break his day what should I gain
By the exaction of the forfeiture?
A pound of man's flesh taken from a man,
Is not so estimable, profitable neither
As flesh of muttons, beefs, or goats,—I say
To buy his favour, I extend this friendship,—
If he will take it, so,—if not, adieu,
And for my love I pray you wrong me not.

Antonio Yes Shylock, I will seal unto this bond.

Shylock Then meet me forthwith at the notary's,
Give him direction for this merry bond—
And I will go and purse the ducats straight[32],
See to my house, left in the fearful guard
Of an unthrifty knave[33]: and presently
I will be with you.

32. Right away.

33. Dishonest man.

Exit

Antonio	Hie thee, gentle Jew. The Hebrew will turn Christian, he grows kind.
Bassanio	I like not fair terms, and a villain's mind.
Antonio	Come on, in this there can be no dismay, My ships come home a month before the day.

Exeunt

A. Reading

Rate this text for readability. Write the word/phrase of your choice into your copy.

VERY EASY ☐   **EASY** ☐   **OKAY** ☐   **HARD** ☐   **VERY HARD** ☐

B. Literacy Questions

1. Examine Shylock's opening speech. Try to explain how he feels towards Antonio. Quote to support your points.
2. List the terms and conditions of the loan.
3. List three awful things which Antonio has done to Shylock.
4. How does Antonio respond to the condition in the loan about the pound of flesh?
5. Guess what happens next in the play. Write 6–8 sentences continuing the story.

C. Oral Language

In groups, dramatise the above scene.

Checklist

- ✓ How many characters are there?
- ✓ Do you need a narrator?
- ✓ Do you need a director?
- ✓ What can be used for props?
- ✓ Consider the costumes that might be worn in a production of this play.
- ✓ What do you need for sound and lighting?

D. Group Work

In groups, compare and contrast the extract from *Romeo and Juliet* with the extract from *The Merchant of Venice*. Use the following headings: genre, themes, basic plot, conflict.

Extracts from Drama Outside the Prescribed List

Read the following extracts and think about which dramatic features they use to tell their stories.

 Leaves *by Lucy Caldwell*

Lucy Caldwell is a successful novelist and dramatist. Born in Belfast in 1981, she studied English at Queen's College, Cambridge, before doing a Master's degree in Creative and Life Writing in Goldsmiths. Her novel *The Meeting Point* (2011) was awarded the Dylan Thomas Prize and *All the Beggars Riding* (2013) was shortlisted for the Kerry Group Irish Novel of the Year. It was also chosen for Belfast and Derry's One City, One Book initiative.

Leaves was first performed at Druid Theatre, Galway, on 1 March 2007, directed by Gary Hynes. It is set in Belfast in the modern day. In the following scene, the Murdoch family is preparing to sit down to dinner. Parents Phyllis and David are both in their forties and have three daughters: Lori, the eldest, is nineteen, Clover is fifteen and Poppy is eleven.

Themes and issues in the play include identity, childhood, relationships and the past. Lori resembles Holden Caulfield, the central character in the classic J. D. Salinger novel *The Catcher in the Rye*. Lori and Holden both wish to return to the safety of childhood and both feel negative about the reality of the adult world. Issues such as war, man's inhumanity to man and the materialism and falseness of society deeply affect the characters. Both feel that nothing ever changes.

The living room.

There is a cheerful fire blazing.

David *is standing watching it.* **Clover** *and* **Poppy** *are sitting close together.* **Poppy** *is cuddled up to* **Clover**.

Phyllis	*(coming into the room)* You've made a fire.

She walks over to **David**. *She leans against him.*

	Oh, love.
David	*(quietly)* I know.
Poppy	Isn't the fire nice? Just once won't hurt the ozone layer, will it, Dad.
Clover	Is there anything we can do to help, Mum, 'cause anything you want us to do, isn't that right, Pops?
David	Thank you, Clover. Poppy. You're good girls.
Phyllis	*(to* **Clover***)* Thank you, love.
Poppy	*(getting up and cuddling into* **Phyllis***)* Mum. Look at the funny shadows on the walls. Doesn't it make the room look like a different place.

Phyllis *puts an arm around* **Poppy**.

David	C'mere, Clover.
Clover	What?
David	'Mere.
Clover	*(reluctantly)* Da-ad –

But she gets up and slouches over to her father.

Silence.

Poppy *reaches for* **Clover's** *hand.* **Clover** *looks at her and squeezes her hand.*

Silence.

David	We're going to be okay.

Silence.

Then **Lori** *comes into the room – bright – brittle – almost feverish.*

Lori	Anything I can do, come on Clovey, Pops. Clovey if you get the cutlery I'll get the glasses, wine, Mum, Dad, would you like a glass of wine, red or white, which would you prefer –

Slight silence.

	Well go on, red or white, would you prefer red or white –
David	Red would be –
Phyllis	There's a bottle of white open in the –
Lori	Well, I'll get both, no problem, come on, Clovey –

She leaves the room. **Phyllis** *and* **David** *glance quickly at each other;* **Clover** *and* **Poppy** *stare at each other;* **Poppy** *skips off first, beaming.*

Poppy	Come on, Clovey –
Clover	Mum, do you think she's –
Poppy	Come on, Clovey –

Poppy *skips out of the room – the sound of laughter from the kitchen – she comes back with a stack of plates.*

Clovey you're to get the cutlery – well, go on –

Clover *leaves the room and comes back with the cutlery. The girls start setting the table;* **Lori** *comes back in with a glass of red and a glass of white wine and hands them to her parents.*

Lori	Here you go, Dad, Mum, here you go. Oh, doesn't it look pretty, I always think how pretty it looks, glasses and cutlery, before they're used, don't you, Mum, hey Dad, will you sing a song, Dad, will you sing one of the songs you used to sing when we were little, will you?

Beat.

David	A song?
Lori	Yeah yeah, go on, please, Dad, one of the ones from – when we were little –
Clover	A song?
Lori	*(to* **Clover***)* Yeah, wouldn't it be, I just thought it would be, hey Pops, you'd like a song, wouldn't you. Go on, Dad. Pops, go get Dad's guitar –

Poppy *leaps up to fetch the guitar.*

David	Lori, I haven't touched the guitar in months, it'll be out of tune –
Lori	Doesn't matter, you can tune it, that doesn't matter go on, Dad –
Clover	Lori –
Lori	Aw, don't be a spoilsport – Clovey, come on, you'd like a song too, I know you would –

During the following speech **Poppy** *comes scampering back with the guitar and hands it to her father, who puts his book down and takes the guitar and starts tuning.* **Lori** *jumps down cross-legged in front of him and* **Poppy** *cuddles in beside her;* **Clover** *hovers for a second and then sits down next to* **Phyllis,** *who puts an arm around her.*

What are you going to sing, Dad, what do you think he'll sing, Clovey – 'mon and sit beside me, Pops, come on, isn't this nice, the fire's lovely, dead cosy, isn't it, Mum, oh that'll do, Dad, it's in tune enough by now, go on, go on –

David *starts to pluck out chords which resolve themselves into a song; he begins to hum along softly and then to sing.* **Lori** *whoops and claps when she recognises it. Her enthusiasm is infectious:* **Poppy** *cheers;* **Clover** *laughs despite herself;* **Phyllis** *smiles too.*

David	Oh, I went down south to see my Sal Singing Polly wolly doodle all the day My Sal she am a spunky gal Sing Polly wolly doodle all the day.

He pauses.

Lori	Oh don't stop –

She starts to hum the chorus, and **David** *plays and sings along:*

Fare thee well, fare thee well
Fare thee well my fairy Fay
For I'm off to Lou'siana for to see my Susyanna
Singing Polly wolly doodle all the day.

Then **David** alone:

Oh my Sal she is a maiden fair
Sing Polly wolly doodle all the day
With curly eyes and laughing hair
Sing Polly wolly doodle all the day.

Poppy	Dad! The verse about the grasshopper, Dad!
David	Oh a grasshopper sittin' on a railroad track Singing Polly wolly doodle all the day A pickin' his teeth with a carpet tack Sing Polly wolly doodle all the day.
Phyllis	David?

ASSESSMENT

Complete this assessment on **page 91** of your **PORTFOLIO**.

Modern Drama Extract

Lovers (Winners and Losers) *by Brian Friel*

The story centres on Margaret (Mag) and Joe, who are both 17 and studying for final summer exams. It is June 1966. Mag is pregnant, so the couple are going to get married in three weeks' time. Joe is determined to study hard and do well. Mag is vivacious and lively. She is a twin but Peter, her brother, died five days after their birth. The following scene takes place on the top of a hill in Ballymore in County Tyrone.

ASSESSMENT

Mag is drowsy with the heat. Her head is propped against her case. Through slitted eyes she surveys the scene below in Ballymore. She is addressing Joe but knows that he is not listening to her.

Mag I can see the boarders out on the tennis courts. They should be studying. And there's a funeral going up High Street; nine cars, and a petrol lorry, and an ambulance. Maybe the deceased was run over by the petrol lorry—the father of a large family—and the driver is paying his respects and crying his eyes out. If he doesn't stop blubbering, he'll run over someone else. And the widow is in the ambulance, all in plaster, crippled for life. *(She tries out a mime of this—both arms and legs cast in awkward shapes)* And the children are going to be farmed out to cruel aunts with squints and moustaches. Sister Michael has a beard. Joan O'Hara says she shaves with a cut-throat[1] every first Friday and uses an after-shave lotion called Virility. God, nuns are screams if you don't take them seriously. I think I'd rather be a widow than a widower; but I'd rather be a bachelor[2] than a spinster[3]. And I'd rather be deaf than dumb; but I'd rather be dumb than blind. And if I had to choose between lung cancer, a coronary[4], and multiple sclerosis[5], I'd take the coronary. Papa's family all died of coronaries, long before they were commonplace. *(She sits up to tell the following piece of family history)* He had a sister. Nan, who used to sing at the parochial[6] concert every Christmas; and one year, when she was singing 'Jerusalem'—you know, just before the chorus, when the piano is panting Huh-huh-huh-huh-huh-huh, she opened her mouth and dropped like a log…

Joe, d'you think *(quoting something she has read)* my legs have got thick, my body gross, my facial expression passive to dull, and my eyes lack-lustre? I hope it's a boy, and that it'll be like you—with a great big bursting brain. Or maybe it'll be twins— like me. I wonder what Peter would have been like? Sometimes when she's very ill Mother calls me Peter. If it were going to be twins I'd rather have a boy and a girl than two boys or two girls; but if it were going to be triplets I'd rather have two boys and a girl or two girls and a boy than three boys or three girls. *(Very wisely and directed to Joe)* And I have a feeling it's going to be premature.

Joe is alerted. His eyes move away from his book, but his head does not move.

Mothers have intuitions about these things. We were premature. Five weeks. Very tricky.

Joe Tricky?

---

1. A very sharp razor.

2. Unmarried man.

3. Unmarried woman.

4. To do with the heart. Heart attacks may be referred to as 'coronaries'.

5. A disease of the nervous system resulting in loss of control of movement and speech.

6. Meaning local. From the word 'parish'; may refer to a local event in a parish.

ASSESSMENT

Mag	Caesarean, as a matter of fact.

Joe *has never heard the term.*

Joe	*(Too casually)* That—sure—sure that's—so was I too.
Mag	*(Delighted)* Were you? Isn't that marvellous! We really have everything in common! Oh, Joe, wait till you hear: I was doing my hair this morning, and d'you know what I found in the comb? A grey hair! I'm old! Two months pregnant and I'm as grey as a badger! Isn't it a scream! I think a young face and silver hair is more attractive than an old face and black hair. But if I had to choose between a young face and black hair and an old face and silver hair I think I'd prefer the young face. *(Gently)* You have a young face. You're only a boy. You're only a baby really. I'll have two babies to take care of. *(She touches his shoe)* Joe, we'll be happy, Joe, won't we? It's such a beautiful morning. So still. I think this is the most important moment in my life. And I think *(she laughs with embarrassment)*, I think sometimes that happiness, real happiness, was never discovered until we discovered it. Isn't that silly? And I want to share it with everyone—everywhere.
Joe	Stupid.
Mag	What?
Joe	A fat lot you have to give.
Mag	I didn't say give!
Joe	You did!
Mag	I did not!
Joe	I heard you!
Mag	Liar! I said 'share'!
Joe	Share what?
Mag	You wouldn't understand!
Joe	Understand what?

Mag *has lost the thread of the argument.*

Mag	Anything! 'Cos you're just a selfish, cold, horrible, priggish[7], conceited donkey! Stuck in your old books as if they were the most important thing in the world; and your—your—your intended waiting like a dog for you to toss her a kind word!
Joe	I only asked.

7. Self-righteously superior.

ASSESSMENT

Mag	You hate me—that's it—you're going to marry me just to crush me! I've heard of men like you—sadicists! I've read about them in books! But I never thought for a second—

She breaks off suddenly and clasps her stomach in terrified agony. At the same time she is pleasantly aware of **Joe's** *mounting panic.*

Mag	Oh, my God—!
Joe	What?
Mag	Ooooooooooh—!
Joe	What—what—what is it, Maggie?
Mag	Joe—!
Joe	Mag, are you sick? Are you sick, Mag?
Mag	*(Formally)* Labour has commenced.
Joe	*(In panic)* Sweet God! How d'you know? What's happening? I'll get help! Don't move! Doctor Watson warned you to stop cycling! How d'you feel? I'll carry you. Don't move—don't move!

In total consternation he searches her face, noting every flicker of every feature. She is gratified at his anxiety. She acts the brave sufferer.

Mag	I… think—
Joe	Don't talk! Don't move! Where did you leave your bike?
Mag	Stay with me, Joe, please. Hold my hand.
Joe	God, this is fierce! On top of a bloody hill! You're all right, Mag, aren't you? Aren't you all right?
Mag	*(She gives him a brave smile)* Dear Joe. I'm fine, thank you, Joe.
Joe	What's happening? Tell me.
Mag	Nothing to be alarmed about. False pains.
Joe	False…?
Mag	*(Cheerily)* Gone again. For the time being.
Joe	They'll be back?
Mag	Oh, yes. But maybe not for a month.
Joe	God, I'm not worth tuppence.
Mag	I'm sorry for calling you names.
Joe	Maybe you should go home, Mag, eh?
Mag	I'm fine. Really. Go on with your work.

ASSESSMENT

Joe	God, I don't know.
Mag	*(Smiling reassuringly)* Please. I'll just rest.

Joe *gropes for something tender to say. But he is too embarrassed.*

Joe	Maggie, I'll. . . I'll try. . . I'll try to be—
Mag	*(A revelation)* I know now!
Joe	Huh?
Mag	No breakfast!
Joe	What are you—?
Mag	Hunger pangs! That's what it was! I'm ravenous!
Joe	Hunger—?
Mag	I could eat the side of a horse!
Joe	But you said you didn't care—?
Mag	Don't be always quoting what I said. There's nothing as detestable as being quoted. I change my mind every two minutes. Or would you rather it was labour?
Joe	*(Totally baffled)* I . . . I . . . *(Resolutely)* I'm going to work.

He begins to study again, **Mag** *opens her case and takes out a packet of sandwiches.*

Questions

1. What is your impression of the character Mag? Explain your answer using quotes for support. (10 marks)

2. What kind of a character is Joe? Explain your answer using quotes for support. (10 marks)

3. Did you find any evidence of humour in the extract? Explain your answer using quotes for support. (10 marks)

ASSESSMENT

Shakespearean Extracts

The Winter's Tale *by William Shakespeare*

One of Shakespeare's final plays, *The Winter's Tale* tells the story of the misguided and jealous King Leontes. The king rashly imprisons his wife, Hermione, having falsely accused her of having an affair. Hermione is expecting their second child and the baby, a girl, is born in prison. She is called Perdita and her father, the king, banishes her from the kingdom because he does not believe she is his child. King Leontes' servant Antigonus abandons the baby (and gold) in the neighbouring land of Bohemia, where she is found by a poor shepherd and his innocent, honest son. They were out searching for firewood when the son spotted the bundle on the ground as a wild storm raged; meanwhile, a ship was wrecked and Antigonus was mauled by a bear.

Note: The shepherd's son is called 'clown', as this was an old word for peasant. It does not mean clown in the modern sense of a clown in a circus.

Enter **Clown**

Clown	Hilloa, loa!
Old Shepherd	What, art so near? If thou'lt see a thing to talk on when thou art dead and rotten, come hither. What ail'st thou, man?

ASSESSMENT

Clown	I have seen two such sights, by sea and by land! But I am not to say it is a sea, for it is now the sky; betwixt the firmament and it you cannot thrust a bodkin's point.
Old Shepherd	Why, boy, how is it?
Clown	I would you did but see how it chafes, how it rages, how it takes up the shore; but that's not to the point. O, the most piteous cry of the poor souls! Sometimes to see 'em, and not to see 'em; now the ship boring the moon with her mainmast, and anon swallowed with yeast and froth, as you'd thrust a cork into a hogshead. And then for the land-service, to see how the bear tore out his shoulder-bone, how he cried to me for help and said his name was Antigonus, a nobleman! But to make an end of the ship, to see how the sea flapdragoned it; but first, how the poor souls roared, and the sea mocked them; and how the poor gentleman roared, and the bear mocked him: both roaring louder than the sea or weather.
Old Shepherd	Name of mercy, when was this, boy?
Clown	Now, now; I have not winked since I saw these sights; the men are not yet cold under water, nor the bear half dined on the gentleman—he's at it now.
Old Shepherd	Would I had been by to have helped the old man.
Clown	I would you had been by the ship side to have helped her; there your charity would have lacked footing.
Old Shepherd	Heavy matters, heavy matters! But look thee here, boy. Now bless thyself; thou metst with things dying, I with things newborn. Here's a sight for thee; look thee, a bearing-cloth for a squire's child; look thee here, take up, take up, boy, open't.

*(The **Clown** picks up the bundle)*

	So, let's see—it was told me I should be rich by the fairies. This is some changeling; open't—what's within, boy?

*(The **Clown** unwraps the bundle)*

Clown	You're a made old man! If the sins of your youth are forgiven you, you're well to live. Gold, all gold!
Old Shepherd	This is fairy gold, boy, and 'twill prove so. Up with't, keep it close; home, home the next way. We are lucky, boy, and to be so still requires nothing but secrecy. Let my sheep go; come, good boy, the next way home.

ASSESSMENT

Clown	Go you the next way with your findings, I'll go see if the bear be gone from the gentleman, and how much he hath eaten. They are never curst but when they are hungry. If there be any of him left, I'll bury it.
Old Shepherd	That's a good deed. If thou mayst discern by that which is left of him what he is, fetch me to th' sight of him.
Clown	Marry, will I; and you shall help to put him i'th' ground.
Old Shepherd	'Tis a lucky day, boy and we'll do good deeds on't.

Exeunt

Questions

1. Do you think that the shepherd and his son are superstitious? Find evidence to support your point. (10 marks)

2. Explain what the shepherd meant when he said 'thou metst with things dying, I with things newborn.' (5 marks)

3. The shepherd says that they will keep their find a secret. Why do you think that he wants to keep it a secret? (5 marks)

The term 'exit pursued by a bear' came into popular use (as a joke amongst actors) thanks to Shakespeare's stage direction in this play, when Antigonus was being chased by a bear.

ASSESSMENT

The Tempest *by William Shakespeare*

Written in 1611, *The Tempest* tells the story of a powerful magician named Prospero. After his own brother, Antonio, conspires against him, Prospero wreaks revenge. The guilty parties eventually admit their errors and are forgiven and all are reconciled. In this scene, on a remote island, Caliban (who is half-man, half-beast) plots with Stephano and Trinculo to murder Prospero. All three are drunk. Caliban is native to the island and he resents Prospero, who arrived on the island 12 years earlier, as his master. Trinculo and Stephano were shipwrecked on the island with a casket of wine.

Caliban	Why, as I told thee, 'tis a custom with him i'th' afternoon to sleep. There thou mayst brain him, Having first seized his books; or with a log Batter his skull, or paunch him with a stake, Or cut his weasand with thy knife. Remember First to possess his books; for without them He's but a sot, as I am, nor hath not One spirit to command—they all do hate him As rootedly as I. Burn but his books. He has brave utensils, for so he calls them, Which when he has a house, he'll deck withal. And that most deeply to consider is The beauty of his daughter. He himself Calls her a nonpareil. I never saw a woman But only Sycorax, my dam, and she; But she as far surpasseth Sycorax As great'st does least.
Stephano	Is it so brave a lass?
Caliban	Ay, lord, she will become thy bed, I warrant, And bring thee forth brave brood.
Stephano	Monster, I will kill this man. His daughter and I will be king and queen—save our graces!—and Trinculo and thyself shall be viceroys. Dost thou like the plot, Trinculo?
Trinculo	Excellent.
Stephano	Give me thy hand. I am sorry I beat thee. But while thou liv'st keep a good tongue in thy head.
Caliban	Within this half hour will he be asleep. Wilt thou destroy him then?
Stephano	Ay, on mine honour.

ASSESSMENT

Ariel	This will I tell my master.
Caliban	Thou mak'st me merry. I am full of pleasure; Let us be jocund. Will you troll the catch You taught me but whilere?
Stephano	At thy request, monster, I will do reason, any reason. Come on, Trinculo, let us sing.
They sing	
	Flout 'em and cout 'em And scout 'em and flout 'em, Thought is free.
Caliban	That's not the tune.

(**Ariel** *plays the tune on a tabor and pipe*)

Stephano	What is this same?
Trinculo	This is the tune of our catch, played by the picture of Nobody.
Stephano (*Calls towards* **Ariel**)	If thou beest a man, show thyself in thy likeness. If thou beest a devil, take't as thou list.
Trinculo	O, forgive me my sins!
Stephano	He that dies pays all debts. I defy thee.— Mercy upon us!
Caliban	Art thou afeard?
Stephano	No, monster, not I.

ASSESSMENT

Caliban	Be not afeard, the isle is full of noises,
	Sounds, and sweet airs, that give delight and hurt not.
	Sometimes a thousand twangling instruments
	Will hum about mine ears; and sometime voices,
	That if I then had waked after long sleep,
	Will make me sleep again, and then in dreaming
	The clouds methought would open and show riches
	Ready to drop upon me, that when I waked
	I cried to dream again.
Stephano	This will prove a brave kingdom to me, where I shall have my music for nothing.
Caliban	When Prospero is destroyed.
Stephano	That shall be by and by. I remember the story.

*(Exit **Ariel**, playing music)*

Trinculo	The sound is going away. Let's follow it, and after do our work.
Stephano	Lead, monster, we'll follow.— I would I could see this taborer; he lays it on.
Trinculo (to **Caliban**)	Wilt come? I'll follow Stephano.

Exeunt

Questions

1. List the methods that Caliban suggests using in order to kill Prospero.

   (10 marks)

2. Explain Stephano's response to the plot. What does he suggest will happen after they kill Prospero? (10 marks)

3. Explain in your own words what the island is like, drawing on Caliban's description. (10 marks)

ONE MILLION DUBLINERS

Every plot has a story

CHAPTER 6

Film:

An International Language

My Learning Expectations

In this chapter I will:

- **Develop** a deeper **understanding** of what film is
- **Learn** about the **different genres** of film
- **Practise filming** and perhaps **create a short film**
- **Understand** the **language/terminology** of film
- **Watch** and **enjoy** some films on my course

Film:
An International Language

A film is a story recorded on camera. The story is told using moving images (visual) and usually sound (audio). Films are made to be shown in the cinema, on TV or online.

Film is an exciting, enthralling way to tell a story. Watching a film transports you to another world – it can make you think about the lives of people in different cultures, times and circumstances. For example, *Beasts of the Southern Wild* is set in an impoverished community in Louisiana, USA, and *Whale Rider* is a story about the Maori people of Whangara, New Zealand, and their legends and beliefs.

A film may also make you think about your own life in a new way. You might identify with characters and events in the film. Maybe the friendship between two characters, like Will and Lee in *Son of Rambow*, reminds you of the relationship you have with your best friend.

You bring your own opinions, tastes, experiences and beliefs to the cinema, so you respond to films in your own particular way. You might feel guilty, sad, upset, annoyed or scared as you watch a film. Or you might laugh out loud non-stop. A trip to the cinema can be a captivating experience.

On **page 97** of your **PORTFOLIO**, tick the boxes to identify your experiences watching any kind of film.

My responses to films	Yes	No	Sometimes
I cried during the film and/or at the end			
At sad parts I remained quiet and stopped myself from crying			
I screamed in fear and terror at the scary parts			
I laughed out loud and really enjoyed the funny parts			
I often had a lump in my throat at the emotional parts			
I shielded my eyes from the gruesome scenes			
I smiled a lot and said 'Aaaaah…' at the cute moments			
My heart was racing during the action scenes			
I fell in love with the hero/heroine			
I wished things would work out for the good guys			
I really enjoyed the music; it was a brilliant soundtrack			
I liked the ending			
I thought the ending was unusual and unexpected			
I was really disappointed with the ending			
I looked forward to seeing to the sequel			
I recommended the film to my family and friends			

Film Posters, Taglines and Blurbs

A film **poster** advertises a soon-to-be-released film. It should be eye-catching and give viewers a good idea of the subject matter and tone of the film. A film poster includes the following features:

- The name of the film, displayed prominently.

- A striking image from the film. This may be of a main character, especially if the film stars a well-known actor.

- Names of the actors, director and other main people involved in making the film.

- A tagline.

A **tagline** is a short slogan designed to get people interested in seeing a film. They usually appear on film posters and on DVD covers. Film taglines should:

- Be a single, short phrase.

- Be catchy and easy to remember.

- Sum up the general plot.

Some examples of taglines are:

Chicken Run	Escape or die frying.
Finding Nemo	There are 3.7 trillion fish in the ocean, they're looking for one.
Bend It Like Beckham	Sometimes, to follow your dreams... you've got to bend the rules!
One Million Dubliners	Every plot has a story.
Son of Rambow	Make believe. Not war.
Jurassic Park	An adventure 65 million years in the making.
The Night of the Hunter	The wedding night, the anticipation, the kiss, the knife, BUT ABOVE ALL... THE SUSPENSE!
Mockingjay	The courage of one will change the world.

A **blurb** is a short description of a film that encourages audiences to see it. A blurb usually includes:

- The name of the film.

- Names of the main actors.

- Persuasive comments on the plot/actors' performances/soundtrack/special effects, etc.

Sample Blurbs

Shaun the Sheep *(G, 85 mins)*

Cute enough for kids, smart and witty enough for adults, *Shaun the Sheep* is a brilliantly crafted comedy from Aardman Animations. Hilarious and heart-warming, this is a must see for all the family to enjoy. Head off to Mossy Bottom Farm to follow cute Shaun the Sheep and his exploits in the city. Wallace and Gromit fans, this one's for you.

Selma *(12A, 128 mins)*

It's 1965. Tensions are dangerously high between black people and white people. In *Selma*, Martin Luther King fights to get voting rights for African Americans in Alabama and the southern states. Archive footage mixed with brilliant cinematography presents a gripping, tasteful, powerful, must-see film. David Oyelowo is an impressively convincing Martin Luther King, pushing President Lyndon Johnson (Tom Wilkinson) to pass legislation allowing African Americans to register to vote. English actress Carmen Ejogo is superb as King's wife Coretta. Oprah Winfrey is brilliant as activist Annie Lee Cooper, a nurse who was fired for trying to register to vote. A clear and focused account of one crucial period in Martin Luther King's life. Don't miss it.

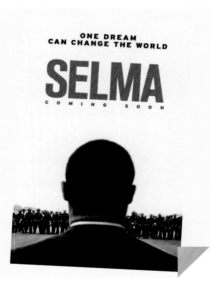

A. Writing

Write a blurb to promote the film that you are studying. Use persuasive language to encourage people to go to see it.

B. Drawing

Imagine that the film you are studying is being re-released. Design a new poster for it. Consider the following features of a film poster:

- Film title: is it in a prominent position?
- Target audience: does the poster cater to them?
- Visuals depicting scenes/actors.
- Use of colour.
- Layout: is it clever and original?

- Tagline: is it catchy?
- Language: is it persuasive?
- Nominations for awards.
- Awards won.
- Star ratings: are there any reviews you can quote?